A FEMINIST POLITICAL ECONOMY OF TRADE

Beyond Free Trade Feminism

Adrienne Roberts and Silke Trommer

BRISTOL
UNIVERSITY
PRESS

First published in Great Britain in 2026 by

Bristol University Press
University of Bristol
1–9 Old Park Hill
Bristol
BS2 8BB
UK
t: +44 (0)117 374 6645
e: bup-info@bristol.ac.uk

Details of international sales and distribution partners are available at bristoluniversitypress.co.uk

DOI: 10.51952/9781529252828

British Library Cataloguing in Publication Data
A catalogue record for this book is available from the British Library

ISBN 978-1-5292-5279-8 hardcover
ISBN 978-1-5292-5280-4 paperback
ISBN 978-1-5292-5281-1 ePub
ISBN 978-1-5292-5282-8 ePdf

Cover design: Liam Roberts Design
Front cover image: Stocksy/James Ross
Bristol University Press uses environmentally responsible print partners.
Printed and bound in Great Britain by CPI Group (UK) Ltd, Croydon, CR0 4YY

FSC
www.fsc.org
MIX
Paper | Supporting responsible forestry
FSC® C013604

Bristol University Press' authorised representative in the European Union is:
Easy Access System Europe, Mustamäe tee 50, 10621 Tallinn, Estonia,
Email: gpsr.requests@easproject.com

Contents

List of Figures, Tables and Boxes

Figures

Tables

Boxes

List of Abbreviations

AfCFTA	African Continental Free Trade Area
AfT	Aid for Trade
AI	Artificial Intelligence
APEC	Asia-Pacific Economic Cooperation
CEDAW	Convention on the Elimination of All Forms of Discrimination Against Women
CPTPP	Comprehensive and Progressive Agreement for Trans-Pacific Partnership
DAWN	Development Alternatives with Women for a New Era
ECLAC	Economic Commission for Latin America and the Caribbean
ECOWAS	Economic Community of West African States
EU	European Union
eWTP	Electronic World Trade Platform
FAO	Food and Agricultural Organization
FTA	free trade agreement
GATT	General Agreement on Tariffs and Trade
GATS	General Agreement on Trade in Services
GVC	global value chain
IGC	International Gender Champions
ILO	International Labour Organization
IMF	International Monetary Fund
IPR	intellectual property rights
ISDS	Investor-State Dispute Settlement
ITC	International Trade Centre
ITGN	International Trade and Gender Network
IWG	Informal Working Group
JSI	Joint Statement Initiative
LDC	Least Developed Country
MSME	micro, small and medium-sized enterprise
NAFTA	North American Free Trade Agreement
OECD	Organisation for Economic Co-operation and Development

RCEP	Regional Comprehensive Economic Partnership
SAP	Structural Adjustment Programme
SDGs	Sustainable Development Goals
TPR	Trade Policy Review
TRIMs	Agreement on Trade-Related Investment Measures
TRIPs	Agreement on Trade-Related Aspects of Intellectual Property Rights
UK	United Kingdom
UN	United Nations
UNCTAD	United Nations Conference on Trade and Development
UNECA	United Nations Economic Commission for Africa
US	United States
WILPF	Women's International League for Peace and Freedom
WSIS	World Summit on the Information Society
WTO	World Trade Organization

Acknowledgements

In early February 2026, as we were finalizing this manuscript for submission, one of our children observed 'Writing a book is hard'. He was not wrong. Thankfully, there have been many people who have helped us along the way.

First and foremost, we would like to acknowledge the central role that Erin Hannah has played in the intellectual development of this work. This project would not have happened without Erin, who was with Silke at the World Trade Organization's 2017 Public Forum, where they first noticed the newfound interest among trade policy elites in women and gender. Tragically, Erin had to step back from the book project to care for her mother who was battling terminal cancer. Nonetheless, our joint research on gender and trade, cited throughout, laid the foundations for much of what comes here.

There have also been numerous other friends and colleagues who have provided feedback on our various drafts and scattered collections of thoughts. These include Ali Bhagat, Andreas Bieler, Chris Clarke, Ellie Gore, Catia Gregoratti, Tian Liu, Laura Macdonald, Marc Palen, Sophia Price, Ben Richardson and Georgina Waylen. Thanks also to the rest of our colleagues in the Global Political Economy Research Cluster at the University of Manchester who have engaged with this work in research seminars and at other times.

We also would like to thank all of the colleagues who have encouraged us along the way, as we presented parts of this research, or discussed gender and trade, on roundtables and at various conferences. These have included the British International Studies Association, the Canadian Political Science Association, the Critical Political Economy Research Network of the European Sociological Association, the European Conference on Politics and Gender, the International Association for Feminist Economics, the International Studies Association, and a number of workshops and invited seminars and lecture series, including at the Austrian Foundation for Development Research, Max Planck Institute for Comparative Public Law and International Law, University of Cambridge, Universidad de los Andes, University of Derby, University of Glasgow, University of Helsinki, University of Warwick and Université Sorbonne Nouvelle. Colleagues who showed invaluable enthusiasm for our project include María Daniela Díaz,

Marzia Fontana, Gavin Fridell, Laura Parisi, Spike Peterson, Elisabeth Prügl, Gabriel Siles-Brügge, René Urueña and Izabella Vergara.

Thanks to Tyler Girard, Lorena Kettle, Aliki Koutlou and Isabel Morrell for research assistance, to Stanley Wilshire for editorial assistance, and to Ursula Mäki for her insights into Maria Mies and 'housewifization'. Thanks also to the team at Bristol University Press for their enthusiastic support for this project, and to our anonymous reviewers. The project was funded by a Social Sciences and Humanities Research Council of Canada Insight Development Grant and Insight Grant.

Finally, thanks to our long-suffering husbands, Chris and Patrick, who have provided intellectual and emotional support throughout this long journey, and to our children, Francis, Jack, Eddie and Leo, who, until this point, have not lived in a world where we were not working towards this book. This is for you.

1

Introduction: Troubling the Gender and Trade Agenda in Global Governance

In October 2017, Silke Trommer attended the World Trade Organization's (WTO's) Public Forum – an event she had regularly attended since 2008.[1] There was a distinct shift in focus at the 2017 event, as numerous sessions were now focused on how trade interacts with gender equality and women's empowerment. From workshops titled 'How Trade Can Help Achieve Sustainable Development Goal #5 – Gender Equality' to discussions on themes such as 'Trade Policy: Unlocking Opportunities for Women', it was clear that gender had moved to the forefront of global trade policy conversations. At the time, two primary narratives appeared to be emerging inside the WTO; one focused on assessing and addressing the gender-differentiated impacts of trade and the other on connecting women – especially entrepreneurs – to global markets (Hannah and Trommer, 2017).

But where did this new focus on gender equality and women's empowerment come from? How is the relationship between gender and trade being understood and addressed within and beyond the WTO? What does this mean for gender-based and other forms of inequality and exclusion in the world economy? What does it mean for our understanding of the role that trade governance plays in the contemporary global political economy? These are the questions that have driven our subsequent research on gender and trade (see Hannah et al, 2018; 2021a; 2022).

A Feminist Political Economy of Trade documents, historicizes and analyses the emergence of the gender and trade agenda within global trade governance that we first noticed in 2017. While there were examples of gender mainstreaming within regional trade governance institutions prior to this period, particularly in the global South (True, 2008; True and Parisi, 2013), feminist and women's civil society groups have long struggled to get the world's most powerful trade institutions to consider trade's impact on gender and intersectional forms of inequality (Liebowitz, 2008; Williams, 2013). According to one feminist activist involved in these efforts, WTO representatives told her at a meeting in 1996 that 'the WTO deals with technical matters' while 'gender is a philosophical matter'. When she and fellow activists proposed a panel on gender for the WTO Public Forum, they were told that they were welcome to attend, but to 'please refrain from bringing up philosophical issues such as gender'.[2]

To critically interrogate the shift towards gender mainstreaming that occurred in global trade governance from the mid-2010s onwards, we develop a feminist political economy framework that allows us to analytically centre the gendered social relations of trade. This framework rests on our understanding that gender inequalities and trade inequalities are co-constitutive in shaping the political economy of trade.

In Chapter 2, we identify the historically and geographically specific ways in which gendered hierarchies have produced and have themselves been reproduced by unequal global capitalist trade relations. Our analysis foregrounds the gendered nature of material trade practices, trade theories, and trade governance structures and mechanisms. Empirically, we focus on the institutional evolution of the gender agenda in global trade governance over the last decade, and on two areas where this agenda is particularly active and which we believe are crucially important from a gender equality perspective: food trade and digital trade.

Our theoretical focus on the gendered social relations of trade allows us to ask how far and in what ways gender mainstreaming agendas in global trade governance identify, challenge and undermine mechanisms of domination and exploitation in global trade relations. We are also attuned to the ways in which they may simultaneously invizibilize, naturalize and/or reproduce the gendered inequalities of global trade. It further enables us to situate the politics of the gender and trade agenda within wider debates and historical processes in the global political economy.

In the book, we focus on the so-called 'business case for gender equality' in global economic governance and on the state of crisis in WTO multilateralism, both of which have their roots in the 1990s. As we show, the business case made a relatively late entrance into global trade governance compared to other areas of economic governance (see also True, 2009; True and Parisi, 2013; Price, 2018; Altan-Olcay, 2020). This belated entrance coincided with the collapse of the WTO's Doha Development Round. At the time of writing, some observers speculate that the WTO, and global governance as we knew it, may be over. This is not least due to the election of Donald Trump as president of the United States (US) for a second term, commencing in 2025 (Döpfner, 2025; Carney, 2026). At this critical historical conjuncture, our feminist political economy of trade perspective allows us to formulate a feminist research agenda for transformative trade governance. It also allows us to draw attention to promising approaches to gender and trade that already exist, for instance within some trade governance institutions and some elements of civil society.

In the remainder of this chapter, we establish how we study and critique the gender and trade agenda in global trade governance. We lay out the main arguments of the book, present our key concepts and theoretical assumptions, and discuss contributions to broader literatures on the business case for gender equality and trade governance. We also review existing research on gender and trade. We end by outlining the chapters of the book.

Free trade feminism

Despite mobilizing against the WTO, the North American Free Trade Agreement (NAFTA) and other free trade agreements (FTAs) on feminist grounds in the 1990s and 2000s (Gabriel and Macdonald, 1994; 2005; Liebowitz, 2008), feminists and women's groups were not primarily responsible for the recent turn towards gender mainstreaming in global trade governance. As we show in Chapter 3, global trade policy elites who were sympathetic to gender equality agendas and who saw an opportunity to bring trade governance institutions into line with gender equality commitments outlined in the United Nations' (UN) Sustainable Development Goals (SDGs) and elsewhere largely drove this top-down agenda.[3]

The *first argument* we develop in this book is that as global trade policy elites in Geneva-based multilateral trade institutions increasingly integrated gender into the mainstream of trade policy and regulation, they constructed a particular consensus around how to 'do gender in trade', which then swept across trade and related governance arenas all around the world. We call this consensus 'free trade feminism'.

While we detail our understanding of free trade feminism in what follows, broadly speaking, we use the term to refer to a trade policy paradigm that is constructed upon and enacts a belief that there exists a 'virtuous circle between increased trade and gender equality' in the world economy (World Bank and WTO, 2020, p 6). As we will see, the belief in the virtuous circle is typically linked to policy paradigms of free trade, economic growth, competitiveness and market-led development. It is also typically accompanied by an understanding that gender inequalities emanate from so-called 'extra-economic' spheres, notably from social norms and laws within countries. It has a particular focus on women entrepreneurs, exporters and traders as the main 'agents' and beneficiaries of the virtuous circle.

In the book, we chart, historicize and critically interrogate the rise of free trade feminism as the dominant approach to gender mainstreaming in global trade governance. As we document in Chapter 3, policy elites within multilateral trade governance institutions (including the WTO, the United

Nations Conference on Trade and Development [UNCTAD] and the WTO–UNCTAD joint agency International Trade Centre [ITC]), regional trade governance institutions and economic and development institutions with a trade mandate (such as the Organisation for Economic Co-operation and Development [OECD] and the World Bank) have actively constructed the policy paradigm of free trade feminism.

They enact free trade feminism by forging and implementing gender and trade policy initiatives around the world that are based on the assumption that a self-perpetuating, circular relationship exists in the global economy, whereby trade liberalization leads to trade expansion, competitiveness, economic growth and development, which lead to women's economic empowerment and gender equality, which encourage further trade expansion, competitiveness, growth and development, and so on. They further tend to assume that women can be empowered to benefit from 'more trade' and 'more gender equality' in their roles as entrepreneurs, exporters (or export-facing workers) and traders so long as governments tackle gender-specific barriers to accessing trade opportunities.

These assumptions resonate with the so-called 'business case' for gender equality – that is to say the idea that gender equality makes good economic sense – that has proliferated across other areas of global economic governance (see for instance Griffin, 2009; Chant and Sweetman, 2012; Roberts and Soederberg, 2012; Elias, 2013; 2020; Calkin, 2015; Roberts, 2015a; Coburn, 2019; Prügl, 2021; Waylen, 2022). The ITC put this clearly when it declared:

> Gone are the days when gender inequality was seen as a purely ethical or moral concern. It is now recognized as a significant challenge to economic development, and achieving the economic empowerment of women has become a compelling business case. The global economy suffers when women – who account for half of the world's working-age population – are not included and are blocked from contributing to growth and development. Inclusive growth is the cornerstone of sustainable development. (ITC, 2020a, p 1)

Free trade feminism has not gone unchallenged, including within the institutions of trade governance. Indeed, we do not suggest that *all* global policy elites that advance free trade feminist agendas endorse *all* of its assumptions *all* of the time. Throughout our analysis, we provide examples of internal inconsistencies, deviations and critiques. Periodically, policy elites make these critiques *at the same time* as their discursive and policy interventions drive forward free trade feminism.

As we document in Chapter 3, when gender considerations started to emerge in trade governance circles, policy makers were engaged in contestations over precisely what gender mainstreaming in trade should entail. While some emphasized the economic benefits of integrating women into existing relations of global trade as producers, consumers and entrepreneurs, others suggested that adequately addressing gender-based inequalities required trade governance institutions to abandon their normative commitment to free trade, address long-standing disagreements between developed and developing countries over issues such as agricultural rules and the role of trade in development, and rectify the economic and political inequalities in the WTO regime. These differences in opinion were expressed within different deliberative spaces, including the WTO Informal Working Group (IWG) on Trade and Gender, in documents published by different trade governance institutions, such as UNCTAD or the UN Economic Commission for Latin America and the Caribbean (ECLAC) and by civil society critics such as the Gender and Trade Coalition. Nonetheless, we argue that over time, and notably since the COVID-19 pandemic, free trade feminism has become the dominant paradigm for making gender governable in trade.

Free trade feminism informs a vast landscape of trade and gender policy programmes in the world today. As we map out in Chapters 3–5, this landscape expands beyond trade governance at global, regional and national levels and increasingly integrates institutions operating on the margins or outside of the trade arena. Examples we cover include the Food and Agricultural Organization (FAO), the International Labour Organization (ILO), a number of international financial institutions and global and regional development banks, UN Women and more. Across the global political economy, free trade feminism is widely accepted today as the only feasible way of addressing the gender-differentiated impacts of trade.

Before discussing our analytical approach, we must clarify the use of key concepts, including 'gender mainstreaming', 'gender'/'gender equality', 'women's economic empowerment', 'trade governance', 'free trade' and the 'developing'/'developed' dichotomy.

We use the term 'gender mainstreaming' to refer to the process of incorporating a gender lens into trade policies, programmes and projects to achieve some measure of gender equality. While the term is contested, this is the core of most gender mainstreaming definitions, which usually fail to spell out what they mean by gender equality (Caglar, 2013, p 338). The ITC offers a general account of how policy elites driving gender mainstreaming in trade governance typically understand it. It notes that gender mainstreaming in trade means 'including gender considerations when trade accords are drafted and implemented' and 'aim[ing] to maximize the positive impact and minimize the negative impact of these pacts for women in trade' (ITC, 2020a, p 2; see also Bahri, 2020, p 11).

For the most part, the policy elites advancing gender mainstreaming in trade governance leave these terms undefined. 'Women' and 'gender' are often used synonymously, especially when it comes to policy interventions. Here, women are generally conceived as a universal and biological category. 'Gender equality' and 'women's empowerment' are also at times conflated, and the latter more commonly evoked as the aim of interventions than the former. For example, in one of the defining policy reports of free trade feminism, *Women and Trade: The Role of Trade in Promoting Gender Equality*, the World Bank and WTO (2020, p 24) define gender as 'the social, behavioural, and cultural attributes, expectations, and norms associated with being a man or a woman'. Gender equality refers to 'how these aspects determine how women and men interact with each other and the resulting differences in power between them'. The report later goes on to say that '[a]lthough gender equality is not explicitly mentioned in WTO agreements, WTO rules help ensure that members interested in adopting policies to promote women's economic empowerment do so in a non-discriminatory, open, and predictable trading environment' (World Bank and WTO, 2020, p 176). This shows how, when it comes to the WTO, the focus on gender equality is largely superseded by a narrower focus on women's economic empowerment. As we will see across our analysis, the focus on the economic empowerment of individual women within the existing market paradigm, as opposed to more collective and transformative understandings of empowerment (Kabeer, 1999), underpins free trade feminism. Thus, for instance, one of the cornerstones of gender mainstreaming at the WTO is the 'WTO Declaration on Trade and *Women's Economic Empowerment*' (WTO, 2017a, emphasis added), signed by 118 members and observers at the 2017 Ministerial Conference in Buenos Aires.

Using Spike Peterson's formulation (2005, p 499), it can be said that free trade feminism is more interested in asking 'how men and women – gender understood empirically – are differentially affected by, and differentially affect' economic exchange.[4] Although the World Bank/WTO definition does not conflate sex and gender, it is nonetheless rooted in a cis-normative understanding of sex as a binary of men/women, and gender as a set of social norms that maps onto this binary. As we will see, many policy actors in the gender and trade agenda recognize intersectional dimensions of inequality, and acknowledge that discriminatory social, political and legal norms structure women's engagement with global trade flows, rules and regulations. They regularly raise other important aspects of gender relations, such as equality in bargaining power within households, access to legal and political rights, responsibility for household and care work and, on occasion, gender-based violence. Nonetheless, free trade feminism is first and foremost interested in using global trade as a mechanism for improving the position of individual women in the economy. Empirical gender and market-centric perspectives dominate how gender equality and women's economic empowerment in trade are conceptualized and measured.[5]

This view differs from our understanding of gender as a social power relation that, in the words of Penny Griffin (2010, p 8), is 'a composite part of the relations of power that drive systems of economic development and growth, global financial flows, and systems of manufacturing and production'. In line with the feminist political economy tradition, rather than asking how trade *impacts* on women and/or gender relations, we elucidate the ways in which trade relations are *co-constituted by* gender relations, which are intrinsically linked to relations of class and race and to capitalism's relationship with nature.

As a broad theoretical approach with roots in Marxist feminism, feminist political economy seeks to understand the interconnections between political, economic and social relations, and the constitutive role that gender-based and other forms of inequality play in the workings of global capitalism (Cantillon et al, 2023). We see gender as a social power relation that is both constitutive of and reproduced by the political, economic and legal relations of global trade (see also Hannah et al, 2021a; 2022; Trommer, 2022). As we lay out in Chapter 2, gendered hierarchies of what constitute valuable economic activities and rationalities are inherent to trade inequalities, and are also connected to intersectional inequalities of class and race and to capitalism's extractivist relationship with nature. Global trade relations have produced and reproduced these hierarchies and dependencies in the historical evolution of capitalism, creating the historically specific context within which gender mainstreaming has emerged. Our conceptualization of gender as a social power relation leads us to explore how these efforts interact with the gendered trade inequalities that are inherent in contemporary global trade governance.

As we document across Chapters 3–5, in promoting women's economic empowerment through trade, free trade feminism takes the existing global trade governance framework as given and immutable. This again differs from our understanding. We see institutional arrangements, relationships between specific actors and the ideational and ideological orientations of global governance as having historically developed through political processes (Weiss and Wilkinson, 2014). Contestations among different political and social forces with different preferences, ideas and interests have shaped these processes (Murphy, 2000; 2014; Avant et al, 2010), with gender relations constituting one axis of contestation (Rai, 2004; Rai and Waylen, 2008).

We analyse trade governance as a global political practice that is rooted in and reproduces the social relations of gender. A wide range of actors participate in global governance, from international institutions and governments to private and civil society interests. Institutional structures, key agents, policy aims and principles, discourses and taken-for-granted ways of going about global governance are all historically contingent, social, legal and political constructs. We are interested in the politics that unfold within their interactions, and in the role that gendered hierarchies play within them (see also Prügl, 2004). While it may be the case that the gender and trade agenda in global trade governance is 'new', its various proponents are enacting their ideas and policy preferences about the links between trade and gender in an *already gendered* terrain of global governance.

A central ideological construct that informs free trade feminism, and trade governance in general, is the concept of 'free trade', which is closely identified with trade liberalization and a normative commitment to continued trade expansion. Since the 1980s and 1990s, this ideological construct, and related discourses about the dangers of protectionism, have shaped the politics of global trade governance (Strange, 1985; Wilkinson, 2009; 2012; Siles-Brügge, 2014; Hannah et al, 2015). Despite challenges from scholars, policy makers and civil society groups, the trade expansion norm has become increasingly taken for granted as a solution to global policy problems in other governance arenas, including food (McMichael, 1997; Margulis, 2014; Clapp, 2017a), public health (Roemer and Roemer, 1982), environment (Gonzalez, 2000; Weber, 2001; Bernstein, 2002), development (Ravenhill, 2014; Trommer, 2014; Selwyn and Leyden, 2022) and, most recently, digital transformation (Azmeh et al, 2020).

We understand free trade and protectionism to be socially constructed economic policy terms that change meaning over time (see, for example, Trentmann, 1998; Lang, 2007; Scott and Trommer, 2024). What policy mixes are thought to fall under free trade has changed considerably across the ages. In the 19th century, for example, the term referred to the dismantling of tariffs and government levies on trade that went beyond governments' revenue needs (Palen, 2016). Unlike in subsequent eras, free trade then *included* the imposition of tariffs insofar as they constituted government revenue. In the embedded liberal era following the Second World War, free trade largely meant lowering such levies while providing for some form of domestic wealth distribution (Ruggie, 1982).

In the neoliberal era, free trade came to be widely understood to entail *both* removing or harmonizing national rules and regulations that limited transnational goods, services and capital flows – for example in financial and banking regulation or social and environmental policy – *and* establishing regulatory frameworks that promoted these flows – for example in service trade or in intellectual property and investment protection. The neoliberal understanding of free trade firmly puts the interests of corporations and investors above those of the wider public (Gill, 1995). The expansion of the trade agenda into other policy domains has also led to much political contestation in trade governance over the past 30 years (Young and Peterson, 2006), not least because it leads to trade laws and rules that support the concentration of economic power and monopoly building (see, for instance, Sell, 2003). This shift has benefited corporate interests and lobby groups who – instead of being unequivocally in favour of trade liberalization *per se* – generally support policies that are 'pro trade' but 'against competition' in the contemporary world economy (van Ommeren, 2025).

As we will see, free trade feminist advocates endorse these neoliberal understandings of free trade and their associated governance mechanisms. They actively create new assumptions about free trade in the 21st century, for example by associating it with women's economic empowerment and gender equality, and by identifying new trade barriers, such as gender discriminations in the (assumed) extra-economic spheres of society and law. Free trade feminism thus legitimizes and lends political weight to the global governance norm in favour of free trade and trade expansion by asserting that liberalization is a prerequisite for gender equality and women's economic empowerment.

Finally, we use the terms 'global South' and 'global North' to refer to how structural inequalities connect different social and geographic regions in the world economy. In using these terms, we aim to look beyond the confines of the nation-state to acknowledge that demarcations between places associated with the global North and South are blurred, and that 'one may exist within the other' (Trefzer et al, 2014, p 1). We variably also use dichotomies such as core/periphery, poor/rich and the expression 'Third World' when engaging with literatures that predominantly use these terms. At the same time, we use the terms 'developed' and 'developing countries' when discussing trade governance dynamics, because these are legal categories within the WTO system. If a WTO member self-identifies as holding developing country status, special dispensations and flexibilities apply to this member, as we clarify in more detail in what follows. Which countries do or do not hold WTO developing country status has provoked political controversy in recent years. The rise of China and other emerging economies into the ranks of the world's top trading nations has by no small measure spurred these controversies (Weinhardt, 2020).

While we use these terms as descriptors of specific sets of relationships among state actors involved in global trade governance, we join critical development scholarship in rejecting standard assumptions that underlie the developed/developing dichotomy. These include hierarchical, Eurocentric ideas about socioeconomic progress, a linear view of history and the erroneous belief that different regions of the world economy historically evolved along separate and separated trajectories, among others (see, for instance, Sachs, 1992; Rosenberg, 2006). Seen through the lens of our feminist political economy of trade approach, structural dependencies and inequalities across the capitalist world economy have historically relied, in part, on the gendered social relations of global trade.

A feminist political economy of trade

We understand and theorize trade as a social and material practice that extends beyond relations of production and exchange to include social reproduction and the life-making work that makes production and exchange possible. Within feminist political economy, most definitions of social reproduction relate to at least three aspects: the biological reproduction of the species, which includes social constructions of motherhood and the conditions under which this work is performed; the reproduction of the labour force (including subsistence, education and training); and the reproduction and provisioning of caring needs (Bakker, 2007, p 541). Others add the reproduction of culture and ideology (Hoskyns and Rai, 2007) or, at a more abstract level, the reproduction of the conditions of social production in their totality, which includes the basic structures of production (Edholm et al, 1977). From our perspective, the important point is not to reify a distinction between production and its outside – or 'the economy' and 'society' – but rather to show how the 'production of goods and services and the production of life are part of one integrated process' (Luxton, 2006, p 36; see also Mies, 1998 [1986]; Bhattacharya, 2017; Hannah et al, 2021a).

While these dynamics have been well established by feminists, trade scholars and policy makers typically (though with some exceptions) consider unpaid labour, reproductive labour and social reproduction processes to lie outside of global trade. They not only reify a distinction between trade, assumed to take place in the so-called 'productive economy', and its outside. They have also failed to ask how trade governance has historically helped to create and perpetuate structural forms of gender inequality, for instance when domestic labour, care work, informal labour and subsistence agriculture are treated as irrelevant or subordinate to 'productive' forms of employment and entrepreneurship.

Our feminist political economy framework builds on two distinct bodies of feminist scholarship to correct these gendered blind spots. First, Marxist feminists have stressed that processes of capital accumulation rest not only on the exploitation of the working class and a global division of labour based on location. They also rest on the reproduction of differences and divisions within the working class, including along gendered and racial lines (Federici, 2004). Notably, in the expansion of capitalism globally, work done by women, as well as by colonized peoples, has been rendered 'natural' and invisible, and been treated as 'freely available like air and water' (Mies, 1998 [1986], p 110), while simultaneously being harnessed to capital accumulation via the mechanism of global trade.

In Chapter 2, we elucidate how global trade relations have historically been entangled with gendered and colonial global divisions of labour and an extractivist relationship with nature that emerged under imperialism and that continues to the present day. To make this argument, we build on feminist scholars who have shown how the devaluation and subordination of types of labour that are considered unproductive gives rise to a gender-based division of labour that in turn enables exploitation and the perpetuation of intersectional inequalities (Mies, 1998 [1986]; Federici, 2004; Bhattacharyya, 2018; Mezzadri et al, 2022). This process is parallel to the exploitation of nature (Mies and Shiva, 1993). It also links to varied experiences of environmental degradation across the world economy (Gonzalez, 2000), which affects the conditions under which social reproduction takes place.

Following Maria Mies (1982; 1998 [1986]), we use the term 'housewifization' to refer to the process whereby value is created in the capitalist world economy by harnessing these hierarchies to transnational economic exchange. From our perspective, capitalist trade relations depend, in part, on gendered and colonial divisions of labour, as well as the appropriation of nature. We would expect feminist trade agendas to identify and work to undo these dependencies.

Second, building on feminist analyses of global economic governance, we further develop our existing critiques of the 'masculinized, elitist and legalized trade orthodoxy' through which housewifization processes and global trade relations in general are governed (Hannah et al, 2021a, p 74; see also Trommer, 2022). Masculinized forms of knowledge that rest on assumptions about 'rational economic man' animate global trade governance (Hannah et al, 2022, p 1371). They normalize efficient resource allocation and productivity maximization as goals of economic governance, and venerate self-interested, calculating and competitive behaviours, as well as masculinized forms of reason, agency and autonomy (Benería, 1999; Folbre, 2001; Ferber and Nelson, 2003; Peterson, 2005).

As we trace in Chapter 2, such trade knowledges and governance techniques have actively feminized (that is to say devalued and subordinated) the work, rationalities and values associated with labour that is presumed to be 'unproductive', and 'freely available' resources. Since the inception of the General Agreement on Tariffs and Trade (GATT) in 1947, international institutions and policy elites have governed trade *as if* the links between trade, unpaid labour, social reproduction, subsistence and environmental conditions were irrelevant – or, at best, second order – to the circulation of goods, and later services, in the world economy.

We refer to such trade knowledges and governance techniques as 'trade productivism'. In Chapter 2, we show that trade productivist theories and governance mechanism are not self-evident or natural, but historically contingent and contested. At the same time, certain trade productivist assumptions and techniques, such as the idea that economic exchange across borders is, at its core, a gender-neutral mechanism, or the political and institutional separation of gender mainstreaming agendas from the (assumed gender-neutral) 'core' of market access negotiations, persist in trade governance today. From our perspective, these are ideational and institutional aspects of gendered inequality in trade that feminist trade agendas must actively challenge.

Our third conceptual device, 'trading on social reproduction', builds on housewifization and trade productivism to capture the gendered social relations of trade in the neoliberal era. It acknowledges the fact that housewifization and trade productivism are not distinct historical processes but interact in the co-constitution of gendered and trade inequalities in the global political economy. We use the concept to refer to a shift in the gendered social relations of trade with the onset of neoliberalism, whereby global trade flows and trade governance are reconfigured in ways that enable corporations and investors to capitalize even more directly on women's labour, on reproductive, subsistence and informal labour, on life-making activities and on nature. This parallels ways that value has been extracted via cross-border trade in goods for centuries.

Structurally, the rise of global value chains (GVCs) was key to these reconfigurations, which saw new waves of underpaid women workers flock onto factory floors, mainly in the global South. This boosted the so-called 'feminization of labour', housewifization and labour informality (Elson and Pearson, 1981; Mezzadri, 2017). In governance terms, the expansion of trade rules under neoliberal free trade enabled capital accumulation to occur within the realm of social reproduction via the mechanism of global trade. Examples include trade in reproductive labour (enabled by new techniques of service trade liberalization), trade in goods essential to reproductive labour (enabled by new intellectual property rights [IPRs] that conferred trade monopolies in living organisms or plant knowledges), and techniques of disciplining the policy space available to governments to regulate in ways that support social reproduction, environmental sustainability and more (enabled by new understandings of trade barriers).

From our perspective, trading on social reproduction helped to create and capitalize on what Isabella Bakker and Stephen Gill (2019) refer to as the 'variegated crises of social reproduction' that are unfolding in interconnected but distinct ways across the world. It is one of the macro-economic mechanisms that contribute to and propel what feminists call the 'depletion' through social reproduction worldwide (Rai et al, 2013; Rai, 2024). We would expect a feminist trade agenda to identify and undermine trading on social reproduction, and to ask how global trade relations can support progressive and sustainable forms of social reproduction around the world (see also Hannah et al, 2021a).

Our analysis of gender mainstreaming in global trade governance in Chapters 3–5 deploys this framework. It draws on eight years of empirical research where we reviewed secondary literatures and official documentation on gender and trade by all multilateral trade governance institutions. We focused specifically on the WTO, UNCTAD and ITC. Because a wide range of international institutions are actively involved in gender mainstreaming in trade, we also reviewed documents and literatures relating to their contributions. They included the World Bank, the OECD, and regional trade institutions, notably the United Nations Economic Commission for Africa (UNECA), the Economic Community of West African States (ECOWAS), ECLAC and the Asia-Pacific Economic Cooperation (APEC). We gathered all agenda-setting gender and trade documents from 2015 onwards, as well as other documents (where relevant for further understanding a particular policy logic), minutes of relevant meetings (primarily those of the WTO's IWG on Trade and Gender) and institutional websites. Given that many governments, corporations, civil society actors and, increasingly, international institutions working in other areas of global governance all around the world participate in this agenda, we also at times draw on their contributions.

We do not understand trade governance institutions to be unitary actors, and make distinctions between the secretariats of institutions and their political organs that bring together member states. By analysing the agendas of specific institutions, the interactions between them, as well as the interactions that they have with other international, regional and national policy elites, we move beyond the common focus in the literature on either the WTO or FTA-based trade governance. By making visible and interrogating the multiple interactions among a wide range of actors, our book contributes to recent scholarly efforts to develop a holistic view of the global trade governance arena (see, for instance, Margulis, 2023).

While gender mainstreaming takes into account many of the traditional sectors of trade policy – such as manufacturing, agriculture, services, investment, and more – we chose to focus our analysis on the historical evolution of gender mainstreaming in the trade governance arena from 2016 onwards, and on two sectors where our research showed the agenda to be particularly active. These are (1) food and agricultural trade and (2) digital trade.

Food and agricultural trade are long-standing contested issues within global trade governance and the governance of trade and development. Food trade is also an important distributive mechanism in the global food system on which the majority of the global population relies for daily subsistence and is central in the response to climate change. Digital trade, on the other hand, is essential to the ongoing digital transformation of the global economy and one of the most recent contentious issues in global trade governance. Digital trade is becoming increasingly relevant for trade across all sectors, and an area where trade rules are, in part, shaping ongoing rapid structural transformations in the global political economy.

We employed document analysis, textual analysis and process tracing to establish how trade policy makers understand trade to be gendered and how policy approaches to 'doing gender' are developed and contested. We triangulated these insights with scholarship from political economy, development studies, law and history to document the wider political economic contestations and processes in which the gender and trade agenda is embedded. Eleven interviews with policy elites and civil society activists conducted between 2019 and 2020 (see Appendix) and regular participation in trade governance settings has further shaped our understanding of the gender and trade agenda. Participation in trade governance settings has included, most notably, the WTO Gender Research Hub and trade policy communities in Geneva and the United Kingdom (UK). While we do not directly draw on or refer to any of these interactions in our analysis, they have nonetheless provided us with direct experiences of the gender and trade agenda and have shaped our view of the policy field.

Based on our analysis, we develop *the second main argument* of the book, which is that in connecting women, especially women in the global South, to global trade relations as they currently exist, free trade feminism works to naturalize and reproduce the gendered inequalities that underpin these relations. It further risks creating new forms of inequality in the global political economy. To be clear, the gender and trade agenda has succeeded in bringing a wide range of feminist concerns into the world's most powerful trade institutions, despite a traditional consensus that such concerns do not belong there. This is no small achievement. It is also the case that we did not study the impact of gender and trade initiatives on the ground, in the various (predominantly developing country) WTO members. Testimonies abound online and in policy documents of individual women, typically from the global South, who explain how trade and gender mainstreaming initiatives have supported their careers and livelihoods. We do not challenge the proposition that these initiatives hold potential to improve the lives of those women that they target, and the lives of their families and communities. Nonetheless, we provide evidence that as free trade feminism has become the dominant approach to gender mainstreaming in trade governance, policy programmes are being legitimated and deployed that leave fundamental gender inequalities in global trade relations intact. In some cases, free trade feminism even promotes new dependencies, by creating new forms of housewifization, trade productivism and trading on social reproduction. This can include the expansion of housewifization and of trading on social reproduction into new geographical or sectoral terrain.

One example of this (elucidated in Chapter 4) is how free trade feminist interventions into the food trade entail the marginalization and devaluation of subsistence agriculture, regardless of the important role this plays in supporting social reproduction. Another example is policy programmes that connect mothers with babies or young children to e-commerce platforms, which allows them to combine the export of domestically produced goods and services with reproductive labour in the home. Rather than seeing this as an intensification of the 'double burden', free trade feminists celebrate it as a new horizon of digitally enabled gender equality. From our perspective, these are not only examples of how and why free trade feminism has limited potential to redress structural inequalities in global trade. The examples also suggest that studying free trade feminism provides lessons about gender equality agendas in global governance, and about global trade governance, at a time when both are under attack.

Locating the emergence of free trade feminism

Our third main argument is that free trade feminism deploys subtle and informal trade governance mechanisms that legitimize and open new spaces for capital accumulation across the world economy, while at the same time significantly narrowing the scope for feminist and other social and environmental interventions in trade governance and politics. The underpinnings of this argument are rooted in existing literatures across feminist and critical political economy, development studies and other related areas that have engaged with, on the one hand, the business case for gender equality, and on the other, the crisis in global trade governance. This allows us to identify the broader political economic context within which free trade feminism has emerged.

Gender mainstreaming in global trade was propelled by the prevalence of the business case for gender equality, or what has more recently been referred to as the 'smart economics' paradigm, circulating within global economic governance (World Bank, 2006; Chant and Sweetman, 2012; Roberts and Soederberg, 2012; Prügl, 2021). Feminist scholars have offered many criticisms of the business case for gender equality that are relevant for our critical engagement with free trade feminism. These include its limited conceptualization of empowerment, the instrumentalization of gender equality, the homogenization and essentialization of women, and the legitimization and naturalization of global capitalism and corporate power.

The early roots of the business case can be traced back to efforts to challenge the masculinist underpinnings of and approaches to development that focused on modernization. Ester Boserup's (1970) influential book, *Women's Role in Economic Development*, made the case that women were being marginalized by development practices, such as the mechanization of agriculture, which separated women's labour from waged agricultural labour and undermined their social status. Subsequent scholarship built on these arguments to say that not only could women benefit from modernization, but that integrating women into the economy would support the achievement of development outcomes. This appeal to modernization and efficiency later became the basis upon which the Women in Development agenda was crafted (Rai, 2018).

The Women in Development agenda has been described as an 'add women and stir' approach, which seeks to integrate individual women into the economy by supporting their education, skills and opportunities to better compete with men in the market, rather than to challenge the broader political economic structures that give rise to gendered forms of inequality. It is also an approach that privileges the male productive norm, while women's roles in social reproduction and their relation to the development process are invisibilized (Kabeer, 1994). Feminists from the global South problematized the colonial and racialized ideas of economic development and linear modernization narratives and called for structural and systemic change to eliminate overlapping inequalities based on class, gender and race, and between countries (Sen and Grown, 1987).

At the UN's 1985 Second World Conference on Women in Nairobi, feminists from what was then called 'the Third World' united in support of an alternative approach to development that was later termed Gender and Development. They criticized 'liberal' approaches to empowerment that focus on individual women who are supposedly motivated by self-interest and whose empowerment is viewed in instrumentalist terms, as a means of achieving economic growth and/or broader development goals (Sardenberg, 2016 [2008], p 19; see also Esquivel, 2016). Instead, they argued for an understanding of empowerment that is contextually specific, and which entails both changes at the individual level *and* forms of structural change made possible by collective action (Sen and Grown, 1987). It was in Nairobi that gender mainstreaming was first discussed, as a strategy that could be used to centre women's issues, rather than adding them on to existing projects.

Gender mainstreaming was formally established as the primary goal for gender equality at the Fourth World Conference on Women in Beijing, held in 1995. Highlighting the need to change not only women, but also institutions, the Beijing Platform for Action called on governments and other actors to apply gender mainstreaming to all policies and programmes. This was a period when the negative impacts of the structural adjustment programmes (SAPs) that were being imposed on many countries in the global South were gaining attention. This ushered in the 'post-Washington Consensus' that recognized the need for social policies, including those aimed at improving gender equality, to accompany free market policies (Prügl, 2021). While creating the institutional space to consider the links between gender equality, economic growth and development (Razavi, 2012; Ferguson, 2015), this largely occurred through a liberal framework that instrumentalized gender equality as being good for economic growth, national competitiveness and efficient development outcomes. According to Chant and Sweetman, from Beijing onwards, 'gender equality and the empowerment of women became increasingly adopted as a goal which made simple economic sense' (Chant and Sweetman, 2012, p 519). The World Bank was key to driving this approach to gender mainstreaming (Bedford, 2005; 2009; Elson, 2009; Griffin, 2009; Berik, 2017; Calkin, 2018) and coined the phrase 'gender equality as smart economics' in a 2006 report.

The World Bank advocated the benefits of investing in women for economic development and poverty reduction, assuming that women would invest more of their money into their families than men (World Bank, 1995). As feminists have pointed out, this line of thinking homogenizes and essentializes women (and girls), who are assumed to possess the feminine virtues of altruism and care, and to be more responsible than men (and boys). It also presumes that women are cis-gendered, heterosexual and part of normative family units (Bedford, 2005; 2009; see also Lind, 2010). At the same time, as post-colonial and decolonial feminists have noted, it led to development interventions that silenced the voices of women from the global South who were projected as victims in need of 'saving' by the World Bank and other Euro-centric global institutions, 'developed' (and often colonial) countries and Western feminists (Mohanty, 1991; Benería, 1999; Bergeron, 2003; Bedford, 2009; Griffin, 2009).

Insofar as smart economics was a development paradigm, it was simultaneously a 'significant communications campaign' that sought to lend legitimacy, or what Prügl calls a 'feminist face', to neoliberalism, especially in the wake of the 2008 global financial crisis (Prügl, 2021, p 470; 2015). From its roots in development policy, the business case became diffused throughout global economic governance, including the International Monetary Fund (IMF) under the stewardship of Cristine Lagarde (Coburn, 2019; Blackmon, 2021), regional development banks (Shields and Wallin, 2015), the World Economic Forum (Elias, 2013), the OECD (Mahon, 2019) and the G20 (Waylen, 2022), among others (Schuberth and Young, 2011; Elomäki, 2015). Private corporations have also come to work in partnership with public bodies and international organizations, adopting the language of gender equality and women's empowerment and positing a win-win scenario for women and the 'bottom line' (Prügl and True, 2014; Gregoratti et al, 2018; Tornhill, 2019). Indeed, a growing coalition of capitalist states, international organizations, non-governmental organizations, academics and others have converged on the smart economics paradigm, giving rise to what Adrienne Roberts refers to as a political economic project of 'transnational business feminism' (Roberts, 2015b). Ultimately, this project seeks to strengthen neoliberal capitalism, and the role of corporations therein, by legitimizing market-based knowledge about women and gender relations and advocating business-driven solutions to much longer-standing, structural, socioeconomic problems (see also Elias, 2013; Griffin, 2013; Prügl, 2015; Tornhill, 2019).

The business case for gender equality, with its underlying assumptions, policy agendas, and coalitions of committed actors, entered into global trade governance relatively late compared to other areas of global economic governance. Similarly to how the smart economics paradigm gained traction in the wake of the 2008 financial crisis, gender mainstreaming in trade gained traction during a period of profound crisis for WTO-based trade governance. Talk of crisis had long been a discursive strategy in driving trade liberalization efforts forward (Wilkinson, 2013). The mid-2010s, however, saw a breakdown in GATT/WTO trade governance, with development questions lying at the heart of irreconcilable political differences, which put an end to extensive multilateral trade liberalization.

On the eve of the emergence of the gender and trade agenda, in December 2015, the US and allies refused to renew the negotiating mandate for the Doha Development Agenda at the WTO Ministerial Conference in Nairobi, triggering the first discontinuation of a multilateral round of trade negotiations in GATT/WTO history (Wilkinson et al, 2016). The Doha Development Round had been launched in 2001 following the 9/11 attacks on New York and Washington, and had initially been expected to redress long-standing grievances about structural imbalances in WTO rules that favour developed over developing country members (Abbott, 2003). Developing countries had raised such structural imbalances in multilateral trade negotiating fora of the 1940s and 1950s (Hudec, 1992; Helleiner, 2014), which eventually led to the adoption of Part IV of the GATT (titled 'Trade and Development'), the GATT Enabling Clause, and also the creation of UNCTAD, in the 1960s and 1970s. Henceforth, GATT rules applied differentially to developing countries, which also did not need to reciprocate trade concessions in negotiating rounds (Hudec, 1992).

The Doha Development Round was fraught by many issues that were linked to concerns over sustainable development and poverty reduction. These included trade rules and market access conditions in agriculture (most famously around domestic support programmes for farmers in exporting nations, some of which distorted world markets, see Clapp, 2006), service and investment negotiations (where developed countries were eager to develop new rules, see Hoekman and Mattoo, 2013), and the state of the WTO Agreement on Trade-Related Aspects of Intellectual Property Rights (TRIPS) (in particular in relation to various public health crisis of the early 2000s, and notably the HIV/AIDS pandemic, see Scott and Harman, 2013).

By the time of the Doha Round, many developing country members had invested heavily in coalition-building and staged effective walk outs, for example during the 2003 WTO Ministerial Conference in Cancún (Narlikar and Wilkinson, 2004; see also Chen, A., 2006). Commentators also suggested that the WTO required institutional and procedural reform to reflect the new global economic realities resulting from the rise of emerging economies, such as China, Brazil and India, to the status of global trade powers (Jones, 2010).

From the 2000s onwards, rule-making activity on global trade began gradually moving into the realm of bilateral and regional trade agreements, as the US adopted 'competitive liberalization' under George W. Bush in 2001 in order to improve its position in the global trading system (Evenett and Meier, 2008). As the WTO negotiating function showed further signs of stalling, many advanced economies in particular started pursuing their trade interests through FTAs (Trommer, 2017). Following further multilateral negotiating collapses, most famously the July 2008 WTO meeting in Geneva, developed country members stood accused of 'maintaining a high level of ambition in areas of interest' to them, 'whilst reducing the ambition in areas of interest to developing countries' (Ismail, 2009, p 580).

In the aftermath of the 2008 global financial crisis, the narrative that 'trade can be an effective tool for reducing poverty and enhancing growth in developing countries' (G20 Seoul Summit Leaders Declaration, 2010, cited in Scott and Wilkinson, 2012, p 17) increasingly gained traction in global governance circles. In the new arena of bilateral trade governance, many of the special rules and exemptions available to developing country members in the GATT/WTO system were gradually removed, and developing countries were increasingly treated as 'equal partners' in North–South trade negotiations (DiCaprio and Trommer, 2010). Such narratives were in part spurred by newly emerging trade and development discourses that saw GVC integration as providing new mechanisms for 'trading out' of poverty (Ravenhill, 2014). In this context, it was argued that the WTO needed to be transformed into an organization that, rather than managing trade between nations, would make rules and regulations that supported the movement of goods, services, money and people with a view to enabling globalized production taking place via GVCs (Baldwin, 2014).

The WTO did not reform to accommodate the new power politics in the world economy, nor to suit the operations of GVCs in the 21st century. Instead, as Kristen Hopewell (2016) has argued, emerging powers such as China, Brazil and India learned to express their own interests and preferences within the WTO system, to the point of 'breaking the WTO'. As Hopewell (2022) cautions, this did not resolve the fundamental inequalities of the GATT/WTO system, as many poor developing countries remained in structurally weak positions vis-à-vis developed and emerging economies. The current trend towards plurilateral, rather than multilateral, decision-making in the WTO has also been critiqued as undermining the ability of developing countries to force a return to resolving outstanding Doha Round issues (Wilkinson, 2017).

At the time of writing, the WTO is widely perceived to be limping from one uneventful Ministerial Conference to the next. Its once powerful dispute settlement system that imposed neoliberal trade rules on governments all around the world has fallen victim to US sentiments that trade multilateralism had gone too far (Condon, 2018). While we do not see a new dawn for the WTO, we nonetheless present a take on multilateral trade governance that is different to the 'downfall of the WTO' perspectives that are common among commentators (Döpfner, 2025).

As our analysis shows, the WTO has retained its position as a central forum of global trade governance, that brings together global policy elites from international, regional and national trade governance, but also from other global governance arenas. Despite a negotiating and adjudication crisis, WTO members continue to make collective decisions through WTO political organs that engage in both formal and informal negotiations (Azmeh, 2024a; Peres, 2024). The Gender Unit in the WTO Secretariat, for example, has agency and influence, in particular working in tandem with member states and other institutions. As we document, it has helped shape trade policy making, in particular in the area of trade and development, across the global economy over the past ten years. To achieve this, it has relied on various forms of formal and informal decision-making, technical assistance and policy review, agenda-setting, and production and dissemination of knowledge about gender and trade policy. While this may be a far cry from being the 'engine of neoliberal globalization', it is also the case that global trade policy elites continue to advance neoliberal trade agendas through the WTO forum.

We suggest that free trade feminism legitimates and advances neoliberal gender equality *and* neoliberal trade governance agendas all around the world, at a time when many commentators assume that neoliberal policy agendas are 'dead'. As we discuss throughout the book, this is problematic from the perspective of more critical and transformative feminist trade politics (Hannah et al, 2021a; 2022) in several respects. For one, free trade feminism's framing of supposedly un- or under-productive labour, including reproductive and subsistence labour, as obstacles to women's empowerment through trade presents a missed opportunity to re-value social reproduction in trade governance and to develop trade policies that support it. By actively working to commodify reproductive and subsistence labour, free trade feminism promotes trading on social reproduction, despite its links to variegated crises and depletion through social reproduction. These approaches present forms of trade and development interventions that corporations and investors can and do support, but that nonetheless cement and even risk expanding gendered forms of inequality across the world economy. Contrary to the assumption that even modest efforts to address gender inequality are useful in opening spaces that may be further wrenched open by others, we show here that free trade feminism forecloses avenues for progressive trade governance and advances neoliberal trade policies, in particular in the trade and development domain, at a time when the 'engine' of neoliberal globalization is broken.

Conceptualizing gender and trade

While free trade feminism is new, the acknowledgement that trade has gendered impacts is not. Here we survey gender and trade literatures across economics, feminist economics, political economy, development studies and legal studies, in order to locate both our own approach and the theoretical underpinnings of free trade feminism.

There has been for some time a range of different conceptualizations of the links between gender and trade, notably between those that focus on gender as an empirical category, versus those that draw attention to gender relations in broader analytical terms and take into account that trade practices and policies are gendered. Within both approaches, there is a further difference between those who tend to see trade liberalization as a means of achieving gender equality (even if some adjustments are needed) and those who see trade liberalization as creating some economic gains while also (re)producing the exploitation and marginalization of certain groups of people, including women and feminized others.

Starting with economics, trade economists have long drawn on Garry Becker's (1971) theory of discrimination to argue that women stand to gain even more than men from trade liberalization (for example, Baldwin, 1995; Busse and Spielmann, 2006; Winters and Martuscelli, 2014). According to Becker's theory, which is frequently cited by free trade feminists, increased competition brought about by trade liberalization makes it costly for employers to maintain wage discrimination among different groups of workers. Neoclassical economists further believe that trade liberalization can improve the position of women across the global economy who earn less and work under worse conditions than men (for example, Wood, 1991).

Where women's employment and wages do not improve under trade liberalization, neoclassical economists have attributed this to factors such as sector-specific skills requirements and technology intensity and endowment, levels of national development and variations in adherence to labour standards (Busse and Spielmann, 2006; Juhn et al, 2013). They believe that tariff reductions can benefit women when they lead to 'blue-collar' jobs being replaced by 'white-collar jobs', that is, as competition leads to investments in new areas and technologies (Juhn et al, 2013). Some studies conducted in poor countries show that there can be both positive and negative impacts of trade liberalization on households. The impact depends on whether households' incomes are generated in export-competing or import-competing sectors (see also Winters and Martuscelli, 2014).

Neoclassical economists predominantly understand and analyse gender empirically, asking how men and women are differentially affected by, and differentially affect, trade flows. This literature understands gender-based discrimination to primarily result from social values, or 'socio-cultural habits' (Busse and Spielmann, 2006, p 363), while trade flows and trade policies are thought to be in and of themselves gender-neutral. Over the years, economists have also increasingly argued that reducing gender inequality in society has positive impacts on trade expansion, and therefore on economic growth and development (Busse and Spielmann, 2006; Ryu and Nam, 2024). As we demonstrate throughout the book, these are assumptions that free trade feminism shares with neoclassical economics.

Feminist trade economists, political economists, legal scholars and others have sought to understand 'how masculinity and femininity – gender understood as a meaning system' (Peterson, 2005, p 499) produce and are produced by global trade relations. Feminist trade economists posit that gender norms and power relations permeate economic spaces, including institutions (Fontana and Wood, 2000; Fontana, 2004; van Staveren et al, 2007). While their work often focuses on how trade impacts women's employment and wages in the 'productive' economy, they also explore the impact of trade policies on reproductive labour, such as household chores and care work (Elson et al, 2007a; Fontana, 2007).

Feminist trade economists challenge the assumption made by neoclassical economists that trade liberalization will necessarily benefit women. They argue that the impact of trade policies on gender relations depends on the pre-existing socioeconomic and political context of a given country (for example, Çağatay, 2005; Chamarbagwala, 2006; van Staveren et al, 2007). These scholars caution that trade liberalization can have negative effects on gender equality (Kucera and Milberg, 2007; Vijaya, 2007) and that social inequality can constitute a comparative advantage in its own right (Elson and Pearson, 1981; Seguino, 2000; Berik et al, 2004; Çağatay, 2005).

When it comes to the productive economy, feminist economists critique the feminization of labour and the feminization of the conditions of work across the global economy. Feminization of labour refers to the phenomenon whereby work forces are mostly made up of women rather than of men, for example, where trade policies encourage gender segmented labour markets in offshore manufacturing (Domínguez-Villalobos and Brown-Grossman, 2010). The feminization of the conditions of work refers to 'informalization, causualization and general disempowerment of workers vis-a-vis capital' (Çağatay, 2005, p 13).

Regarding the reproductive sphere, Diane Elson and colleagues (Elson et al 2007b) argue that any loss of government revenue (such as through a reduction of tariffs) may impact users of public services, a disproportionate share of whom are women (as well as the poor and specific marginalized groups), as public services are often scaled back during fiscal contraction. Feminist economists argue that service trade liberalization and the embedding of IPRs in trade relations are feminist concerns (Armah, 1995a; 1995b; Williams, 2007), because regulatory shifts towards market-based public provisioning tend to benefit middle- and high-income social groups, which tend to be male, white and middle-aged on aggregate (Elson and Çağatay, 2000).

Feminist economists also draw attention to the wider impacts of trade liberalization on the lives of women. In the absence of additional resources, reproductive labour may be cut back as women enter into the formal labour force, which can lead to decreasing levels of care work performed overall (Melanson, 2005; Fontana, 2007). While for some women export-oriented factory employment can support personal liberation from family structures (Wolf, 1992), others are pressured into factory work by patriarchal structures and family interest (Pearson, 1998). Women's increased involvement in paid work following trade liberalization can create a violent backlash in the household, usually from household members who hold firm to patriarchal norms (Melanson, 2005). A small number of studies explore how gendered forms of inequality intersect with other inequality dimensions such as class and race under trade liberalization (Armah, 1995a; 1995b).

Free trade feminism shares an awareness of women's reproductive labour and of the subordinated position of women in patriarchal societies. However, as we argue throughout, it does not acknowledge nor directly address how trade policies interact with these forms of inequality, which are understood as emanating from social and cultural relations and as obstacles to women's participation in global trade.

The politics and governance of global trade have been studied by feminists working in global politics, political economy, development studies and international law. These scholars place emphasis on how gendered social norms and power relations interact with trade institutions, policy processes and outcomes. They share a broad consensus that the gendered effects of trade are palpable across the spheres of production, consumption and reproduction. This literature critiques how gendered dichotomies of state/market, economy/society, production/social reproduction, economic law/human rights law, and so on, generate false notions that trade governance can and should be separated from its human, social and environmental impacts (Pahuja, 2000; True, 2009; Choudhury, 2012; Hannah et al, 2021a; Bahri and Amaral, 2024).

While much of the existing feminist research in this area focuses on women, some scholars have made explicit their concern for the intersectional dimensions of inequality (Mengesha, 2008; Gammage and Momodu, 2020; Kuhlmann, 2021; Price, 2025). A small number of contributions focus on LGBTQIA+ rights (for example, Bhala and Wood, 2018), gender identity and sexual orientation protections in trade agreements (for example, Galbraith and Lu, 2019) or use queer theory to study trade governance (for example, O'Hara, 2022). To date, there is very little scholarship that focuses on the racial politics of global trade, or on the intersections of gender and race in trade governance (for exceptions see Singh, 2017; 2021; Helleiner, 2023a; Price, 2025).

Recent research on gender mainstreaming in global trade governance focuses on the new 'gender chapters' and gender-related clauses and provisions that have been integrated into a growing number of FTAs. Legal scholars in particular critique the limited potential of these measures to redress the gendered inequalities of trade, not least because they are not legally enforceable, and are often not accompanied by the financial resources needed to make implementation meaningful (Zakaria, 2018; Bhala and Wood, 2018; Bahri, 2019; 2020; 2025; Bahri and Boklan, 2022). Beyond legal provisions, gender and trade policy initiatives often lack 'concrete measures to ensure women's equality in the workplace and in society more broadly' (Price, 2018, p 120). Overall, these scholars argue that efforts to 'gender' trade governance are political in nature and are unlikely to produce tangible economic outcomes (Williams, 2007; True, 2008; Price, 2018; Goff, 2021; Hannah et al, 2022).

Some scholars are concerned that gender and trade initiatives may instrumentalize gender goals (Altan-Olcay, 2020; Price, 2025). For example, where policy makers separate a focus on gender and trade from labour and trade concerns, they risk perpetuating neoliberal policy projects (Macdonald, 2024; Price, 2025). This scholarship is divided between those who believe that gender mainstreaming in trade governance is flawed but something that can and should be salvaged (for example, Acharya et al, 2019; Bahri et al, 2023; Bahri and Amaral, 2024; Bahri, 2025) and those, including ourselves, who believe that redressing gender imbalances requires a radical restructuring of current global trade arrangements and modes of trade governance (for example, Hannah et al, 2022; Trommer, 2022; Price, 2025). Free trade feminism sides with the former position and aims to redress gender imbalances in trade while preserving the liberal global trade order.

The literature on feminist and women's civil society organizations mobilizing around trade issues reveals that despite the recent prominence of gender in trade governance, feminist and women's voices have tended to remain on the margins of trade. Female representation in trade policy making and governance continues to be poor (Bandele, 2016). Feminist contestations of economic globalization have also typically failed to influence trade policy making (Macdonald, 2002) and alter-globalization and anti-free trade movements have traditionally not engaged with gender issues (Rice, 2010). This situation persists despite the fact that feminist and women's civil society groups have been actively involved in campaigns designed to influence the politics of global trade from the very start. Even when women are afforded a presence in trade governance settings, as occurred during the

2003 WTO Ministerial Conference in Cancún, this has perpetuated the exclusion of certain groups of (non-elite) women, with the division between 'insiders' and 'outsiders' mapping onto both class and colour hierarchies (Liebowitz, 2008, p 224).

While we draw on many of the insights outlined here, we also depart from existing gender and trade literatures. Empirically, our study is unique in looking across global trade governance to document and analyse the rise of free trade feminism. We also situate this within wider developments in the global political economy, historically and up to the present. We develop and apply an original feminist political economy framework that highlights the role of gender norms and power relations in producing and reproducing capitalist trade relations globally, including their historically specific modes of operation and wider societal, economic, political and environmental effects. This allows us to make sense of how gender became governable in trade institutions, what the gender and trade agenda implies for challenging inequality in the global economy moving forward, and what feminist alternatives to free trade feminism should and do exist.

Chapter overview

The next chapter outlines our feminist political economy of trade perspective. It tells the story of the evolution of global trade relations over the past few centuries, going back to the colonial period. But we tell this story from a unique feminist political economy vantage point, demonstrating the co-constitutive nature of gender and global trade relations. We organize this discussion around three conceptual devices – housewifization, trade productivism and trading on social reproduction – which allow us to show how gender inequalities are entangled with trade inequalities historically and up to the present. These conceptual devices are used subsequently to make sense of free trade feminism.

Chapter 3 details the rise of gender mainstreaming in trade in the mid-2010s, and shows how and why free trade feminism gradually came to replace alternative approaches, most notably in the wake of the COVID-19 pandemic. We identify how specific actors, particularly gender units within the Secretariats of the WTO, UNCTAD and the ITC, formulated the case that free trade and gender equality are mutually conducive, and drove gender mainstreaming initiatives that focused narrowly on empowering women entrepreneurs and women exporters via market-centric and neoliberal policy tools. We further show how this marginalized alternative views.

Chapter 4 focuses on free trade feminist interventions in the food trade. We show how free trade feminism perpetuates a trade productivist approach to food by focusing on how to improve the productivity of women working in food and agriculture, which generally involves commercialization and integration into agricultural value chains. The counterpart to this is the housewifization of a host of labour relations that are considered to be un- or under-productive from the perspective of capital, including subsistence labour, despite what this means from the perspective of life-making. We argue that this approach overlooks important, and long-standing, controversies over agricultural trade, including regarding 'the trade-ification' (Clapp, 2017a) of food security and sustainability, which have contributed to the current deadlock in multilateral trade governance. They do so while creating new profit-making frontiers for food corporations and investors.

Chapter 5 turns its attention to the digital trade arena, which is reshaping some of the traditional assumptions about what is traded, how, and with whom, with profound implications for relations of production and social reproduction. We show how free trade feminism overwhelmingly focuses on how best to integrate women into the digital economy, namely by connecting them to e-commerce platforms and supporting digital inclusion. We argue that this approach is overly narrow in its focus and works to depoliticize the expansion of the digital economy, to fuel the digital housewifization of women's labour, and to deepen and legitimize the commodification, privatization and digitization of social reproduction. We suggest that free trade feminism supports the current approach to digital trade governance that is being driven by corporate interests, and backed by the US, China and the European Union (EU). In so doing, it is helping to fuel corporate power and deepen existing inequalities between countries, between capital and labour, and along gendered lines while marginalizing feminist alternatives.

The concluding chapter argues that it is necessary to move beyond free trade feminism and towards feminist ontologies of global trade in order to challenge the ways in which global trade produces and reproduces global inequalities. We argue that free trade feminism has remained surprisingly resilient in the face of the challenges that Donald Trump is posing to the existing multilateral trading system. But, there is and must be another way forward. The path that this will take is uncertain, but possibilities abound, both in the ideas and actions of the more structurally oriented trade governance institutions and in the alternative, transformative, feminist visions of trade that have been outlined by civil society and social movements, including in the areas of food and digital trade.

2

Gender, Inequality and Global Trade

Free trade feminism assumes that women are excluded, or insufficiently integrated, into global trade. Despite acknowledging that gender-based inequalities in global trade relations exist, free trade feminism largely understands the economy and society to constitute separate, if interlinked, spheres. The trade policy elites enacting free trade feminist ideas and policy initiatives typically assume trade to be a transnational exchange mechanism that creates economic growth and distributes resources efficiently. Gender-based inequalities in trade are presumed to derive from societal and cultural norms and values and are believed to hinder the proper workings of (in principle efficient) transnational economic exchange.

Our understanding of the links between gender, inequality and global trade differs radically from this view. At the heart of our feminist political economy of trade lies the insight that the historical evolution of global trade relations has unfolded on gendered terrain. Rather than thinking of women as historically being excluded from trade, we understand gendered hierarchies and exploitations to be intrinsic to the unequal trade relations of global capitalism. Put differently, we see gendered power relations as foundational features of how global trade relations have been forged historically, and global trade relations as inherent to the historical production and reproduction of gendered inequalities.

In this chapter, we provide a detailed discussion of our theoretical premise that unequal gender relations and unequal trade relations are co-constitutive in the world economy, in ways that are specific to space and time. We organize our discussion around three conceptual devices that capture our ontological understanding of how gendered social relations have shaped and have been shaped by global trade. In epistemological terms, the three concepts point to the main ways in which we understand historically contingent gendered power relations to permeate trade governance today.

The concepts inform our analysis of gender and trade agendas in global governance in subsequent chapters.

The first concept is 'housewifization' (Mies, 1998 [1986]). We use housewifization to refer to the structural entanglements of global trade relations with gendered and colonial global divisions of labour that emerged under imperialism, and that continue on to the present day. The concept allows us to see how global trade, from the colonial period onward, has depended on the naturalization, invisibilization and exploitation of women's work in the capitalist core and the exploitation of gendered and racialized labour in the colonies. It also allows us to see how these processes are structurally linked to each other, and to the appropriation of nature.

Second, we develop the concept of 'trade productivism'. Relying on scholarship that highlights the gendered hierarchies underpinning trade theories and governance mechanisms (for instance, van Staveren et al, 2007; Hannah et al, 2021a; 2022), we document the historical construction of the mistaken idea that trade is gender-neutral, and the creation of political institutions that govern trade accordingly during the Bretton Woods period. We juxtapose the masculinist trade theories and governance techniques of this era with public and scholarly trade debates of the 19th century. Nineteenth-century debates actively incorporated concerns for the impacts of trade on social relations, including the social relations of gender and imperialism, and the voices of 'free trade feminists' of the era (Palen, 2024). This allows us to see how trade productivism is a construct of the immediate post-Second World War period, when gender and broader social concerns, as well as women's voices, were actively disappeared from trade theory and policy making.

Finally, our concept of 'trading on social reproduction' combines the structuralist/materialist emphasis of housewifization and the ideational/institutionalist emphasis of trade productivism, showing how the gendered dimensions of the political economy of trade are interwoven and co-constitutive in practice. We use trading on social reproduction to highlight how the neoliberal restructuring of the global economy in the 1970s and 1980s created new forms of gendered trade dependencies and exploitations across the global political economy. On the one hand, it did so by intensifying and expanding housewifization (Elson and Pearson, 1981; Mezzadri, 2017). On the other hand, novel trade laws and regulations were designed to enable neoliberal restructuring. As we show, the 'new trade politics' (Young and Peterson, 2006) of the neoliberal era enabled the commodification, financialization and trade of social reproduction across borders. Corporations and investors could now rely on global trade as a mechanism for directly capitalizing on reproductive, subsistence and informal labour and on life-making work, in parallel ways to how they historically capitalized on transnational production. Trading on social reproduction created new forms of exploitation, as global commodity chains and care chains relying on gendered and racialized divisions of labour became *both* ever more entangled *and* ever more central to the world economy. It also further normalized capitalism's extractivist relationship with nature.

As we will show in later chapters, despite presenting trade governance agendas that combine women's empowerment with trade expansion as the solution to gender inequality, free trade feminism usually works with partial understandings at best of how the material, ideational and institutional dimensions of global trade are structurally related to gender-based and other forms of inequality. These insights give us reason for concern that free trade feminism in global governance works to legitimize and propel forward structural inequalities in the global political economy.

Housewifization and colonial trade relations

Today's unequal global trade relations find their historical origin in the central role that commerce played in European imperialism and settler-colonialism, which expanded across the world between the 15th and the 20th centuries. As dependency and world systems theorists have argued, the history of world trade is not a story of organizing economic exchange in support of 'mutual benefit' or 'comparative advantage'. It is a history of hierarchical integration, whereby trade has been structured, from the colonial period onwards, in ways that enrich the core countries at the expense of an exploited periphery, and perpetuate economic dependence and underdevelopment (Frank, 1967; dos Santos, 1970; Amin, 1974; Wallerstein, 1974).

While we largely agree with this analysis, we aim to overcome the gender-blindness of this scholarship. Building on arguments made by Maria Mies and others in the 1980s and 1990s, we are not only concerned with how waged and coerced labour was integrated into European-dominated global trade circuits that promoted imperialism. We also foreground the role that embodied, non-waged and subjugated labour played in this historical process. The divides and hierarchies between productive/reproductive, masculinized/feminized, free/unfree, colonizer/colonized labour that were created across these centuries live on in the present-day gendered power relations of global trade.

Trade and colonial divisions of labour

To begin with the more familiar part of the story, the European world economy was formed during what Immanuel Wallerstein (1974) called 'the long 16th century', lasting from roughly 1450 until 1640, when the Spanish and Portuguese empires dominated European trade with the so-called 'New World'. By the 17th century, trading companies, particularly those associated with the Dutch and the British, exercised trade monopolies and expanded the mercantilist system across the world economy. Imperial states granted them trading rights, as well as the ability to make war and peace, and to exercise rights over colonized peoples. This included profiting from the slave trade and the trade of goods produced by forced labour (Alessandrini, 2022, p 627). In the 18th and 19th centuries, trading companies were also increasingly concerned with territorial conquest and rule (Zeleza, 1993). Trade in human beings was a central feature of imperial trade relations, entailing the enslavement and transportation of millions of Africans who were forced to work in extractive industries and plantations in the Americas. This also facilitated the appropriation of indigenous land and resources.

Between the 16th and 19th century, such trade was organized into commodity chains, which were 'network[s] of labor and production processes whose end result is a finished commodity' (Hopkins and Wallerstein, 1986, p 159). Imperial powers obtained raw materials from trading with colonies and created dependent markets for industrial and manufacturing outputs (Zeleza, 1993; Watson, 2017; Bhambra, 2020). Colonial policies often actively identified which primary commodities were to be resourced from which regions, laying the foundations of persisting 'comparative advantages' in these commodities (Barry, 1971; Zeleza, 1993). For example, in West Africa, the French colonial administration determined cocoa to be the focus of agriculture in Ivory Coast, peanuts in Senegal, cotton in Mali, and so on. Trade with the periphery was also of interest from the perspective of capital accumulation, because the return to labour in these places was less than what it would be in the centre (Amin, 1974, p 13).

In their analyses, world systems theorists have largely focused on how waged and coerced labour are foundational to the extraction of value through trade inequalities and dependencies. They have shown that unequal trading arrangements rested on colonial divisions of labour, which shaped unequal core–periphery relations in the world economy, as well as inequalities within countries (Frank, 1967; dos Santos, 1970; Wallerstein, 1974; Mies, 1998 [1986]). They also recognized that these arrangements involved many different types of labour, including waged labour, household labour, share labour, slave labour, serf labour and other coerced labour (Hopkins and Wallerstein, 1986, p 166). Yet, it was feminist scholarship that took up the task of emphasizing the role that household labour and reproductive labour more broadly have played in constructing unequal relations of exchange across the world economy.

In her landmark contribution, *Patriarchy and Accumulation on a World Scale*, Mies (1998 [1986]) offers a feminist account of how the expansion of colonial trade established relations of dependency between capital and the unpaid reproductive labour of women, in both the core and the periphery of the world economy. A key dynamic here is what Mies calls housewifization.

Housewifization describes the process through which capitalist patriarchy harnesses various types of non-waged work to capital accumulation across the global economy, while simultaneously externalizing, naturalizing and devaluing this work. The non-waged reproductive labour performed in households and the non-waged labour performed in the colonies are thus structurally connected, and fundamental to how global trade was historically put into the service of capital accumulation (Mies, 1982; 1998 [1986]).

Trade and housewifization

Mies first used housewifization in her book *The Lace Makers of Narsapur* (1982), which was based on ethnographic research with women producing lace for export in the Andhra Pradesh region of India. These women, who worked long hours for no or low pay, created value for capital at the same time as this work accelerated their pauperization. Their work was systematically disguised as housework, which served to justify low pay and exclusion from formal labour statistics and protections (see also Mezzadri, 2017).

Building on Rosa Luxemburg's insight that capital accumulation depends on the continued exploitation of 'non-capitalist' relations, Mies (1998 [1986], pp 74–77) argues in *Patriarchy and Accumulation on a World Scale* that the emergence and expansion of global capitalism involved the violent subjugation of women and colonized others, and the invisibilization of a wide range of unpaid, informal, subsistence-oriented, forced and non-standard labour (see also Mies et al, 1988; Federici, 2004; Von Werlhof, 2007). These processes of subjugating and exploiting the 'general production of life' (Mies, 1998 [1986], p 48) have operated alongside proletarianization and land and labour expropriation to provide the material foundations for trade from the commodity chains of the colonial era up to the present.

For Mies (1998 [1986], p ix), as for feminist scholars involved in the so-called 'domestic labour debates' of the 1970s and 1980s (Dalla Costa and James, 1972; Federici, 1974; Davis, 1983), the process of deriving value from the general production of life rests on the ideological construction of women as mothers, wives and housewives. Silvia Federici, for example, writes that with the demise of the subsistence economy in Europe,

> the unity of production and reproduction which has been typical of all societies based on production-for-use came to an end, as these activities became the carriers of different social relations and were sexually differentiated. In the new monetary regime, only production-for-market was defined as a value-creating activity, whereas the reproduction of the worker began to be considered as valueless from an economic viewpoint and even ceased to be considered as work. (Federici, 2004, p 75)

The active devaluation and naturalization of the labour associated with women and feminized others is thus central to global capital accumulation. Mies (1998 [1986], p 110) explains that housewifization involves 'the externalisation, or ex-territorialisation of costs which otherwise would have to be covered by the capitalists. This means women's labour is considered a natural resource, freely available like air and water'.

From our perspective, Mies usefully highlights how the conditions of domestic labour in Europe and labour in the colonies are structurally linked, as they emerged together through colonial trade expansion. This is not to suggest that there is an equivalence between the domestic labour in Europe and labour in the colonies. Rather, the conditions in which this labour is performed are structurally connected by virtue of the historical unfolding of capitalism (Bhattacharyya, 2018, p 41). According to Mies, housewifization unfolds in the colonies through their externalization, or ex-territorialization. Colonizers see colonized subjects as lying outside 'civilized society', assume colonized lands to be 'virgin territory', and declare the land and people 'as wild, savage nature, waiting to be exploited and tamed by the male civilizers' (Mies, 1998 [1986], 75). As her later work with Vandana Shiva (Mies and Shiva, 1993) further stresses, capital accumulation thus also depends on the exploitation of nature, which is subjected to similar processes of feminization, naturalization and devaluation, including through trade governance mechanisms.

Conceptualizing housewifization

Our conceptualization of housewifization is informed by Mies' (1998 [1986], p 48) insight that value creation under capitalist trade involves 'the superexploitation of non-wage labourers (women, colonies, peasants) upon which wage labour exploitation then is possible'. We derive from Mies the understanding that the contemporary global trade order emerged through a long historical process whereby capital accumulation came to rely, and largely continues to rely, on actively constructed divides and hierarchies among productive/reproductive, free/unfree, colonizer/colonized labour, as well as economy/nature. Our theoretical lens emphasizes how the exploitation of gendered and racialized work performed in different parts of the world economy is structurally linked through global trade, which is one essential dimension of co-constitutive gender and trade inequalities.

At the same time, we depart from Mies' conceptualization of 'women' as a sex-based, universal and biological category and do not share her critique of what she calls 'gender ideology'.[1] As post-colonial and decolonial feminist scholars have argued, part of the colonial project entailed the creation of sex binaries and the imposition of heteronormative, cis-normative and hetero-patriarchal structures of power (Federici, 2004, pp 110–112; Lugones, 2007). We understand these impositions to be part of the historical process of housewifization and, as explained in Chapter 1, understand sex and gender to be social and historical constructs.

Our theoretical and conceptual perspective aligns with the emphasis that Diane Elson and Ruth Pearson (1981) place on the interconnectedness of gendered, international and class-based inequalities in global production networks. They argued that as competitive pressures to increase productivity in the 1970s drove capital to move production to the 'Third World', women were seen as being 'naturally' inclined to work in the world factory. Women were seen as ideal workers because they 'are considered not only to have naturally nimble fingers, but also to be naturally more docile and willing to accept tough work discipline, and naturally less inclined to join trade unions, than men; and to be naturally more suited to tedious, repetitious, monotonous work' (Elson and Pearson, 1981, p 93). These women were paid less than men, which was linked to their secondary status in the labour market – itself connected to the socially constructed sexual division of labour, or as Mies would put it, to their housewifization. This then reinforced the devaluation and subordination of the contributions that women, as well as other feminized and racialized groups, make to production and social reproduction. As Spike Peterson (2005, pp 507–508) observes, 'feminisation devalorises not only women but also racially, culturally and economically marginalised men and work that is deemed unskilled, menial and "merely" reproductive'.

Our understanding of housewifization is also informed by wider scholarly traditions. Marxist and decolonial feminist scholars have used the concept to explain how a wide range of un/under-paid activities, from domestic work, sweatshop work and certain forms of gig work to commercial surrogacy, are connected by virtue of being deemed unproductive or reproductive (Vertommen, 2025). Feminist political economists have documented that feminization and devaluation can be observed across the global political economy (Standing, 1999; Peterson, 2005; Bakker, 2007; LeBaron and Gore, 2020; Mezzadri, 2021). Racial capitalism scholarship has shown how the hierarchical positioning of workers in capitalism is rooted in colonialism and relies on the rendering of racialized populations as 'disposable' (Shilliam, 2018; Robinson, 2021 [1983]), and on the 'reproduction-production nexus' (Bhattacharyya, 2018; Gore, 2025).

Our understanding of housewifization also incorporates insights from decolonial economic history scholarship that has highlighted how pre-colonial forms of economic exchange persisted across the imperial era and operated alongside colonial trade in varying relations of cooperation and conflict (Zeleza, 1993). Pre-colonial traders and their trading networks typically dated back many centuries, covered vast geographical distances, supported pre-colonial political economies of wealth creation, life-making and social organization, and were embedded in pre-colonial political orders.

Extending Mies' framework, we can say that the pre-colonial trade relations of colonized peoples were themselves housewifized in the historical process of capitalist trade expansion. Their externalization and ex-territorialization occurred as pre-colonial traders and trading networks in the colonies were gradually pushed outside of the remit of the colonial state and its officially sanctioned economy that was dominated by colonial traders and corporations (Zeleza, 1993). Examples of such practices included the denial of credit and overseas trade to local traders by colonial administrations (Harding, 1992). However, pre-colonial traders and their trading networks persist into the present day (Meagher, 2009) and women often occupy key positions within them (see, for instance, Marfaing and Sow, 1999). As we will see in later chapters, their existence appears promising to free trade feminist agendas of empowering women through trade but poses difficult challenges to Western-centric trade thinking and policy making.

This points to the intersections of housewifization with how gendered ideas, norms and power relations shape trade theory and governance. We qualify the currently dominant mode of thinking and governing trade through our concept of trade productivism, which we discuss next.

Trade productivism and the Bretton Woods era

As feminist trade economists have shown, trade theory and trade policy making are 'shaped by the system of gendered power in which they are formulated and implemented' (Elson et al, 2007a, p 1). This includes not only the gendered labour relations that we discussed in the previous section. It also includes gendered assumptions about what economic activities, rationalities and aims are of value to society that underlie different forms of theorizing and governing the economy. Notably, there exist hierarchies in economic theorizing and policy making between masculinized economic activities, rationalities and values that are venerated and promoted (such as profit-seeking and risk-taking), and feminized economic activities, rationalities and values that are devalued, marginalized or fully excluded (such as altruism and care) (Benería, 1999; Ferber and Nelson, 2003).

Our second concept, trade productivism, refers to trade theories and governance techniques that are dominated by masculinist rationalities and values. We trace its historical origins by showing how, in the immediate post-Second World War period, trade theorists and policy makers considered unpaid labour, reproductive labour, social reproduction and the social relations of gender to be practically entirely irrelevant to transnational commercial exchange.

These ideational and governance approaches, dominant across the 1940s, 1950s and 1960s, were far from self-evident. Instead, scholarly and public concern for how trade interacted with women's roles in society, reproduction of the working class and 'social progress' were actively disappeared from trade debates with the emergence of neoclassical trade theory and embedded liberal trade governance. Trade productivism's false notion that trade is, in and of itself, gender-neutral, and its governance technique of eclipsing or marginalizing gender relations in trade law and policy making, are thus historically contingent ideational and institutional dimensions of the present-day gendered power relations of global trade.

Trade and post-Second World War global economic governance

To discuss trade productivism, we recall again the more familiar part of the story. We begin with the 1944 Bretton Woods Conference, where Allied nations discussed the post-Second World War global economic order. The conference provided momentum for wide-reaching dismantling of protectionist tariff regimes, particularly in industrial and manufacturing products, through newly created trade governance institutions, most famously the GATT. Many of the institutions created over the next decades actively participate in the gender and trade agenda in global trade governance today (see Table 2.1).

During the Bretton Woods decades, the global economy witnessed considerable trade expansion. This trade growth was due in part to the lowering of industrial and manufacturing tariffs through consecutive rounds

Table 2.1: International organizations with a trade mandate created between 1944 and 1969

Year of creation	International organization
1944	International Bank for Reconstruction and Development*
1947	General Agreement on Tariffs and Trade*
1948	Economic Commission for Latin America and the Caribbean*
1948	Organisation for Economic Co-operation and Development*
1949	Council of Mutual Assistance
1958	European Economic Community*
1958	United Nations Economic Commission for Africa*
1963	Organization of African Union
1964	United Nations Conference on Trade and Development*
1964	International Trade Centre*
1965	Caribbean Free Trade Association
1967	Association of South Asian Nations
1969	South African Customs Union Agreement

Note: * Institutions that we study as participants in gender mainstreaming in trade of GATT negotiations, but also due to a logistics revolution that took hold at the time (Hoekman and Kostecki, 2009).

From the 1960s onwards, containers and long-distance jet airliners became standard modes of transport in global trade, which made items tradable that could not previously be traded at profit. The so-called 'containerization' of global trade allowed for a dramatic up-scaling of trade volumes, enabled the geographical expansion and slicing up of production processes, and undermined the power of organized labour to disrupt trade flows (Bernhofen et al, 2016; Broeze, 2017; Connors et al, 2020). Given that containerization emerged from industrial countries, it also perpetuated their 'particular vision of world ordering' (Quiroga-Villamarín, 2020, p 461).

John Ruggie (1982) famously characterized the GATT trade governance regime that enabled these forms of world ordering as being informed by 'embedded liberalism'. He used the term to describe an international economic order that balanced free trade with the need for domestic social and economic stability. Under embedded liberalism, policy makers recognized that trade liberalization and the global reordering of production caused social disruptions that required intervention. It was assumed that international trade policies ought to be accompanied by state interventions, not only to secure balance of payments at the time, but also to provide for trade adjustment, domestic welfare states and/or development planning policies, including, at the time, Soviet planning models (Graz, 2016).

Political challenges to the GATT regime mainly came from the newly independent countries that emerged from the 1950s and 1960s decolonization movement and other global South countries, which contested the Bretton Woods trade order from the start (Helleiner, 2014). Yet, the dominant understanding of social justice in the embedded liberal era revolved around class-based and international inequalities (Graz, 2016) and did not extend to questions of gendered inequalities or gender relations. As Eric Helleiner (2023a, p 1704) has shown, participating governments in fact actively marginalized feminist voices and women's groups at Bretton Woods. Working with the perfectly gender-blind trade theories of the era, male experts and policy makers constructed Bretton Woods trade institutions to be perfectly gender-blind.

The trade productivism of Bretton Woods

We start by elucidating the gender-blindness of key academic theories on trade during Bretton Woods times, before showing how this productivist and masculinist thinking also permeated embedded liberal approaches to trade policy and governance. We focus here on neoclassical, Keynesian and Marx-inspired theories. Irrespective of scholars' theoretical commitments, during the Bretton Woods decades, these trade theories all narrowly focused on largely male-dominated and masculinized industries and formal, paid labour, that is to say on labour that was considered to be 'productive' in an economic sense. They assessed the economic impacts of trade in terms of highly abstracted categories – such as return on investment and wages for productive labour. They entirely excluded concerns for social reproduction, gender relations and all types of labour considered 'unproductive' – including much subsistence labour and life-making work – from the purview of trade theory (see also Price, 2025).

Evolving in the early 20th century from the marginalist school in classical political economy, neoclassical trade theory assessed the effects of international trade in terms of individual utility, accounted for as economic gains and losses (understood as return on investment and wages) under trade liberalization (Çağatay, 1994). Individual utility considerations operated on the gendered assumption that economic rationality entails making cost–benefit calculations that serve one's own interests (Benería, 1999; Ferber and Nelson, 2003). These assumptions were modelled on an archetype of 'rational economic man', that imagined the individual as separate from others and denied the significance of community and collective experiences to economic processes. They ignored a wide array of activities, values and rationalities that make seemingly 'rational' behaviour possible – not least the care and domestic work involved in reproducing life and labour (Folbre, 2001; England, 2003).

These economic theories elevated the utility-maximizing reasoning associated with 'rational economic man' above forms of economic reasoning guided by values, such as care or altruism, that are associated with femininity and judged to be 'irrational' or 'backward' (Benería, 1999, p 72). They also fused essentialist dichotomies of male/female, rational/irrational, economic/social, Western/non-Western, which led rationality and individualism to appear as attributes of white (Western) men – views that later came to permeate modernizationist development paradigms (Charusheela and Zein-Elabdin, 2003).

Neoclassical theory further assumed that trade took place in an a-political, a-historical sphere, which reproduced methodological masculinism and a blind-spot for gendered and colonial divisions of labour. In the 1930s, Eli Heckscher and Bertil Ohlin famously revitalized the debate around Ricardian comparative advantage and began developing the neoclassical reading of Ricardo, which bears only partial resemblance to his original texts (Picchio, 1992; Çağatay, 2005; Watson, 2017).

To recall, David Ricardo is credited today with having developed a mathematical example of the welfare effects of free trade between nations. His example relies on a heavily reduced model of commerce, operating on the basis of two countries, two products and one factor of production (namely: labour). He showed numerically that specialization and exchange are advantageous for both countries, even if one country uses more labour in the production of both products. This is because, so the argument goes, if countries trade in those products that they are relatively better at producing than their trading partner, global welfare will increase. Based on *relatively* lower production costs (measured in labour time), Ricardo's comparative advantage theory replaced Adam Smith's absolute advantage theory as the main intellectual argument for free trade.

Like their marginalist precursors, neoclassical advances of Ricardo's comparative advantage theory were masculinist in that they valued rational economic man over and above feminized economic rationalities and values and fully ignored reproductive labour (see also England, 2003, p 36). They also ignored political relations among and within trading nations, including the history of colonialism.[2] Heckscher and Ohlin, for example, attributed a country's specific comparative advantages and disadvantages to assumed 'natural' endowment in capital, labour and land, without inquiring what the historical roots of such endowments may be. Wolfgang Stolper and Paul Samuelson (1941) showed that the remuneration of factors of production increases or decreases under trade liberalization, depending on factor endowment and intensity in production. They concluded from this observation that the losers of trade liberalization ought to be compensated for their losses to maintain a societal consensus in favour of free trade. This idea found political expression in the embedded liberal compromise of the Bretton Woods decades but was perfectly focused on the productive economy alone.[3]

Keynesian and Marxist scholars challenged neoclassical trade economics for its blindness to political and social relations, including (imperial) history. They did not, however, escape masculinist and productivist biases. Instead, they also focused primarily on relations in the productive economy without considering how trade was entangled with the social relations of gender and with relations of social reproduction.

Keynesians insightfully argued that neoclassical trade theory obfuscates the role of foreign investment in the global economy and were critical of neoclassicals' a-temporal theories (Robinson, 1973). In contrast, Keynesian trade theory focused on the role of firms, their market power and their role in bringing about the aim of (full) employment in the productive economy (Burbidge, 1979). Despite acknowledging the importance of power relations for the workings of the economy, Keynesian and post-Keynesian theories nonetheless upheld a number of assumptions about market relations that 'limit its capacity to think about gender: an undersocialised entrepreneur as the maker of investment decisions; a market/nonmarket divide that ignores and devalues household activity; a neutral, powerful state and law of contract' (Danby, 2004, pp 56–57).

Like Keynesianism, dependency and structuralist trade theories were concerned with how the passage of time structured economic exchange (see Prebisch, 1950). Despite a focus on the social relations and structures of production (Kvangraven, 2021), they did not consider how women experienced particularly gendered forms of marginalization in production, how they were simultaneously exploited in the reproductive realm, nor how these processes were foundational to imperial trade relations. Instead, in the Bretton Woods decades, scholarship in the dependency tradition tended to subordinate all forms of struggle to class struggle (Antunes de Oliveira and Kvangraven, 2023, p 1684). Notwithstanding their emancipatory focus, Marxist scholarship of the era remained 'based on masculinist conceptions of the development of history, human labour and gender divisions' (Villegas Plá, 2024, p 1328; see also Scott, 2021).

This nearly universal trade productivism in economic thought found institutional and political expression in the trade governance institutions of the Bretton Woods decades. Here, we focus in particular on the GATT, as the cornerstone of the Bretton Woods trade order and the institutional precursor to the WTO.

Trade governance under the GATT regime mirrored the masculinist and productivist biases of trade theory. It focused on trade in industrial and manufacturing sectors of the economy (Hudec, 1990), that is to say on productive labour that was generally male-dominated and masculinized. It further showed no recognition for reproductive labour and worked with and propelled masculinist economic rationalities and values – notably productivity, efficiency, financial reward and self-interested behaviour (Benería, 1999, p 65).

The GATT regime also gave rise to a distinct trade governance technique that separated the regulation of trade from the regulation of other public policy domains (Keohane and Nye, 2003), including social policy. In the embedded liberal spirit, the economic mechanisms of trade were to be managed through international negotiations under GATT. The social relations underlying trade, including processes of social reproduction, were managed domestically, a task for which the GATT gave legal and political leeway to governments.

At the time, many capitalist countries tasked domestic welfare states with supporting the reproductive labour and social reproduction processes that enabled the harnessing of productive labour to capital accumulation through trade. Welfare states, where they existed, shifted some of the costs of social reproduction onto capital and the state (Bakker, 2003; Moos and Gonalons-Pons, 2024). Nonetheless, they were also designed around a productivist male-breadwinner gender order, that tied the most generous benefits to paid employment and reinforced women's dependence on men and/or the state (Nelson, 1984; Fraser, 1989; Orloff, 1993; O'Connor et al, 1999). These systems were highly exclusionary, often denying racialized groups as well as unmarried and non-heterosexual women and others access to the most generous benefits.

At the same time, the GATT regime offloaded the costs of creating domestic stability in capitalist countries onto poorer countries (Ruggie, 1982; Muzaka and Bishop, 2015). It perpetuated colonial divisions of labour that structurally disadvantaged former colonies, while favouring the trade interests of capitalist countries and deepening trade dependencies in industrialized goods (Alessandrini, 2022). GATT negotiations and rules excluded areas such as agriculture and textiles, where many poor countries held comparative advantages, often resulting from imperial trade policies.[4] The GATT was designed and evolved in a way that privileged the pursuit of industrial states' interests at the expense of the interests of developing countries and continued tying the latter into global trade in an inferior position (Wilkinson and Scott, 2008, p 475; see also Hudec, 1990; Ostry, 1997; Alessandrini, 2022).

In response, many newly independent countries adopted the import substitution policies recommended by dependency and structuralist trade theorists and launched a series of global governance initiatives designed to address structural trade inequalities that we discussed in Chapter 1. The initiatives led to the launch of the New International Economic Order, the creation of UNCTAD in 1964, and the creation of 'nonreciprocity' and 'special and differential treatment' in the GATT system (Alessandrini, 2022, p 631). Expressing his views of the problems with the GATT at UNCTAD in 1964, Che Guevara, then minister of industry for Cuba, argued:

> GATT, for its part, by establishing equal treatment and reciprocal concessions between developed and under-developed countries, helps to maintain the status quo and serves the interests of the former group of countries, and its machinery fails to provide the necessary means for the elimination of agricultural protectionism, subsidies, tariffs, and other obstacles to the expansion of exports from the dependent countries. (UNCTAD, 1964, p 165)

Nonetheless, developmentalist trade governance initiatives were also exclusively focused on commodity trade (Rothstein, 2015), ignored its gendered dimensions and were embedded in patriarchal political institutions (Wright, 1995). While feminists from the global South had some influence in shaping developmentist thought in broad terms, gender concerns were not apparant in their approach to trade governance initiatives of the Bretton Woods decades.

Instead, both the GATT and UNCTAD enjoyed limited women's representation and almost never acknowledged economic issues specific to women or to feminized types of labour.[5] For example, for much of the population in the formerly colonized world, trade remained an essential part of the subsistence economy. Yet, these forms of economic exchange, women's specific roles within them, and their relationship to state-sanctioned forms of trade remained largely unrecognized by the international and development communities of the era (Wright, 1995). Under the GATT's so-called 'club-model' of decision-making, trade policy making was further treated as a technocratic exercise that was deliberately separated from public debate and democratic control (Keohane and Nye, 2003). Masculinist trade governance techniques and knowledges that invisibilized and normalized housewifization were thus shielded from political contestation.

Although embedded liberalism eventually gave way to neoliberalism, trade productivism became deeply embedded in common sense knowledge about global trade. The WTO (2017b, p 1), for example, explained in its 2017–2019 *Trade and Gender Action Plan* that 'for decades, it was agreed [in the WTO] and never challenged that trade rules are gender neutral'. The statement shows just how taken-for-granted trade productivist thinking is in trade governance circles, given that women's groups and feminists did challenge the WTO in the 1990s and early 2000s. Yet, trade productivism is far from inescapable. As economic history teaches us, the trade productivism of the Bretton Woods era resulted from an active removal of questions of reproduction and women's roles in society and of early free trade feminists from trade theory and governance.

Disappearing reproduction, women's roles in society and early free trade feminists

In contrast with the Bretton Woods era, trade debates of the 19th and early 20th century were actively concerned with how trade could support what was then called 'social progress', and with the social reproduction of the working class in imperial countries. Women and gender relations factored into these debates in ways that reflected prominent attitudes towards gender (and race) at the time. 'Free trade feminist' activists projected the views of liberal, 'Listian'[6] and socialist feminists into public and policy debates on trade well into the inter-war period (Helleiner, 2023a; 2023b; Palen, 2024). By the time of Bretton Woods, these concerns and voices all but disappeared from trade theory and governance. This intellectual history matters because it shows how trade productivism arose as a gendered ideology that helped to create and legitimize gendered trade orders across space and time.

Ricardo, like many of his contemporary classical political economists, did not theorize trade policy in isolation from its social underpinnings. Although eclipsed from neoclassical readings of his 1817 *Principles of Political Economy and Taxation*, Ricardo's support for free trade rested on his explicit normative commitment to supporting the social reproduction of the working class in industrializing Britain (Picchio, 1992). Working with a labour theory of value, Ricardo saw low import costs as beneficial from the perspective of what this meant for workers, or what we understand as the social reproduction of the working class. In *Principles*, he explained that the reproduction of labourers, 'and the family which may be necessary to keep up the number of labourers, does not depend on the quantity of money which he may receive for wages, but on the quantity of food' that those wages will afford (Ricardo 1817, cited in Picchio, 1992, p 17). The desire to reduce the costs of the reproduction of labour in Britain motivated Ricardo to support free trade. He expected free trade to decrease the cost of corn via cheaper European imports and therefore ultimately to boost industrial production in Britain (Robinson, 1974; Walsh, 1979).

As seen in this quote, Ricardo offered a masculinist understanding of industrial labour as being the realm of men. His choice of the pronoun 'he' when writing about labourers contrasts starkly with the fact – doubtlessly known to Ricardo – that large numbers of working-class women and children were systematically pushed into industrial production and employed under appalling conditions in the early years of the industrial revolution. This practice undermined the social reproduction of the working class and caused moral outrage at the time (Fraser, 2016).

Instead of following Ricardian modelling, many classical scholars in fact examined trade policies in relation to their understanding of 'social progress' (for example, Powers, 1888; Taylor, 1903; see also Trommer, 2014). They saw trade policy first and foremost as a social problem (Levasseur, 1892; Poinsard, 1893) and recognized 'private' and familial relations (and thus implicitly gender relations) as part of its context. The French political economist Léon Poinsard, for example, insisted that trade analysts should not only pay attention to 'increases or decreases in trade flows and their effects on the movement of wealth'. They must also consider 'the developments that free trade or protection can bring in the conditions of individuals, to the constitution of the family, in the situation of public powers, in one word in the private and public life of the nation' (Poinsard, 1893, p 3, translation by authors). When assessing tariff questions, classical political economists took into account demographic developments and considered societal practices and dynamics including agricultural traditions and growing methods, labour conditions, mortgage rates, and more (Powers, 1888; Taussig, 1889; Keasbey, 1898).

At the same time, classical political economists did not extend their analysis to the various forms of labour that were subjected to housewifization processes, nor to the gendered and colonial hierarchies underpinning trade. Despite showing some awareness of the social relations of trade, classical political economists thus legitimated and perpetuated housewifization. They did so by, in the words of Paula England, 'failing to see how much child rearing, household work, and volunteer work contribute to "the wealth of nations"' (2003, p 36).

Furthermore, as Matthew Watson (2017) has detailed, Ricardo's model showing the advantages of specialization and exchange actively disappeared the 'actual historical social relations of production' underlying trade. Ricardo's calculation demonstrated the welfare-creating effects of England and Portugal trading cloth and wine. The calculation omitted the fact – also doubtlessly known to Ricardo – that, in his time, the 'real England and Portugal' were heavily involved in forging the imperial world economy, including as leading nations of the transatlantic slave trade (Watson, 2017, p 268).[7] Despite criticizing colonial trade in the *Principles*, what Ricardo opposed were the disadvantageous terms of trade that settler colonialists faced, not the implications of colonial trade for colonized peoples. These normativities persisted throughout the 19th century, when socially embedded analysis of the trade policies of imperial nations was underpinned by the sexist and racist epistemologies and values widely held in Europe at the time (see, for instance, Poinsard, 1893; Keasbey, 1898).

Problematic as classical concerns for the reproduction of the working class and for the societal impacts of trade had been, they were gradually removed from the purview of economic theory in the late 19th and early 20th century. The methodological choices of emerging marginalist and neoclassical economists broke with classical understandings of trade as being inherently connected to the reproduction of the working class and to families, gender relations and social organization more broadly. Instead, they placed commercial and corporate interests above concerns for societal welfare and 'social progress' in trade theory.

As indicated earlier, marginalism was masculinist in its assumptions about economic value and rationality, which included treating economic relations in isolation from their social and historical context. Frank William Taussig (1904), an American economist credited with laying the foundations of neoclassical trade economics, strengthened the productivist biases of trade theory when he influentially recommended using the impact of tariffs on a country's industries as the proxy for assessing the impact of tariffs on all of society (see also Trommer, 2014). By the time of the seminal theorems of neoclassical trade economics, such as Heckscher-Ohlin and Stolper-Samuelson, questions of reproduction of the working class were theoretically subsumed under the narrow question of wages, or what neoclassicals called the renumeration of the labour factor of production. This meant that the scope of the impacts of trade on societal welfare was now narrowly understood to refer to rising or falling wages in productive sectors of the economy – with the latter being imagined to be devoid of social power relations.

Neoclassical methods constituted a clear and deliberate departure from how trade and tariff matters had been politically debated in the 19th century. These debates had raised questions about how trade policy could be used in support of social reproduction, gender equality, anti-imperialism, the abolition of slavery and world peace. So-called 'Manchester School' liberals saw advantage in how lowering the price of food via free trade lowered the subsistence costs of the British working class (Palen, 2016; 2020; see also Chase-Dunn et al, 2023). Richard Cobden, John Bright and the Anti-Corn Law League fervently supported free trade in early- to mid-19th century Britain.

Cobden critiqued British imperialism and believed that international free trade would bring about domestic prosperity as well as political emancipation and world peace. So-called 'Cobdenites' became leaders of the transatlantic abolitionist and peace movements (Palen, 2016). Their ideas regarding the benefits of free trade drew wide support within Europe and North America. They also influenced liberal thinkers in Latin America, South Asia and Africa, who revised these ideas in ways that connected free trade to liberty, sovereignty and anti-imperialism (for more, see Helleiner, 2023b, pp 38–50). Such causes also came to be associated with women's suffrage and, in the wake of the First World War, free trade became integral to feminist peace and anti-imperial activism (Palen, 2024, p 121; see also Helleiner, 2023b, pp 168–174).[8]

The economic historian Marc Palen (2024) uses the term 'free trade feminism' to refer to 19th and early 20th century women's and feminist activism in support of free trade.[9] Networks of female and feminist free trade activists stretched 'from the Victorian world of Harriet Martineau and Florence Nightingale to the interwar networks of the international women's peace movement' (Palen, 2024, p 120). It included both liberal and socialist feminists, who shared a belief in the benefits of free trade, albeit for different political reasons.

The liberal free trade feminist and influential political economist Harriet Martineau (1837), for example, assumed that free trade would bring benefits for the working population.[10] She advocated for free trade, alongside women's access to education, property rights for married women and improvements in women's working conditions and wages (Helleiner, 2023b, p 168). Martineau was critical of slavery and of British free-trade imperialism, although she also sometimes expressed support for imperialism as a 'civilizing' mission, for instance, regarding British colonial rule in India (Palen, 2024, p 123). The Women's International League for Peace and Freedom (WILPF) pointed to the negative effects of protectionist tariffs on women as the household's main consumers (Helleiner, 2023b, p 169; see also Palen, 2016, pp 2014–2015).

Socialist feminists such as Louise Zietz, head of the German Social Democratic Party's women's movement, also expressed support for free trade, though not with the same political motives as liberals (Palen, 2024, pp 127–128). In what Palen calls the 'Marx-Manchester tradition', support for free trade came from the belief that it would bring about the proletarianization of the world, hastening the socialist revolution (Ghorashi, 1995; Palen, 2020; 2024).

Nineteenth-century concerns for the effects of trade on women were often imbued with upper-class ideas about women's roles in society and relied on gendered stereotypes that subordinated women and feminized types of work to men and masculinized work. The nineteenth-century British women's journal, *Women's Herald*, for example, described the negative impacts of protectionist tariffs on household purchases and pledged to support 'women who indulge in *that feminine mania, shopping*' (Women's Herald, 1892, cited in Palen, 2016, p 215, emphasis added). In his 1859 *Principles of Social Science*, Henry Carey argued that free trade fostered a deterioration in women's working conditions and displaced women's employment in industrial and agricultural production. He declared: '*Unfit to dig the earth*, [women] find themselves driven from the light labor of conversion, in every country subject to the system [of free trade] ... What, then, remains to them? In millions of cases, *little else than prostitution*' (Carey, 1859, cited in Helleiner, 2023b, p 182, emphasis added).

Although politicians and the publics of various nations 'hotly debated' the connections between trade policy, 'social progress' and imperialism at the time (Palen, 2016, p xvii), as Mies (1998 [1986]) documented, the expansion of imperial trade produced patriarchy and capitalism on a world scale. In political terms, all imperial nations experimented with variations of protectionist and free trade policies to support the continued annexation of territories into their realms of influence, whether in the American West, the Pacific, Latin America, Asia or Africa (Palen, 2016).[11]

Women's and feminist voices became marginalized in public and political debates on trade in the first half of the 20th century. In 1915, the liberal free trade feminist Jane Addams – who would later become the first president of WILPF – called for the 'formal organizations of international relations' to consider 'those primitive human urgings to foster life and to protect the helpless, of which women were the earliest custodians' (Addams, 1915, cited in Helleiner, 2023b, p 170). In 1944, the ILO requested, in its Declaration of Philadelphia, that the architects of the post-war global order would 'explicitly judge their designs for the postwar international financial order according to the principle that "all human beings, irrespective of race, creed or sex, have the right to pursue their material well-being and their spiritual development in conditions of freedom and dignity, of economic security and equal opportunity"' (Helleiner, 2023a, pp 1702–1703).

Such requests went unanswered. In the same year, feminists, in particular Latin American feminists, who argued that women's rights should underpin post-war economic institutions, were not included among the region's delegates to the Bretton Woods Conference (Helleiner, 2023a, p 1704). By now, academic and public commentators had ceased seeing trade policies as standing in direct relation to social reproduction or to the role of women in society. Under embedded liberalism, trade policy was further seen to be invariably international in nature (because it concerned economic exchange across national borders), while social policy was now firmly understood to be a national concern.

The trade productivism of the Bretton Woods decades would soon be challenged by the material and institutional transformations associated with the neoliberal era. Neoliberal restructuring also brought the voices of feminist activists and scholars back into trade debates, albeit often in marginalized positions. In the final section, we develop our third analytical concept of trading on social reproduction by examining the gendered social relations that characterized the rise of GVCs from the 1970s onwards and the shifts in trade politics that enabled this rise.

Trading on social reproduction in the neoliberal era

From the 1970s onwards, the expansion of GVCs at previously inconceivable scale (Gereffi, 1994; 2015) reconfigured global trade relations, including their gendered underpinnings. In the neoliberal era, free trade was increasingly understood to require, in principle, regulations that actively supported the transnational flows of goods, services and capital (Gill, 1995; Young and Peterson, 2006; Lang, 2011). These new types of trade regulations and governance mechanisms were one important driver of the rise of globalized production (Alessandrini, 2022, p 632).

Our third analytical concept of trading on social reproduction captures how these transformations both reconfigured and intensified gender and trade inequalities. As we show in what follows, they did so by expanding and introducing new forms of housewifization, and by modifying trade governance techniques in ways that actively incorporated reproductive labour, social reproduction processes and life-making activities into the realm of trade law and regulation.

At the same time as they overcame the traditional exclusive focus on trade in the productive economy, global trade policy elites did not, however, re-value reproductive labour, social reproduction processes and life-making activities in trade governance. They remained committed to trade productivist principles, such as economic growth, competitiveness and efficiency, false ideas about the gender neutrality of trade, and governance practices that subordinated reproductive, unpaid, subsistence, informal and otherwise irregular labour, as well as nature, to the productive economy. Neoliberal reconfigurations of the world economy opened up social reproduction as a new sphere of capital accumulation via trade.

Women's and feminist activists and scholars challenged neoliberal trade relations practically from their inception. As we will argue in the concluding chapter of the book, it is from such resistance that feminist visions for transformative trade governance must emerge.

Trade and the rise of global value chains

We start once more with a familiar story, that is the rise of globalized production from the 1970s onwards. A combination of containerization, technological advances in communication and information technology and broader macroeconomic transformations – notably the liberalization of foreign direct investment and novel approaches to trade law and regulation – made globalized production possible. In structural terms, the expansion of GVCs fuelled export-oriented and often labour-intensive manufacturing in many countries of the global South (for example, in textiles and electronics sectors). Many of these jobs were lost in the global North, as low-paid, often female, labour represented a comparative advantage of global South countries (Elson and Pearson, 1981; Çağatay, 2005). As we saw in Chapter 1, these developments led neoclassical trade economists to study the links between trade liberalization and women's employment and wages (Wood, 1991; Baldwin, 1995), a question they had not previously considered.

In governance terms, the new approaches to trade law and regulation that enabled globalized production were founded on 'a revolution in social ontology' (Drake and Nicolaïdis, 1992, p 38; see also Lang, 2011). When the WTO replaced the GATT as the world's multilateral trade governance body on 1 January 1995, it introduced novel types of trade regulations, notably in relation to services and investment and intellectual property protection. It also for the first time brought agricultural trade systematically under multilateral trade disciplines. The GATT had excluded agriculture from negotiations, and advanced economies, notably the US and the EU, operated protectionist trade policies and domestic support systems that disadvantaged agricultural producers in the global South (Josling, 2012).

These new rules and governance techniques had been developed with the intention to promote and at the same time regulate the globally integrated world economy. They were developed in FTAs such as NAFTA, negotiated between 1988 and 1992, the GATT Uruguay Round, negotiated between 1986 and 1994, the European Single Market negotiated between 1986 and 1992, and across the various SAPs that international financial institutions imposed on Latin American, African and East Asian countries as well as on the post-communist states of Eastern and Central Europe in the wake of 1980s/1990s public debt crises.

The so-called 'servicification' of global trade (Lodefalk, 2017) provides one example of how material *and* ideational/institutional reconfigurations of global trade relations brought about a re-politicization of trade governance in the neoliberal era. Servicification refers not only to the increasing importance of service trade flows in overall growth terms from the 1980s onwards, but also to the fact that in the economic model underpinning GVCs, service trade became integral to goods trade. To understand this, it is important to recognize that technological advances and financial liberalization allowed for the spatial separation of the provision and consumption of services at scale. By the 1980s, growth in transnational business services trade – including accounting, finance, human resource or customer services – began overtaking growth in manufacturing trade (Sauvant, 1993). The rise in service trade in part resulted from the fact that corporations were now able to spatially separate the production side from the business services side of their operations at profit.

The material shift from a goods-based international trading system to a goods-and-services-based global production system prompted, and was promoted by, a shift in 'how governments thought about the nature of services, their movement across borders, their roles in society, and the objectives and principles according to which they should be governed' (Drake and Nicolaïdis, 1992, p 38). Failing to agree on a workable definition of services, trade policy makers (often working together with corporate interests) established a governance norm across various sets of trade negotiations in the 1980s and 1990s that services, unlike goods, would be liberalized by how they crossed borders (Benz, 1985).[12] Four modes of cross-border service delivery were agreed upon in negotiations towards the WTO General Agreement on Trade in Services 1994 (GATS). The modes focused on the behaviours of service providers and consumers, that is to say of the persons (both legal and human) involved in the service economy, and free service trade was understood to mean, in principle, their free movement across borders. Domestic laws in other public policy areas – from migration rules and professional qualifications to capital mobility and foreign direct investment laws – thus came to be seen as barriers to global services trade.

At the same time, neoliberal trade regulatory innovations in investment and intellectual property protection strengthened the economic rights of corporations and investors. While narrow in scope, the WTO Agreement on Trade-Related Investment Measures (TRIMs) of 1994 secured protections for foreign investors by preventing governments from taking investment measures that impede on trade in goods flows. Investment protection in trade governance was created in parallel to then-existing international systems of investment protection, such as Investor-State Dispute Settlement (ISDS) mechanisms going back to the 1960s. The WTO TRIPs Agreement of 1994 introduced IPRs such as patents, trademarks and copyrights into international trade law. It provided exclusive use and commercialization rights for registered products, product characteristics or production/commercialization methods to the rights holder and became increasingly uniform and weighted in favour of investors (May and Sell, 2005).

While trade agreements in the neoliberal era expanded corporate and investor rights, an ever-growing number of public policy areas were simultaneously drawn into the scope of trade governance through expanding logics of what constituted a trade barrier (see Table 2.2). All these regulatory innovations encountered resistance from civil society groups and social forces that challenged their implications for social and environmental regulation, inequality, development and democracy (von Bülow, 2010; Kay and Evans, 2018).

When it became apparent in the early 2000s that the WTO was unable to produce substantial new trade rules, trade negotiations increasingly shifted from the multilateral arena into the domain of bilateral and regional FTAs (Trommer, 2017). Here, the trend of expanding corporate and investor rights while including an ever-wider range of public policy areas into trade governance continued (see Table 2.2).

Seen through our feminist lens, these transformations in global trade relations produced shifts in how global trade related to social reproduction

Table 2.2: Evolution of regulatory content of international trade agreements

Trade agreements and governance frameworks	Policy areas
GATT 1947 GATT Rounds 1947–1979 (that is, Geneva 1947, Annecy 1949, Torquay 1950–1951, Geneva 1956, Dillon 1960–1961, Kennedy 1964–1967, Tokyo 1973–1979)	Tariffs, non-tariff measures
GATT Uruguay Round 1986–1994 NAFTA 1994 WTO 1994 (including the GATS, TRIPs and TRIMs)	As above and: services, intellectual property protection, dispute settlement, textiles, agriculture, investment, environmental law, labour law
WTO Doha Round 2001– FTAs 2003–	As above and: trade facilitation, competition policy, procurement, food security, state trading enterprises, consumer protection, energy, health, human rights, taxation, data protection, audiovisual, anti-corruption, innovation, industrial cooperation, small and medium-sized enterprises, cultural cooperation, information society, illegal immigration, nuclear safety, mining, money laundering, illicit drugs, visa and asylum, terrorism, political dialogue

Source: Authors' compilation based on Hofmann et al (2017) and Hoekman and Kostecki (2009).

and to the social relations of trade, both structurally and in governance terms, which our concept of trading on social reproduction makes visible.

Neoliberal trade and trading on social reproduction

From our feminist perspective, what changed in the neoliberal era was that corporations and investors could now directly capitalize on social reproduction through trade, in parallel ways to how they had capitalized on production through trade for centuries. This was made possible because: global trade relations in the neoliberal era continued to rely on gendered and colonial divisions of labour; commodified, financialized and made tradable reproductive labour; disciplined government policies that supported social reproduction; and promoted corporate monopolies over, and extractivist relationships with, nature.

In structural terms, neoliberal trade perpetuated housewifization. GVCs intensified the feminization of labour and the feminization of the conditions of work globally, which included 'a deep process of informalization of labour' (Mezzadri, 2017, p 25; see also Ossome, 2015; Price, 2025). The spread of 'the global factory' (Mezzadri, 2017) incorporated more and more women – and workers in developing countries more broadly – into the workforce at the same time as the conditions of work were becoming increasingly informalized, casualized and disempowering for workers *vis-à-vis* capital (Standing, 1999).

GVCs often extended to paid and unpaid, free and unfree, productive and reproductive labour that was performed by women, among others, outside of factory walls (Gore and LeBaron, 2019; LeBaron and Gore, 2020; Alessandrini et al, 2022). By the early 2000s, an estimated 300 million homeworkers were producing for globalized production by working from the home. The bulk of this household-based global workforce (which extended across global South and global North countries) were women who were 'denied a living wage, safe working conditions, basic decent living standards, and recognition as workers' (Delaney, 2004, p 22). Informality further expanded globally with the development and expansion of the gig economy and crowd work (Mezzadri, 2019, p 38) and the retreat of social provisioning systems and welfare states.

Neoliberal trade governance encouraged such retreat of social provisioning and of the expansion of global informality. SAPs provided one example of this. The tariff removals imposed via conditions attached to loans issued to developing countries by the IMF and World Bank resulted in public revenue loss.[13] This created severe budgetary constraints in countries where governments had limited alternative revenue sources. In the wake of the economic and social crises induced by SAPs, populations in debtor countries increasingly relied on informal economic activities to assure their social reproduction. In these contexts, informal cross-border trade and subsistence agriculture – where women traditionally occupy central responsibilities and positions (Wright, 1995) – became increasingly important.

In institutional terms, the WTO continued within the spirit of the GATT's productivist governance practices, which included a commitment to masculinized market rationality, false ideas about the gender neutrality of trade, and a lack of consideration for the wider social relations of trade. In contrast with the GATT, the WTO was heavily legalized and technocratic. Its de facto binding system for adjudicating trade disputes among members 'entrench[ed] rights for investors and corporations, deter[ed] deviation from market principles and insulate[d] market transactions from public scrutiny and social and environmental regulation' (Hannah et al, 2022, p 1371).

Neoliberal trade governance techniques also created regulatory frameworks that allowed value to be extracted from trading reproductive labour across borders, while simultaneously discipling government policies that supported social reproduction processes (on 'disciplinary neoliberalism', see Gill, 1995). Central here are the service trade liberalization techniques introduced during the 1980s. As indicated earlier, professional services were the initial focus of service trade negotiations. The decision to liberalize services by mode of delivery (rather than in any other way) meant, however, that paid reproductive labour, such as that performed in education institutions, hospitals, nursing homes, retail, hospitality and beyond, could also in principle be brought under the emerging service trade disciplines. Consequently, domestic policies that supported this reproductive labour (for instance by protecting services from market imperatives) now appeared to be trade barriers that required removal or harmonization in the name of free trade. The reformulated understanding of free trade implied that many public policy areas central to supporting social reproduction – such as labour, environmental or migration law, public utilities or transport, or national health and education systems (Benz, 1985; Footer, 1993; Hocking and McGuire, 2004) – were now, in principle, targets of trade liberalization.

The global health services trade provides one example of how neoliberal trade governance has actively supported the creation of an international division of reproductive labour. While data on health services trade is not systematically recorded and difficult to obtain, it is nonetheless clear that the global health services trade is primarily centred around large economies such as the US, the UK, Europe, Japan, China and India. Central America and Asia have been integrated as governments have adopted policies to promote their countries as medical tourism hubs (Smith et al, 2009). There are strong investment flows related to private healthcare groups and hospitals among these regions. For both physicians and nurses, there are strong cross-border movements from developing into developed regions of the global economy, and notably into private healthcare provision in rich countries. The global health services trade has created 'knock-on effects down the chain to public sectors within wealthy nations, private and public sectors in low-income countries, and ultimately the rural areas within poorer countries' (Smith et al, 2009, p 598). In sub-Saharan Africa, located at the bottom of the health services value chain, the migration of health professionals has, for example, become a factor in endemic health crises (Smith et al, 2009).

Beyond formal employment by reproductive service providers, better off women in wealthier countries also hire women – often migrant women from poorer countries or regions – into their households to perform reproductive labour such as childcare, elder care, cleaning and cooking. While the employers are able to enter into the formal labour market, domestic workers are paid low wages and face various vulnerabilities that stem from the intersection of their gender, race/ethnicity and legal status as migrants. This international division of reproductive labour is upheld by the stereotyping of certain groups of (racialized) women as being natural caregivers and of their labour as unskilled and undeserving of high wages or formal protection (Parreñas, 2001; Yeates, 2004; Kofman and Raghuram, 2015). Alongside these processes of housewifization, the labour that goes into caring for the families of the migrants is also naturalized and often invisibilized in policy discourses that extol the benefits of the expansion of care markets and the trade in reproductive services, such as health services. Instead, trading on social reproduction contributes to fuelling, while also capitalizing on, forms of depletion (Rai et al, 2013) and 'variegated crises of social reproduction' that have been unfolding globally in historically and geographically specific ways (Bakker and Gill, 2019).

The creation of investment and IPR protections in trade agreements provided further avenues for capitalizing on social reproduction while simultaneously limiting the possibilities available for governments with regards to social provisioning. Feminists and other critics have argued that investment protection, and the incorporation of ISDS into FTAs in particular, produced chilling effects on government regulation in areas related to social reproduction, ranging from public health and consumer laws to environmental and social protection (United Nations High Commissioner for Human Rights, 2015; Roberts et al, 2019, p 10). At the same time, they extend political power to foreign investors by providing them with channels for private legal recourse not available to any other group, including women, and for defining the permissible range of public policy exceptions to free trade rules (Roberts et al, 2019, p 11).

Ecofeminists have also forcefully argued that TRIPs disciplines and their strengthening in many FTAs across later decades allowed corporations and investors to assert ownership over life itself (that is, over plants, animals and human genes) and over knowledges and techniques that are essential to reproductive and life-making work (Mies and Shiva, 1993; Mies, 1996, p 359). This allowed corporations and investors to capitalize on so-called 'biopiracy', whereby traditional knowledge, genetic resources and biological materials are patented from, and in some cases re-sold to, indigenous communities and farmers who remain un- or under-compensated (Mies and Shiva, 1993; Shiva, 2001; 2005). Concerns about how IPRs contributed to price hikes and curtailed access to medicines, in particular for poor countries and marginalized populations (Baker, 2016; Friel et al, 2015), also featured prominently during the HIV/AIDS epidemic in the 1990s, as well as during the COVID-19 pandemic (Roberts and Trommer, 2026). The patenting of seeds became a key battle ground between peasant movements and food value chains, which relied on TRIPS provisions, alongside other neoliberal trade rules, in order to organize what, from our feminist perspective, is capitalizing on life-making through trade (Downes, 2004; see also Shiva, 2005; Gonzalez, 2006).

These are all examples of how neoliberal trade governance techniques have limited the possibilities for governments to engage in social provisioning and protection, while simultaneously enabling corporate profits to be drawn directly from life-making work and social reproduction processes. In the neoliberal era, these new trade governance techniques contributed to the intensification of gendered and colonial inequalities of global trade, commodified reproductive labour and nature, and expanded corporate and investor rights while actively promoting restraint on government policies that support wider social and public policy goals. As we shall see in later chapters, free trade feminism furthers many of these trends.

Contesting global trade governance and the rise of gender mainstreaming

A wide range of actors at different sites and scales, including feminist and women's rights organizations, contested neoliberal reconfigurations of global trade. In response to SAPs, transnational feminist solidarities began to flourish 'in multiple spaces from the local grassroots movements and community-based [non-governmental organizations] to national and transnational feminist networks' (Desai, 2002, p 15). The growing feminist advocacy in relation to trade reflected a broader political shift whereby groups were demanding a voice in a wide range of economic and social policy-making arenas, for instance at the launch of the Beijing Platform for Action.

Feminist and women's movements actively mobilized alongside trade unionists, environmentalists and decolonial critics around the WTO's early Ministerial Conferences in the late 1990s and early 2000s. They participated in the emerging political battles over trade and development, trade and labour, and trade and environment that erupted in response to neoliberal trade governance. Many feminist civil society groups with an interest in trade worked through and alongside the International Trade and Gender Network (ITGN). The ITGN aimed to bring a feminist perspective to trade policy and WTO governance (Williams, 2013). In the 1990s and 2000s, feminists campaigned around issues such as NAFTA and the failed Free Trade Agreement of the Americas (Gabriel and Macdonald, 1994; Domínguez, 2002), the WTO's 1999 'Battle of Seattle' (Smith, 2001; Wood, 2020), the TRIPS access to medicines campaign, and many North–South trade agreements (such as during the negotiations for FTAs among the EU and African, Caribbean and Pacific countries; see Trommer, 2014).

Some regional trade institutions in the global South, as well as certain UN agencies and non-trade specific global or regional governance bodies, began acknowledging the relationship between trade and gender from the 1980s/1990s onwards (see Table 2.3). They generally focused on women in trade and development and on trade and women in the labour force. From the 2000s onwards, dedicated gender and trade work programmes began emerging within global trade governance institutions. They had a specific focus on women in relation to trade and development questions, while the language of *gender*, trade and development also became more prominent at the time, reflecting the broader gender mainstreaming trends outlined in Chapter 1.

Nonetheless, policy makers within the most powerful trade governance institutions continued to insist on the trade productivist credo that trade is gender neutral. By the 2010s, many women's groups had lost access to public sources of funding. The ITGN, for example, ceased operating around this time. Others turned their attention to different issues. They included in particular, in the wake of the 2008 global financial crisis, the issue of financial regulation, as well as climate change (Gabriel and Macdonald, 2005; Williams, 2013).

Strikingly, this was the point in time when global trade governance institutions, notably the WTO, began abandoning their traditional opposition to tackling gender concerns in trade governance. In the next chapter, we trace the roots of this surprising shift and show how free trade feminism emerged as the dominant way of making gender questions governable in contemporary global trade governance from 2016 onwards.

Conclusion

In this chapter we have developed three conceptual devices – housewifization, trade productivism and trading on social reproduction – that allow us to show how relations of social reproduction, gender and gender-based inequalities, and colonialism and its afterlife stand in a co-constitutive relationship with global trade relations. Our feminist political economy of trade illuminates how unequal global trade relations rely on and reproduce hierarchies and distinctions between productive/reproductive labour, paid/unpaid labour,

Table 2.3: Gender and trade governance initiatives, 1983–2015

Year	International organization	Initiative
1983	Economic Community of Central African States	Obliges members to engage in research on the economic, social and cultural status of women in rural and urban areas with a view to improving their integration in development activities
1993	Common Market for Eastern and Southern Africa	Women and Development Chapter
1993	ECOWAS	Women and Development Chapter
1993	East African Community	Women and Development Chapter
1994	NAFTA	Gender-specific labour provisions
1995	Beijing Declaration and Platform for Action	Asked governments to ensure that national policies relating to trade agreements do not adversely affect women's economic activities
1999	UNCTAD	Expert workshops on trade, sustainable development and gender
2002	ECLAC	Integration of gender perspectives into trade programmes
2003	UN Inter-Agency Network on Women and Gender Equality	Task Force on Gender and Trade, comprised of UN agencies and regional commissions, including UNCTAD, World Bank, WTO, OECD and Commonwealth Secretariat
2002	APEC	Trade-specific gender mainstreaming
2005	Commonwealth Secretariat	Trade-specific gender mainstreaming
2005	WTO	Aid for Trade (AfT) launch declares gender as integral to it
2006	WTO	AfT Taskforce recommends focus on women entrepreneurs
2010	WTO Secretariat and International Trade Centre	Roundtable on gender mainstreaming in AfT
2010	UNCTAD	Dedicated work programme on trade, gender and development
2012	EU-Central America Association Agreement	Incorporates International Labour Organization Conventions 100 and 111 on equal pay and non-discrimination in employment and a provision envisaging cooperation on equal participation and opportunities from men and women in all sectors of economic, political, social and cultural life
2015	World Bank and WTO	Joint report on *The Role of Trade in Ending Poverty* contains section on 'Women Trade and Poverty'

Source: Compiled by authors based on ECLAC (2002), UNCTAD (1999; 2021a), True (2008), Hannah et al (2018), WTO (2017b; 2019a) and Monteiro (2021).

masculinity/femininity as well as economy/society and economy/nature. These hierarchies permeate not only material trade flows, but also different trade knowledges and governance mechanisms. At the same time, gender inequalities and the unequal relations of trade have been fundamentally interwoven in ways that were, and continue to be, historically and geographically specific.

We have also shown how trade governance has come to take on its current gendered form, which is historically contingent and therefore not inevitable. By doing so, we have laid the foundations for our critical engagement with gender mainstreaming efforts in global trade governance today. Our understanding of how gendered hierarchies are entangled with trade governance through housewifization, trade productivism and trading on social reproduction is key to why we deem free trade feminist governance agendas to be wrong-headed. Treating trade governance as a technocratic exercise of aligning trade expansion with women's economic empowerment agendas may well benefit women recipients across the world economy in their day-to-day lives. However, free trade feminism masks the fact that trade governance is a site of social and political contestation that is fundamentally intertwined with the pursuit of gender justice. It risks reproducing and even expanding on the social hierarchies upon which global trade relations are built, including their gendered dimensions.

3

The Rise of Free Trade Feminism

As we saw in Chapter 2, the 2010s marked a low point in feminist activism around trade governance. Nonetheless, interest in the links between trade and gender moved from the margins into the centre of global trade governance in this decade. The story that we outline in this chapter is one whereby ideas about the business case for gender equality that had been formulated in other areas of global economic governance much earlier made a belated entrance into the leading fora of trade governance in the mid-2010s. We show how global trade policy elites actively constructed free trade feminism and how they successfully worked to elevate it into the position of the only feasible approach to trade and gender mainstreaming.

We chart the rise of free trade feminism and its relationship to gender inequalities across two distinct phases in the gender and trade agenda. We show how, in the mid- and late 2010s, policy elites in institutions such as the WTO, the World Bank, the OECD and the ITC actively constructed and promoted free trade feminist approaches to gender mainstreaming in trade. These approaches built on trade productivist ideas. First among them were the assumed proven benefits of (masculinist) free trade theories, which these policy elites connected to policy paradigms of economic growth, competitiveness and market-led development. They also included ideas about the (supposedly 'extra-economic') roots of gender discrimination in trade and a particular focus on women exporters and entrepreneurs. While this political project found much support in the international community, various states, regional trade bodies of the global South and civil society actors also challenged it. Some of these critics echoed longer-standing concerns over the global feminization of labour processes, and, in some cases, also over housewifization and trading on social reproduction.

Things changed during the COVID-19 pandemic from 2020 onward, when free trade feminism came to be *the* taken-for-granted approach to trade and gender mainstreaming in global trade governance, and in regional and national trade policy approaches to gender questions all around the world. The WTO and UNCTAD both proved instrumental to establishing the intellectual and political hegemony of free trade feminism over alternative trade and gender mainstreaming approaches that had existed in the early days. The WTO was able to exert global influence given its standing as an informal agenda-setter and thought-leader in trade policy making around the world. UNCTAD, on the other hand, gradually downscaled its traditional concerns over the feminization of labour, housewifization and trading on social reproduction around the time of the pandemic. Following the 2021 Bridgetown Covenant, where internal contestations over its gender, trade and development approach became apparent, UNCTAD began actively promoting free trade feminist discourses and policy initiatives in global trade governance, and in trade and development policy programming around the world.

By the mid-2020s, free trade feminism had been widely diffused into all levels of trade governance and had also entered and found allies in other areas of governance, for example in finance, development, food security, labour rights and more. At the time of writing, free trade feminism is widely accepted in trade governance circles around the world as being without alternative when it comes to redressing the gender-differential impacts of trade. This hegemonic standing was forcefully demonstrated when free trade feminism withstood US government attacks on equality, diversity and inclusion programmes, on free trade, and on multilateralism under the second Trump administration in 2025.

Given our theoretical understanding of the imbrications of trade and gender inequalities, the rise of free trade feminism gives us reason for concern that gender mainstreaming in trade reproduces and expands upon many of the gendered hierarchies and exploitations inherent in global trade relations that we identified in Chapter 2.

Contesting gender mainstreaming in trade governance

The year 2016 was a pivotal one for gender mainstreaming in global trade governance. In 2016, some of the world's most powerful global trade governance elites configured a gender and trade mainstreaming agenda that superseded existing but dispersed gender and trade initiatives in regional trade governance (see Chapter 2). Various sets of actors, including certain states and civil society groups, openly opposed this agenda, arguing that gender mainstreaming had no place in global trade governance. Nonetheless, the WTO proudly proclaimed in 2017 that 'today, no WTO Member is questioning the importance of this theme [of gender and trade]' (WTO, 2017b, p 1).

Over the next few years, different trade institutions advanced their preferred approaches to gender mainstreaming in trade. In this section, we show how the Secretariats of the WTO, the ITC and UNCTAD all provided global policy leadership on trade and gender. They did so by relying on the various mechanisms for consultation, transparency and deliberation that each of these Secretariats has at their disposal. They all also used their organizations' mandates over development policy programming and development finance to roll out gender mainstreaming initiatives in trade and development policy via donor and recipient countries globally. As UNCTAD Deputy Secretary-General Isabelle Durant explained at an UNCTAD/WTO co-organized workshop on 'Gender Considerations in Trade Agreements' in March 2019, such 'high-level gatherings to discuss trade and gender would have been quite unthinkable even just a few years ago' (UNCTAD, 2019a).

During these early days of the gender and trade agenda, the three Secretariats promoted varied and at times incommensurable ways of conceptualizing and addressing the gendered impacts of trade. The WTO in particular supported the development of a free trade feminist gender mainstreaming paradigm. UNCTAD, on the other hand, was a leader among institutions that remained true to more structuralist policy perspectives on trade and showed better recognition of how gender inequalities are co-constitutive of trade inequalities.

2016: Gender goes mainstream

The Trade Impact Working Group of the International Gender Champions (IGC) played a pivotal role in bringing gender concerns into the heart of global trade governance. Established in 2015, the IGC is a highly exclusive international leaders' network, 'bring[ing] together decision-makers determined to break down gender barriers and make gender equality a working reality in their spheres of influence' (IGC, 2025a). IGC members must be the head of an international organization, permanent mission or civil society organization in Geneva, New York, Vienna, Nairobi, The Hague or Paris – all of which are among the world's global governance capitals. They must commit 'to advanc[ing] gender equality in their organization or programmatic work' (IGC, 2025a).

Led by the ITC, Sierra Leone and Iceland, the IGC Trade Impact Group devised a work plan in 2016 that targeted the WTO's Ministerial Conference planned for 2017, inviting then-ITC Executive Director and IGC member Arancha González to participate (Women at the Table, 2025). It drafted the WTO Declaration on Trade and Women's Economic Empowerment (herein: 'the WTO Declaration'), which was adopted as a plurilateral declaration at the 2017 Ministerial Conference and established the foundations for the WTO's gender work (IGC, 2025b). The ITC also made its *SheTrades* programme operational in 2016 (ITC, 2022), following a 'Trailblazers Call to Action'. Issued in September 2015, the ITC's Call to Action aimed 'to bring … one million women entrepreneurs to market' (ITC, 2025a).

In line with his IGC pledges, then-Director General of the WTO and IGC member Roberto Azevêdo created a 'gender focal point' in the WTO

Secretariat in 2016 (WTO, 2021a). A general interest in gender resurfaced among the WTO policy community that year (see Figure 3.1). It occurred in the context of a broader global policy trend towards so-called 'inclusive economy' and inclusive trade[1] following the adoption of 'inclusivity' as one key objective of the 2015 SDGs (Fukuda-Parr, 2023). The year 2016 also witnessed a spike in the integration of gender provisions in FTAs. Until 2015, specific gender-related provisions in FTAs had remained limited and had narrowly focused on women in employment relations or women in development. From 2016, not only did the number of provisions increase significantly, but this was also the year that a dedicated stand-alone gender chapter first appeared in an FTA (Monteiro, 2021). The gender chapter in the Chile–Uruguay FTA included provisions on domestic policies, international agreements, intergovernmental cooperation and institutional arrangements, but did not result in enforceable legal obligations (Hannah et al, 2022).

While gender questions were new to most trade governance elites in 2016, two distinct approaches to tackling gender had been evolving under multilateral trade and development efforts for some time. The WTO's Aid for Trade (AfT) Task Force had promoted women entrepreneurs and value chain integration through trade and development financing since 2006. AfT is a global trade and development policy framework that allocates significant portions of globally available overseas aid funds and informs the trade and development policies of donor and recipient countries globally. Between 2006 and 2022, the international donor community committed AfT funds 'that finance[d] trade-related technical assistance, trade-related infrastructure, and aid to develop productive capacity' (Dorsey, 2007) worth 'a cumulative total of US$648 billion' (WTO and OECD, 2024, p 7).

In 2006, the AfT Task Force recommended a focus on women entrepreneurs in trade and development aid (WTO, 2019a, p 5). Through regular AfT reporting exercises organized by the WTO and OECD, programming gender objectives into trade and development aid was gradually mainstreamed in the first decades of the 2000s. While in 2007, less than 20 per cent of donor countries and a negligible number of recipient countries reported a gender-lens in their AfT activities, numbers rose to 84 per cent and 85 per cent respectively in 2019 (WTO, 2019a, p 4). From 2013 onwards, AfT donors and recipients were also increasingly promoting value chain integration and women's economic empowerment as compatible policy agendas (WTO, 2019a).

UNCTAD's work programme on trade, gender and development, established in 2010, took a different approach. Rather than conflating 'women' and 'gender' as occurred in WTO circles, UNCTAD focused on generating evidence regarding the effects of trade policies on men, women, boys and girls. Instead of orienting development finance towards integrating women entrepreneurs into value chains, UNCTAD worked on identifying and addressing gender-based constraints to so-called 'inclusive

Figure 3.1: World Trade Organization Public Forum session titles, 2001–2024

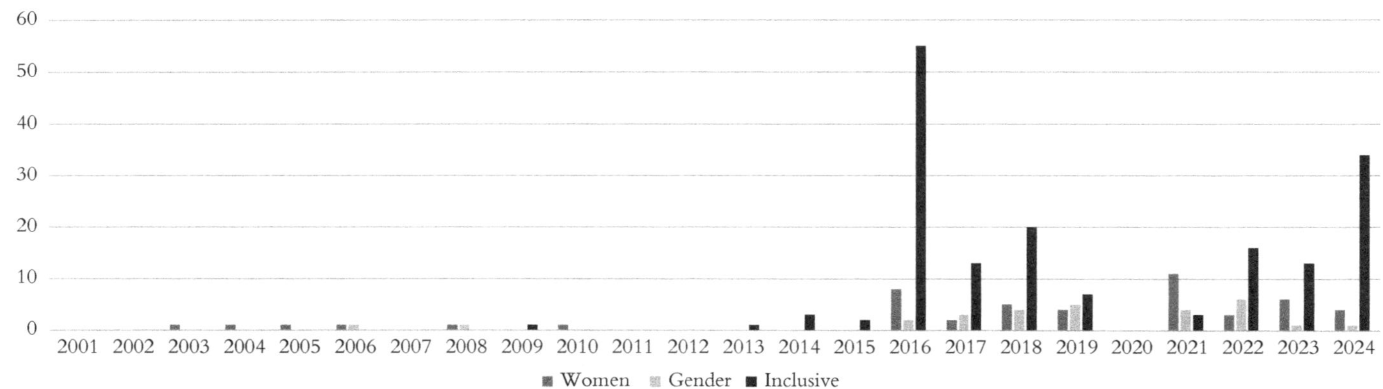

Source: Authors' own calculations of Public Forum session titles using 'women', 'gender', 'inclusive', 'inclusivity' and 'inclusion' based on WTO Public Forum programmes, retrieved from WTO (2025a). There is no data available for 2020 as the Public Forum was cancelled due to the COVID-19 pandemic.

development'. It sought to foreground gender as a social power relation and to strengthen the capacity for member states to mainstream and implement gender in trade policy. This included in-country interventions focused on specific issues, such as those related to cross-border trade (UNCTAD, 2021a, p 2), which, for reasons that we traced in Chapter 2, is often informal and women-dominated in many developing countries.

As global trade policy elites formulated the business case for gender equality in trade governance in the second half of the 2010s, they expanded upon these two approaches to gender, trade and development.

Formulating the business case for gender equality in trade governance

In the early days of the gender and trade agenda, many multilateral and regional trade institutions issued reports in which they made their case for gender mainstreaming in trade (see, for instance, ECOWAS, 2014; 2015; UNCTAD, 2015a; 2017a; UNECA, 2017; WTO, 2017b; APEC, 2019; ITC, 2020a; 2020b). In these reports, most institutions echoed the business case for gender equality. They expressed the belief that greater gender equality in trade should be supported *because* it will lead to good economic outcomes and produce a 'win-win' for gender equality, economic growth and sustainable development. All institutions also linked gender mainstreaming in trade to other international gender equality commitments, including the 1979 Convention on the Elimination of All Forms of Discrimination Against Women (CEDAW), the 1995 Beijing Platform for Action and the UN's SDG 5, to achieve gender equality and empower all women and girls.

SDG 5, in particular, lent legitimacy to the claim that promoting gender equality in trade leads to sustainable forms of development. As different institutions formulated their case for gender mainstreaming in trade, profound differences over how they saw trade and development as linked, and how they understood gender equality to relate to the long-standing trade and development debate, became apparent.

In their reports, many institutions sidestepped the question of what constitutes 'sustainable development' and perpetuated well-established, if contested, trade governance norms about a straightforward relationship between trade liberalization, competitiveness, growth and development (see also Wilkinson, 2012; Trommer, 2014), 'adding gender' into these pre-existing norms. The WTO (2017b; 2021a), the OECD (2021), the World Bank (World Bank and WTO, 2020), ECOWAS (2014; 2015) and UNECA (2017; 2021a), for example, all declared that support for gender equality in trade would lead to growth and sustainable development and benefit poverty reduction more broadly. Some reports (see for instance ITC, 2015) also argued that gender equality in trade supports human capital creation (namely because women are more likely to invest in their children and families) and leads to women's empowerment in other areas, including in social and political life.

Several global South institutions, on the other hand, drew on long-standing critiques of how trade and trade governance perpetuate underdevelopment, and saw gender equality as inherent to development. They tended to ask what trade policies can contribute to both goals. UNCTAD (2015a; 2017a; 2022a), for example, articulated broader aims of gender-equitable development and the reduction of multiple inequalities, including those based on gender. APEC (2019) further emphasized the impacts of trade on decent work, highlighting the problems with focusing exclusively on the expansion of employment without considering how the conditions of this work may be feminized. ECLAC (2022) was the only institution to consider how gender mainstreaming in trade could be used to support social reproduction, or what it referred to as the 'care society'.

The WTO, together with the World Bank and the OECD, actively constructed the free trade feminist belief in the 'virtuous circle' between trade expansion and gender equality in their reports (see World Bank and WTO, 2020, p 6; OECD, 2021). To do so, the institutions built on neoclassical theories which predicted that trade liberalization would result in higher wages and employment for women, better opportunities for female entrepreneurs, and a depression in consumer prices. They largely ignored well-established feminist scholarship showing how trade liberalization plays out, for better *and* for worse, on gendered terrain. Such insights about the links between trade liberalization, employment and income loss, and global feminization of labour processes tended to be expressed in the reports of global South trade governance institutions, which provided gender mainstreaming alternatives to free trade feminism at the time (see UNCTAD, 2016; 2019a; APEC, 2019; UNECA, 2021a; ECLAC, 2022).

We begin our discussion of the underlying assumptions of the 'virtuous circle' with the question of women's wages. In their joint report *Women and Trade: The Role of Trade in Promoting Gender Equality*, the World Bank and WTO built on what they called Gary Becker's 'canonical model' of discrimination (2020, p 6). The model assumes that increased competition brought about by trade liberalization makes it costly for employers to discriminate between different groups of workers, thereby putting downward pressure on the wages of 'privileged' groups. Similarly, in its flagship report, *Trade and Gender: A Framework of Analysis*, the OECD (2021) asserted that the competitive pressures resulting from market openings would make gender-based wage discrimination 'less affordable', despite recognizing that evidence on the links between trade openness and gender equality in the labour market was mixed (2021, pp 17–18).

In other words, these institutions maintained that trade liberalization reduces gender gaps by lowering men's wages relative to women's. From the perspective of the World Bank and WTO, these are positive developments, as they render countries more competitive globally: '[c]ountries that do not allow women to fully participate in the economy are less competitive internationally—particularly those countries with export industries that globally have high female employment rates' (2020, p 48).

From a feminist perspective, these dynamics feminize the labour conditions of male workers. In their reports, global South institutions outlined these and other concerns with trade liberalization. UNECA, for example, pointed out that 'increased trade may, in fact, widen the inequality gap between men and women and further marginalize women' (2021a, p 2). It noted that '[w]hile trade liberalization may, in the long term, bring net benefits overall, it is also clear that its benefits and associated costs are not evenly distributed across economic sectors, and fundamentally, between genders' (2021a, p 1; see also ECOWAS, 2014). UNCTAD (2016, p 1) asserted that '[t]he relationship between trade policies and gender is complex, and there is no clear-cut evidence on the effects of trade liberalization on women. Liberalization can be instrumental in providing new opportunities for women, yet may also, in certain cases, contribute to exacerbating existing gender biases and discrimination'. It warned that '[t]he existence of a well-functioning multilateral trading system will not in itself guarantee economic growth that is equitable among and within countries' (UNCTAD, 2015a, p 4).

Constructing further claims in support of the 'virtuous circle', the World Bank and WTO (2020) and the OECD (2021) posited that trade liberalization creates jobs and economic opportunities for women, who they believe also benefit from lower consumer prices driven by import competition. They argued these dynamics would be especially beneficial for female entrepreneurs and exporters. In relation to the effects of increased exports, the World Bank and WTO asserted that trade creates better jobs for women, as exporting sectors employ more workers 'formally' (2020, p 4), and that trade liberalization may create incentives for expanding women's legal rights and access to resources such as education and technology (2020, p 6).

The OECD declared that smaller sized women-owned enterprises 'benefit even more than larger firms from the removal of barriers to trade, greater transparency in trade regulations and administrative processes and trade facilitating reforms' (2021, p 38) and that trade liberalization, particularly in services, can ameliorate women's over-representation among informal and involuntary part-time workers. This may result, for instance, as trade liberalization furthers the expansion of services and may enable women to purchase services to assist with domestic work (OECD, 2021, p 20).

In relation to increased imports, the OECD defended what it called the 'conventional wisdom' that trade is generally pro-poor, because trade liberalization lowers consumer prices which disproportionately benefits those with lower incomes (2021, p 22). Given that women are over-represented among the poor globally, this is then presumed to be good for them. The World Bank and WTO similarly argued that women and female-headed households are more likely to benefit from tariff reductions as consumers, including of foodstuffs (2020, p 5).

The institutions identified expanding trade sectors as particularly promising from the perspective of women's economic empowerment in trade. Highlighting the growth of trade in services, the rise of GVCs and the adoption of new digital technologies as key trends in the global economy, the World Bank and WTO declared that 'in all three of these areas, women have the opportunity to increase their share of the labour force, increase their own skills and wages, and find ways to achieve better work-life balance' (2020, p ix). These three promises rest on the predictions that masculinist trade theories make about the links between trade liberalization and wages, employment/entrepreneurship opportunities, and consumer prices. These theories have very little to say about how paid employment relates to other opportunities and areas of life, including care, although, in line with the post-Washington Consensus (see Chapter 1), the World Bank and WTO did advocate the need for governments to invest in women's human capital via investment in education, health systems and infrastructure (see, for instance, World Bank and WTO, 2020, p 12).

Contrary to this emerging free trade feminist perspective, in their reports, global South institutions expressed concerns over the effects of import competition on employment, wages, and the ability to consume products and (public) services. UNCTAD, for example, warned that trade liberalization could disrupt sectors where women are concentrated in the workforce, increase competition from imported goods and lower the price of the commodities that women produce (2017a, p 1). It identified connections between trade liberalization and low wages, segmentation in labour-intensive industries, volatile forms of employment and the loss of jobs due to foreign competition (UNCTAD, 2014). It also pointed to the fact that women workers tend to be concentrated in lower segments of value chains and in labour-intensive employment where working conditions remain poor. They also risk being most affected when economic 'upgrading' leads to the de-feminization of employment (UNCTAD, 2015a, p 4). It highlighted the negative impacts of tariff removals on government budgets, which could lead to increases in taxation and unpaid labour (UNCTAD, 2019a, p 5). For all of these reasons, UNCTAD stressed that 'apart from tapping the potentialities of trade, its possible adverse effects also need to be addressed' (2015a, p 4).

Put differently, global South institutions pointed out that the femininization of labour was not a 'win win' for gender equality, economic growth and development, but rather a structural feature of the expansion of the world market and the deepening of the power of capital over labour. ECLAC went further by connecting these processes to the devaluation of reproductive labour and social reproduction, which it suggested needed to be re-valued in trade governance. In its 2022 report *The Care Society*, it pointed to 'the interdependence that exists between production and social reproduction processes', which, it argued, 'highlights the need to rethink the dominant development pattern' and 'to mainstream gender in macroeconomic, trade and development policies, while recognizing and redistributing care' (ECLAC, 2022, p 128). It recommended diversifying the structure of production and trade, so as to create 'more and better employment opportunities for women' and to support their economic autonomy (ECLAC, 2022, p 131). ECLAC also saw these needs in a wider context of global inequalities, pointing out how Latin American and Caribbean countries were particularly 'exposed to the vagaries of international trade, commodity price fluctuations and financial market volatility', and advocating a shift to more regionally focused trade (2022, p 127).

Taking a very different approach, the WTO, the World Bank and the OECD saw care and reproductive labour more broadly as trade barriers for women. This assumption is another defining feature of free trade feminism. Socio-cultural attitudes that cause gender-based discrimination and discriminatory laws (which are believed to be related but not fundamental to economic processes) were similarly seen as trade barriers. Thus, these institutions reiterated the trade productivist standpoint that 'the recognition of unpaid work and care' (OECD, 2021, p 40) or women's reduced access to legal rights and resources (World Bank and WTO, 2020) lay 'clearly outside the realm of trade policy' (OECD, 2021, p 40). They characterized these issues as being 'trade-related' – trade policy jargon for second-order problems in global trade – and declared them to constitute 'obstacles that prevent or hinder [women] from accessing [trade] opportunities' (World Bank and WTO, 2020, p 82).

The understanding that gender inequalities reside in 'extra-economic' spheres replicated trade governance techniques that recognize reproduction while continuing to subordinate it to production, and assuming economic exchange to be gender-neutral. The World Bank and WTO, for example understood limited access to education, difficulties in accessing finance, and '[i]ngrained gender bias for domestic tasks such as child rearing' that 'limits women's flexibility and mobility' (2020, p 82) to be obstacles to women's participation in trade. The ITC similarly saw 'cultural and regulatory barriers, time constraints due to unpaid family care workload, and education choices', as well as issues of limited access to finance, land, information and networks as key reasons for why women benefited less from trade openness than men (2015, p xiii; see also ITC, 2020a, p 1).

With the exception of ECLAC, the emerging free trade feminist construction of reproductive labour as a trade barrier was not effectively countered by global South institutions, which remained true to traditions of paying limited systematic attention to housewifization, that is to say the process through which global trade relations extract value from unpaid, underpaid, invisibilized and unfree labour in the world economy.

Meanwhile, a number of governments and civil society organizations rejected gender mainstreaming in trade governance entirely. For instance, India, South Africa and the US were among the most vocal of the 32 WTO members who chose not to support the WTO Declaration in 2017.[2] India and South Africa's positions in particular show how the gender and trade agenda was contested from the outset inside the WTO along the lines of the trade and development debate. Indian officials reportedly raised concerns that advanced economies would use 'their higher standards in gender-related policies' for protectionist purposes and would target development policies that 'incentivis[e] their women citizens' (Arun, 2017). South Africa's WTO Ambassador expressed concern that the WTO's non-discrimination principles might work against positive discrimination policies in the global economy and highlighted the burdens imposed by new gender monitoring mechanisms on already stretched developing country governments (WTO, 2019b). The Ambassador called for global trade reform in order to 'deliver outcomes for women', in particular in relation to agriculture – given domestic support for agricultural sectors in developed countries – and in relation to the WTO TRIPS and TRIMs Agreements, which she stated 'constrain the ability of governments to really drive the development agenda' (WTO, 2019b).

Civil society organizations and women's movements also asserted that gender mainstreaming in trade required radical reform of the existing trading system. In 2018, in response to the WTO Declaration, civil society groups and women's organizations, many of which had previously been connected to the ITGN, established the Gender and Trade Coalition. They highlighted the negative impacts of global trade on developing countries generally, on women in developing countries, and on a wide range of public policy areas from public health to environmental protection. They also asserted that gender and trade questions needed to be approached from the perspective of gender relations and human rights.

They put forth an alternative set of feminist demands, arguing that 'gendered exploitation is at the heart of the free trade agenda' and 'an international trade system that works for women' requires 'overhaul[ing] our approach to trade' (Hardefeldt, 2017). Ranja Sengupta of Third World Network India called for gender mainstreaming in trade to 'take a comprehensive look' at how trade 'affects women's lives', taking into account 'women everywhere, who do not even trade, who do not even know about trade policy and [that] are getting impacted nevertheless' (WTO, 2019b).

The Gender and Trade Coalition remains a vocal opponent of gender mainstreaming in trade governance (see for instance GTC, 2025), but its demands are typically not heard by trade policy elites. In the process of implementing gender mainstreaming in trade governance, the various institutions not only promoted their particular views on what it entailed, but also all developed concrete trade policy agendas to put their visions into practice. The WTO proved to be particularly apt at leading the agenda.

Implementing gender mainstreaming in trade in the World Trade Organization

Even with the WTO's negotiation and adjudication functions in crisis, its Secretariat had the political clout, international networks and institutional capacity to actively shape global and national gender mainstreaming agendas. Once the decision had been made that the WTO would engage in gender mainstreaming, as expressed by 'the DG [Director General]'s political stance' (WTO, 2017b, p 1) and the plurilateral endorsement of a gender and trade agenda at the 2017 Ministerial Conference, the Secretariat effectively worked to orient gender mainstreaming agendas to align with its emerging free trade version of the business case for gender equality.

The *WTO Action Plan on Trade and Gender* (herein: 'WTO Action Plan'), issued by the WTO Secretariat in October 2017 in the run up to the adoption of the WTO Declaration (WTO, 2017b), was very clear in this respect. Driven by Canada, Ghana, Sierra Leone, Sweden, the EU, the Gambia, the Netherlands and Zambia, the report set out four objectives and five related actions that the WTO Secretariat could take in order 'to frame and structure the WTO's actions on trade and gender' (WTO, 2017b, p 1). These included data-gathering, mapping policy trends, developing training programmes for public officials and women entrepreneurs, and building knowledge and awareness among trade policy communities and the general public.

The WTO Action Plan further discussed how the WTO could leverage its existing administrative, political and technical procedures to implement these actions. It identified as appropriate policy tools the integration of gender-specific questionnaires in AfT monitoring, in the WTO Trade Policy Review (TPR) - an obligatory, regular review exercise of domestic trade policies for all WTO members – and in WTO accession negotiations (WTO, 2017b, p 6). It also identified using the WTO's e-learning programme and its Institute for Training and Technical Cooperation to develop and deliver developing country-focused training courses on trade and gender for government officials, and modules on trade rules for women entrepreneurs (WTO, 2017b, p 8). The WTO Action Plan recognized that the WTO Secretariat could not achieve this alone, and advocated cooperation with other actors.

In addition to these implementation channels, the WTO Action Plan identified a set of 'key political messages' that 'will help explain to WTO Staff and Members why the WTO is focusing on gender, why this issue is important, why there is space in the WTO to integrate gender focused activities and what are the gains of doing so' (WTO, 2017b, p 3). Reflecting emerging free trade feminist assumptions and the wider business case for gender equality, the plan announced that '[t]rade can create opportunities for women's employment and economic development', that '[e]mpowering women means economic efficiency' and that '[t]rade can be a force driving economic empowerment' (WTO, 2017b, pp 3–4).

The Action Plan was agreed when WTO members signed the WTO Declaration in December 2017 and a seminar series was established, focusing on women's entrepreneurship, financial inclusion and trade financing for women traders, the inclusion of women-owned business in value chains and 'the identification of barriers that limit women's participation in trade' (WTO, 2017a). The Declaration's preamble expressed free trade feminist worldviews, declaring 'that international trade and investment are engines of economic growth for both developing and developed countries, and that improving women's access to opportunities and removing barriers to their participation in national and international economies contributes to sustainable economic development' (WTO, 2017a). Taken together, the WTO Action Plan and the WTO Declaration created a sense that a coherent gender mainstreaming agenda oriented around free trade feminist principles constituted 'low-hanging fruit' for multilateral trade governance at a moment when the WTO was in profound legitimacy and political crisis.

WTO-based gender mainstreaming was also diffused through WTO technical and institutional mechanisms such as AfT monitoring and TPR. As noted earlier, gender had increasingly been mainstreamed into AfT programming across the world from the mid-2000s onwards. By 2021, major donors, such as the EU, reported that 'gender equality is mainstreamed into all Aid for Trade programming' (WTO, 2021a). By actively encouraging this trend, the WTO Secretariat embedded free trade feminist assumptions in AfT discussions and gave clear steers that gender mainstreaming should follow free trade feminist principles.

On Women's Day 2018, the WTO Secretariat, for example, issued a leaflet titled 'Aid for Trade and Women's Economic Empowerment: It's an Easy Win and It Works'. The leaflet actively promoted, but did not substantiate, three free trade feminist claims among the wider AfT policy community. It claimed that: 'Aid for Trade contributes to the 2030 Sustainable Development Agenda, gender equality and women's economic empowerment', that '[d]eveloping services capacity in low income countries has a particular impact on women's economic empowerment' and that '[e]-commerce provides economic opportunities for women' (WTO, 2018a, p 1). Using AfT for this messaging was effective for two reasons. The vast majority of governments around the world are, in one way or another, involved with trade and development assistance, and AfT is one of the trade governance mechanisms that brings many financial institutions – including the IMF, the OECD, the World Bank and regional development banks – into the trade governance arena.

TPRs constituted another springboard for implementing and diffusing the free trade feminist vision for the gender and trade agenda. The WTO Secretariat began asking members questions about their gender and trade policies in these reviews in the mid-2010s. According to the Secretariat, 111 TPRs conducted from 2014 to 2018 revealed that 77 members had implemented at least one policy aimed at women's empowerment (WTO, 2019c). It identified 30 different types of women's empowerment policies, finding that, overall, policy activity focused on a narrow range of policies, namely 'financial and non-financial incentives to the private sector and women-owned/led Micro, Small, and Medium Enterprises', agriculture and fishery, and government procurement (WTO, 2019c, p 2).

Gendered effects stemming from housewifization and trading on social reproduction were not considered in TPRs. In her feminist analysis of TPRs, Caroline Dommen finds that they rarely focus on how trade and trade rules impact men and women differently and tend to focus on women exclusively in their economic roles as workers, business owners and at times consumers (rather than as carers, taxpayers, users of public services, and so on) (see also Hannah et al, 2018). She notes that

> no reference was found to possible negative impacts of trade and trade rules on gender equality, to indirect impacts of trade on women not engaged in trade, or to steps taken to identify or minimise possible gender inequality impacts of new rules under negotiation at the WTO. None refer to gendered impacts of regulatory measures such as those relating to intellectual property, government procurement, or domestic regulation of services. Another gap is the lack of evidence of Members having considered the impact of commitments made in services schedules on gender equality, or on governments' policy space to implement measures in favour of gender equality. (Dommen, 2023, pp 12–13)

In this way, WTO gender mainstreaming efforts reproduced rather than undermined the invisibilization of social reproduction and the multifaceted gendered impacts of trade – both positive and negative. From our perspective, these are key limitations of free trade feminist empowerment initiatives, to which we will return in subsequent chapters.

Gender mainstreaming beyond the World Trade Organization

The WTO Secretariat found support from the ITC in its political project of promoting free trade feminist worldviews and implementing gender mainstreaming in trade in accordance with free trade feminist principles. As indicated earlier, *SheTrades*, the ITC's flagship women's empowerment programme, was consolidated in 2016 within the spirit of the wider business case for gender equality, namely to grow the global economy through women's participation in trade (ITC, 2025a). The ITC developed gender mainstreaming strategies that it implemented in a range of different global South countries, typically collaborating with different state and non-state development policy partners. These strategies generally relied on a mix of information gathering, and capacity building and financial inclusion programmes for women entrepreneurs in developing countries with the intention of connecting them to global markets (see Box 3.1). With a portfolio of around US$54 million between 2015 and 2022, the ITC actively prioritized women and businesses that it considered to be 'near-export ready' over more marginalized groups of women (ITC, 2022).

Box 3.1: *SheTrades* offerings

SheTrades.com. A website acting as a 'one-stop-shop' for women entrepreneurs, offering them information about and access to the programme, news features and success stories.

SheTradesOutlook. An interactive data tool used to assess, monitor and improve women's participation in trade.

SheTrades Academy. A 'virtual learning space' with close to 200 training videos for women entrepreneurs/business owners.

ITC SheTrades Hubs. Resource centres for women-led businesses, policy makers, business organizations and the private sector that are co-implemented with national and regional institutions. There are 15 in-country and two regional hubs across Africa, Asia, Latin America, the Caribbean, and Middle East and North Africa region.

SheTrades Invest. A programme building connections between investors and women seeking funding, to build the capacity of women entrepreneurs to become investment ready, and to promote the field of gender-lens investing.

SheTrades Global Events. Trade fairs connecting women entrepreneurs who are export-ready with potential buyers, investors and partners. Events were held in Ethiopia, the UK, Turkey, Brazil, Rwanda, Mexico and China, and purportedly generated over US$80 million of new business for women entrepreneurs.

SheTrades Projects. Micro-level support for women entrepreneurs and women-owned MSMEs in different countries or regions. Most projects last 1–2 years and involve funding of less than US$1 million.

SheTrades Partnerships. According to the ITC, more than 200 partnerships have been developed with funders, business services organizations, the private sector and policy-making institutions. The website lists a number of active partnerships, mainly with private sector partners, including partnerships with UPS, Mary Kay, Visa and Unilever.

Policy Advocacy. This occurs under the umbrella of *SheTrades* projects and Hubs, but also under lone initiatives such as the *SheTrades* Trade Impact Group funded by the EU Directorate-General for Trade, contributing to gender mainstreaming in trade governance through research and partnerships, including in the WTO Informal Working Group on Trade and Gender and the International Gender Champions Trade Impact Group.

Source: This box is based on information available on the *SheTrades* website (last accessed 2 March 2025), and a similar list published by the ITC (2022, p 3). Updated figures can be found at shetrades.com.

Departing from the WTO/ITC approach, in the early years of gender mainstreaming in global trade, the UNCTAD Secretariat and a number of regional institutions employed a broader view of the gendered impacts of trade. These institutions sought to develop trade policy agendas that would take into account and work to address, at least to some extent, the structural hierarchies and exclusions that we outlined in Chapter 2. Like the WTO and the ITC, the UNCTAD Secretariat and its Trade, Gender and Development Programme in particular relied on capacity building, information sharing and advocacy to promote its preferred mode of gender mainstreaming in trade (UNCTAD, 2015a). However, UNCTAD had fewer direct levers for shaping or delivering trade and development finance at its disposal when compared to the WTO or the ITC. Nonetheless, in the mid-2010s, the scope and scale of UNCTAD's activities was such that it presented a credible global alternative to free trade feminism in gender mainstreaming.

UNCTAD's distinctive approach to gender mainstreaming in trade emphasized the need to consider the wider economic, social and political contexts of each country and was not categorically for or against trade liberalization. In 2015, for example, UNCTAD launched its online trade and gender training courses for international and national civil servants, and members of global policy communities working on trade and development. Some 104 participants from 51 countries attended the first ever course to discuss 'the conceptual, theoretical and empirical links between trade and gender' (UNCTAD, 2015b). Subsequent courses across 2016–2020 focused on how trade liberalization affected women versus men, and how gender could be mainstreamed in trade policy (UNCTAD, 2025). It published numerous studies on gender and trade in different countries and regions and distilled its findings in numerous policy briefings. The studies integrated not only trade but also labour market dynamics and considered complementary policies to support gender equality and women's empowerment (UNCTAD, 2015a, p 1).

In 2017, UNCTAD launched its *Trade and Gender Toolbox*, which prescribed a methodology for ex-ante assessments of the gendered impacts of trade policies. While still based in part in the business case for gender equality, the Toolbox departed from free trade feminism in important ways. It asserted, for instance, that '[t]rade liberalization can have either a positive or negative impact on women and gender inequalities', that '[t]his matters both for equity concerns and for long-run growth' and that '[t]he gender impact is context-specific and needs to be evaluated on a case-by-case basis' (Piovani, 2017, p 3). The *Toolbox* asked analysts to begin by assessing gender inequalities and the economic context of the country being considered before engaging in quantitative analysis of the expected consequences of trade policies on the economy and women's participation therein. It supplemented quantitative assessments with a checklist for gender-sensitive accompanying measures and monitoring indicators. The checklist included unpaid labour and care work, and pointed to the need to assess, for instance, whether export promotion policies included support for childcare and whether reductions in public expenditures and increases in taxation affected access to public services and the burden of care work (UNCTAD, 2017a, p 28).

While the *Toolbox* has been used in the impact assessment of the Economic Partnership Agreement between the EU and the East African Community (UNCTAD, 2017a) and certain governments showed initial interest in it (see, for instance, Shaw and Jobes, 2019), we have found little evidence that it has been widely discussed or applied in trade policy circles. This is despite the fact that gender and trade policy communities regularly reviewed UNCTAD reports in the context of trying to identify best practices for gathering gender-sensitive trade data (see, for instance, WTO, 2021b). Instead, free trade feminist agendas gradually displaced more structuralist approaches to gender mainstreaming in trade towards the late 2010s. In its review of gender-based impact assessment methodologies, the OECD (2021) does not even mention the UNCTAD *Toolbox*.

Yet, this displacement was not a given at the time. The COVID-19 pandemic starting in late 2019 drew unprecedented public attention to the fundamental interconnections between social reproduction and other economic processes. The rapid evolution of a public health crisis into a generalized economic crisis made clear that people – especially those engaged in care work and other so-called 'essential work' – are at the centre of all economic activity (Stevano et al, 2021). As Tithi Bhattacharya explained, the COVID-19 pandemic 'clarified what social reproduction feminists have been saying for a while, which is that care work and life-making work are the essential work of society' (Jaffe, 2020).

During the pandemic, policy elites actively searched for ways of creating prosperity and more equitable societies for the post-pandemic era (UN, 2020). Counterintuitively, perhaps, it was in this context that free trade feminism became the dominant gender mainstreaming paradigm in global trade.

Free trade feminism rises

The 2020–2023 COVID-19 pandemic led to the loss of millions of lives, the overburdening of healthcare systems, widespread economic disruption, and the exacerbation of socioeconomic inequalities within and between countries. The pandemic also caused the world's biggest trade contraction since the 1930s Great Depression (Baldwin, 2020) and threatened to throw gender equality back by four decades (UNCTAD, 2021a). Highlighting some of these dynamics, the WTO explained in an information note in August 2020 that:

> [t]he temporary closures of schools and childcare facilities has had a significant impact on working families, with the resultant burden falling disproportionately on working mothers. Some have had to change their work schedules, reduce their working hours or take unpaid leave. Stay-at-home orders have also increased incidences of domestic violence against women and children. In parallel, women who lose their jobs or are required to reduce working hours also face lower opportunities than men of finding jobs, in part because employers may believe women have more limited flexibility due to greater housework and childcare responsibilities compared to their male counterparts. Given that, on average, women continue to earn less than men, income losses due to the COVID-19 recession may further increase poverty among women. (WTO, 2020a, p 4)

These insights, however, did not lead policy elites to rethink the general goals and policy orientations of trade governance (Trommer, 2022; Roberts and Trommer, 2026). Instead, as we show in what follows, they further consolidated and reinforced the business case for gender equality. Most significantly, in the midst of the pandemic, divisions around the gender and trade agenda became visible in UNCTAD. These divisions were ostensibly eventually settled in favour of free trade feminism, a fundamental shift in UNCTAD's position that deprived those actors who favoured more structuralist approaches to gender mainstreaming in trade of their most powerful institutional voice and ally in global trade governance.

At the same time, the WTO's gender and trade work expanded during the pandemic years, as newly formed committees and informal groups within the WTO – that included not only many global North and South governments from around the world but also actors from other areas of global governance – further developed, promoted and implemented free trade feminist principles. We argue in this section that despite sustained critiques from a small number of WTO members, civil society groups and institutions such as ECLAC, policy makers in global trade governance, regional and national trade governance and, increasingly, in other global governance arenas, widely accept free trade feminism as the common-sense approach to gender mainstreaming in trade today.

COVID-19, UNCTAD and the hegemony of free trade feminism

Global policy elites framed the COVID-19 pandemic as an event that provided new urgency to gender mainstreaming in trade and embedded free trade feminist principles in their concrete policy recommendations for the COVID-19 policy response. The World Bank and the WTO, for example, explained that the research underlying their *Women and Trade* report was conducted prior to the COVID-19 outbreak, but that the pandemic made its conclusions and policy recommendations 'more relevant than ever' (World Bank and WTO, 2020, p ix). In an information note published in August 2020, the WTO echoed the spirit of the report, arguing that '[m]aintaining open markets during the recovery period is key to building faster and more inclusive growth', and that '[o]pen markets need to be accompanied by appropriate labour and education policies as well as legal and social reforms to support women workers, consumers and traders' (WTO, 2020a, p 9). Reportedly, policy elites agreed that women's empowerment through trade had become an 'important issue' for the WTO 'as a result of the disproportionate impact of the COVID-19 pandemic on women' (Geneva Trade Platform, 2023).

Gender mainstreaming programmes now concentrated even more narrowly on women's economic performance in the productive economy. ITC *SheTrades*, for example, ceased integrating the power to make and act on economic decisions, including in the household, in its understanding of women's empowerment, and began articulating it narrowly in terms of advancing economically in the market (ITC, 2022, p 4). The OECD put forward a framework for governments to assess 'the impact of their trade policies on women'. In contrast with the UNCTAD *Toolbox*, the OECD took a narrow focus on 'sectors in which women work and own businesses' (OECD, 2021, p 51). Although recognizing problems with 'gender balance in trade policy participation', it recommended, in line with free trade feminist principles, that accompanying policies to trade liberalization should tackle 'barriers to women's participation in trade'. It listed these as lacking 'access to credit and finance', 'shallow business networks' and 'lack of time' due to 'unpaid work undertaken by women' (OECD, 2021, pp 54–57).

In WTO discussions, members and observers made clear that their gender mainstreaming efforts were primarily concerned with 'the *trade and women's economic empowerment nexus* and how this issue is integrated into Members' trade and trade policies' (WTO, 2021b, p 1, emphasis added). When various members and observers reported their COVID-19-specific trade and women's economic empowerment initiatives to the WTO in 2021, the Asian Development Bank, Mauritius, Peru and Vietnam's initiatives were entirely focused on women entrepreneurs and women-owned MSMEs (WTO, 2021b, pp 8–9). Korea also reported 'financial support for family care', and Australia reported programmes 'support[ing] women's economic empowerment, leadership, ending violence against women and girls, and access to sexual and reproductive health and rights'. ECLAC again stood out by stating that 'international trade should be reoriented towards the transformative social economic recovery with gender equality' in order 'to mitigate the COVID-19 impact on women in Latin America' (WTO, 2021b, p 8).

The rising dominance of free trade feminism was also startingly apparent in the COVID-19 TRIPS waiver debate at the time. The TRIPS waiver debate was one of the most highly visible trade policy controversies of the COVID-19 years. In October 2020, India and South Africa proposed in the WTO that members should suspend patents and other TRIPS provisions in relation to IPRs on all medical products required to fight the pandemic. The goal was to temporarily suspend these provisions to facilitate the global production and distribution of essential medical products. While over 100 countries backed the proposal, including, in a narrowed down version, the US, it was opposed by other countries, including the UK and the EU, who argued that IPRs played a 'positive role' in supporting medical innovation (Manley, 2021).

From our feminist perspective, IPRs enable corporations and investors to capitalize on life-making work and knowledge through trade. Explaining the gendered effects of IPRs, the Gender and Trade Coalition asked the European Commission in a public letter to support the TRIPS waiver because:

> [g]iven the relative lack of power of women and gender non-conforming people economically, socially, and politically, including on the basis of race, caste, class, sexuality, ethnicity, religion, migratory status, whenever there is limited supply of essential products, including critical medical products, they face the greatest barriers to access. If medical diagnostics, treatment, and care are expensive, women and gender non-conforming people often give up use, voluntarily or

> involuntarily, in order to save household resources and ensure supply for the male members. (GTC, 2020)

Yet, such concerns were left outside of extensive and high-profile WTO negotiations on TRIPS provisions during the COVID-19 pandemic. More strikingly, we also encountered perfect silence around the TRIPS waiver debate in the countless documents on gender mainstreaming that we analysed for our research, and in our numerous direct observations of gender and trade policy events. As the waiver negotiations in the TRIPS Council drew considerable global public attention to WTO-based trade multilateralism and to problems with global 'vaccine equity' (Hannah et al, 2021b), gender mainstreaming discussions taking place *within the same building* focused narrowly on women's employment and entrepreneurship and their contributions to economic recovery and growth.

In trade productivist fashion, global trade policy elites were separating what they considered to be the 'hard core' of trade law strictly from their gender mainstreaming efforts, even where existing trade rules and governance mechanisms had been shown to negatively affect marginalized genders, intersectional inequality, and the conditions in which reproductive labour and social reproduction take place. Free trade feminism and its political project of fostering trade expansion and removing obstacles to women entrepreneurs' participation within *existing* global trade rules and arrangements seemed to have entirely overtaken the WTO – ironically within the context of a global pandemic in which global policy elites expressed concern for gender relations, women's work and reproduction.

Furthermore, during the COVID-19 pandemic, UNCTAD gradually began dropping its structuralist objections and alternative approaches that had been informed by more critical feminist analyses of trade. In part, UNCTAD had long-standing programmes that were a 'natural' fit with free trade feminism. For example, UNCTAD's entrepreneurship programme, Empretec, was established in 1988, but increasingly focused on women entrepreneurs and women-owned MSMEs as gender went mainstream in global trade governance (UNCTAD, 2015c). UNCTAD also had a well-developed work programme providing training and capacity building for women engaged in cross-border trade, which was also focused on women entrepreneurs and increasingly on those involved in e-commerce. It provided, for instance, training related to tackling gender-specific obstacles at borders, trade rules and procedures, and entrepreneurial and business skills. In 2019, UNCTAD launched the *eTrade for Women* Initiative to support female entrepreneurs in developing countries working in e-commerce and the digital economy, and to bring their voices into policy processes at the local, regional and global levels (see, for instance, UNCTAD, 2025).

Tensions between those within UNCTAD that subscribed to its traditional structuralist perspective on gender and trade and those that aligned with free trade feminism became evident during UNCTAD's inaugural Gender and Development Forum in 2021. Taking place in the context of its Bridgetown Covenant, at which UNCTAD renegotiated its mandate, the Forum was spearheaded by host country Barbados in collaboration with various feminist groups, civil society organizations, academics and activists. Echoing UNCTAD's traditional concerns with global feminization of labour processes, UNCTAD Deputy Secretary-General Isabelle Durant explained at the Forum that the jobs that trade liberalization had created for women, even in the context of South–South trade agreements, had been 'mainly in simple tasks that do not include management or supervisory responsibilities'. She stated: 'they are not empowering jobs' (UNCTAD, 2021b).

Other speakers presented free trade feminist arguments that governments had to 'help create virtuous circles that empower women and allow them to take advantage of new economic opportunities', citing access to finance and to land titles and core labour standards in trade agreements as key supporting policies (UNCTAD, 2021b). Finland's trade and development minister, Ville Skinnari, stressed that in order for women to benefit from trade opportunities, governments had to tackle domestic 'gender-based obstacles'. In her closing remarks to the meeting, UNCTAD Secretary-General Rebeca Grynspan articulated the free trade feminist view that women's empowerment through trade required increasing women's participation in trade and removing obstacles through domestic policies (UNCTAD, 2021b).

The outcome document of the Bridgetown conference signalled that these tensions had been resolved in favour of free trade feminism, and that perspectives that framed gendered inequalities as structurally entangled with global trade inequalities and environmental degradation were losing sway within UNCTAD. Notably, within the outcome document, UNCTAD called for enhanced trade liberalization to tackle global problems and encouraged gender mainstreaming and support for 'women's economic empowerment, economic security and rights' and the enhancement of their digital skills and opportunities (UNCTAD, 2022a, pp 37–43). It also reaffirmed its commitment to 'an open, transparent, inclusive, non-discriminatory, rules-based, multilateral trading system under the World Trade Organization' (UNCTAD, 2022a, pp 36–37). It did not, however, reiterate concerns over how the WTO system interacts with international and gender inequalities, which it had raised in previous trade and gender publications (for example, UNCTAD, 2015a).

Official documents submitted for the Bridgetown Covenant reveal considerable internal contestations around these revised goals, suggesting that in 2021 UNCTAD was embroiled in a wider struggle over its mandate. Supported in its position by civil society groups (see, for instance, Civil Society Declaration, 2021), China and the G77 group (made up of developing countries members) argued that UNCTAD needed to set 'a developmental narrative' that acknowledged and addressed global challenges, including international inequalities, climate change, escalating debt crises, commodity dependence, food insecurity, lack of basic services and infrastructures, growing coercive unilateralism and more (UNCTAD, 2021c). The Gender and Development Forum called out the narrow focus on economic empowerment and on entrepreneurs put forward during the Covenant and argued for the need to promote a radical restructuring of the global political economy in line with feminist and ecological principles. These included a prioritization of gender justice and the respect for life and ecosystems above the economic aims of trade and investment agreements (UNCTAD, 2021c). It noted that:

> [f]undamentally, the state of the global political economy is based on inequitable and uneven power relations between States in which countries of the global South continue to experience an extractive relationship, which minimizes the value of primary commodities and reduces countries to net importers of goods and services. These extractive relations which are the basis of privatized profit by the few are at the heart of the existential climate crisis that we all face. And we recognize the parallel undervaluing of women's labour within the household, community and national economies which mirror and reinforce the extractive and unequal relations between countries of the global North and the global South. (UNCTAD, 2021c, p 2)

Critics accused a block of developed countries, led by the EU, to be largely responsible for the outcome document's clear commitments to trade liberalization and to the credo that trade expansion is central to achieving sustainable development (see James, 2021). The Gender and Trade Coalition provided evidence of pressuring tactics long familiar from WTO negotiations (Jawara and Kwa, 2004), when it reported that the EU tabled a proposal whereby 'UNCTAD publications shall always undergo an established peer review process with relevant UN and other entities, as well as … incorporating existing academic research and reports of relevant international organizations' (GTC, 2021, p 4; see also Civil Society Declaration, 2021, p 2). While this was hollowed out in the outcome document, the episode suggests that there were significant behind-the-scenes struggles over who set the narrative of sustainable development and in line with which priorities within UNCTAD. The outcome helped set the tone for the UNCTAD Secretariat to further align its gender and trade work programme with free trade feminism.

UNCTAD's active participation in the many informal working groups, committees and special expert groups that the WTO Secretariat set up during the global pandemic and which fostered the global diffusion of free trade feminism provides further evidence of this gradual alignment. It is to these informal governance mechanisms that we turn next.

The global diffusion of free trade feminism

During the pandemic years, the WTO successfully established itself as the main global governance hub for trade and gender mainstreaming. The WTO Secretariat and WTO members created various networks and groups, which further developed and implemented free trade feminist policy approaches to gender mainstreaming and from where free trade feminism diffused to regional and national trade governance levels and beyond. During this period, WTO-based gender mainstreaming predominantly involved international organizations, states and business representatives, think tanks, academic experts and researchers, while civil society voices found themselves increasingly marginalized. We discuss specifically the WTO Gender Research Hub and the WTO IWG on Trade and Gender.

The WTO Secretariat launched the Gender Research Hub in 2021 as a follow-up to the 2017 WTO Declaration and the Action Plan. Conceived as 'an international network of trade and gender researchers working in academia and international organizations' (WTO, 2022a, p 5), its aim is to foster and disseminate research on gender and trade, and to provide WTO members interested in gender questions with state-of-the-art research and scholarship. At the time of writing, the Hub is comprised of researchers from the WTO Secretariat, ECLAC, IMF, ITC, OECD, UNCTAD, UNECA and the World Bank, as well as four WTO Chairs (Mexico, Chile, Barbados and South Africa) and eight universities (WTO, 2025b).[3] The Gender and Trade Coalition has expressed dismay that the Hub does not include women's groups or civil society organizations, which it sees as reflecting a lack of a plurality of voices, 'especially those from developing countries and working at grassroot levels, in the whole process' of WTO gender mainstreaming (GTC, 2022, p 1).

In addition to its function as a knowledge leader on gender questions inside the WTO, the Hub organizes regular, public-facing seminars and conferences. It typically works together with UNCTAD staff, although representatives of the ITC, the World Bank, UN Women, and WTO Ambassadors, academics and entrepreneurs have also participated. These events have included the 2022 World Trade Congress on Gender, a 2023 Youth Trade Summit and public discussion sessions 'Think Up!', published on the WTO Conference Services YouTube channel.[4] Sessions are typically curated around topics such as gender-based research data, women's economic empowerment, women entrepreneurs and traders, e-commerce, investment, trade finance, trade in services, digital trade and trade diagnostics. They are committed to the business case for gender equality to the point of framing gender-based violence as 'an economic crisis and a trade cost',[5] or asking young participants, typically students, to make individual pledges on gender mainstreaming in trade.

The WTO IWG on Trade and Gender (hereafter: 'the IWG') has been the most influential policy network in terms of legitimating, advancing and implementing free trade feminism. IWGs are typically set up by sub-groups of WTO members to hold structured discussions around controversial issues that other members block from entering the negotiating agenda (Brodsky et al, 2021).[6] Established in September 2020 to meet the commitments made in the Action Plan and the Declaration (WTO, 2025c), the IWG on Trade and Gender stood out from other thematic IWGs 'thanks to its exceptionally large membership, clear goals, and defined roadmap' (Brodsky et al, 2021).

Beginning with membership, 130 out of 164 WTO members are active in the IWG (WTO, 2024a), making it a group that is dominated by developing country members. International organizations working in global economic governance on themes such as debt and finance, development, or IPRs, as well as organizations working in wider areas, such as gender equality or food, also participate in the IWG (see Table 3.1), while non-state interests are for the most part excluded. Exceptions to this have been made over the years for a narrow set of actors, including the self-declared non-feminist, women-only trade policy think tank 'Trade Experettes', women's entrepreneurship advocates such as Sheela Bide (India) and UKODER (Turkey), a handful of academics, and the global logistics corporation UPS. Some active members, such as long-standing IWG Co-Chair El Salvador, perform poorly on the World Population Review's Gender Equality Index.

In terms of goals, the IWG has successfully promoted women's entrepreneurship and financial inclusion agendas as key policy tools that can deliver on the free trade feminist vision of expanding gender equality through increased trade. While we found repeated concerns for structural inequalities and conditions of reproductive labour in publicly available IWG documents, the conversations overall have nonetheless narrowly focused on economic empowerment via entrepreneurship (see Figure 3.2). The IWG's International Prize for Gender Equality in Trade, launched on International Women's Day in 2024, also predominantly recognized policy programmes that aligned with these themes, including projects focused on women's entrepreneurship, rights in the workplace, trade facilitation and gender-lens investing in Chile, Pakistan, Spain, Colombia, Brazil, Ghana and the Dominican Republic (WTO, 2024b).

In terms of roadmap, the IWG has continually advanced gender mainstreaming in the WTO at Ministerial Conferences, in AfT and TPRs, and in other WTO bodies and committees (WTO, 2021b). In 2023, it further began joint work with the WTO IWG on MSMEs on access to finance

Table 3.1: Chairs and invited presenters of Informal Working Group meetings, 2020–2025

IWG co-chairs	Invited presentations by WTO members	Invited presentation by international organizations	Invited presentations by non-state groups or individuals
Australia (11/2025–) Botswana (12/2020–12/2023) Cape Verde (7/2023–) El Salvador (4/2021–) Iceland (12/2020–6/2023) UK (7/2023–10/2025)	Australia Brazil Canada China Chile Colombia Dominican Republic Ecuador El Salvador EU The Gambia Iceland Korea Mauritius Mexico Mongolia New Zealand Nigeria Norway Pakistan Peru Russian Federation Saudi Arabia Spain Turkey UK US	CEDAW ECLAC Enhanced Integrated Framework (EIF) FAO Islamic Development Bank ITC OECD Secretariat for Central American Economic Integration (SIECA) UNCTAD United Nations Development Programme (UNDP) United Nations Economic Commission for Europe (UNECE) United Nations Economic and Social Commission for Asia and the Pacific (UNESCAP) Universal Postal Union (UPU) UN Women World Customs Organization (WCO) World Intellectual Property Organization (WIPO) World Bank WTO Secretariat	Amrita Bahri, Mexico Autonomous Institute of Technology Centro por la Justicia y el Derecho Internacional Elisa Fornalé, World Trade Institute Eylla Laire Gutierrez, Asian Institute of Management IGC Trade Impact Group Sheela Bhide Trade Experettes UKODER UPS

Source: Compiled by authors based on documents available online at WTO (2026b).

and financial inclusion (WTO, 2023a) and on trade and investment policy (WTO, 2024c). This shows an emerging governance consensus that financial and digital inclusion constitute key policy tools that can support women's empowerment through trade and deliver on the free trade feminist promises of increased gender equality, growth and development through increased trade exposure – ideas that we will encounter again in subsequent chapters.

At the 2024 WTO Ministerial Conference in Abu Dhabi, the two IWGs officially launched the *Compendium of Financial Inclusion Initiatives for Women*

Figure 3.2: Discussions in Informal Working Group meetings, 2020–2025

Source: Derived using an NVivo word frequency query based on publicly available IWG documents, 2020–2025.

Entrepreneurs (WTO, 2023a; see also WTO, 2024d) as a gender mainstreaming tool for trade policy makers around the world. They also released a 'Joint Statement on Promoting Inclusive and Sustainable Trade Growth through Gender Equality and Building a Gender-responsive WTO' (WTO, 2024a). The statement highlighted, *inter alia*, that the IWGs engaged with the WTO's Trade and Environmental Structured Discussions, indicating an increasing merging of free trade feminism with liberal environmental politics – a development that we will also return to in the subsequent chapters. Together with the ITC, the WTO Secretariat also launched the *Women Exporters in the Digital Economy (WEIDE) Fund* at the Ministerial Conference. Supported by the United Arab Emirates and the FIFA World Cup Qatar Legacy Fund, WEIDE provides US$50 million for 'unlock[ing] opportunities in international trade and digital trade for women entrepreneurs', notably through policy initiatives that promote access to finance and to digital platforms, export performance and competitiveness (ITC, 2025b). All of these initiatives reflect the normalization of the proposition that the interests of women in trade converge with the interests of small-scale entrepreneurs in trade, and that lack of access to finance represents a key barrier faced by both groups.

Finally, the IWG has played a key role in keeping the gender agenda alive in the WTO and beyond, despite continued opposition. During the WTO's 2022 Ministerial Conference, for example, a small number of WTO members successfully opposed the adoption of an updated WTO Declaration on Trade, Gender Equality and Women's Economic Empowerment (Dommen, 2022).

Nonetheless, the outcome document of the 2022 and 2024 Ministerial Conferences recognized that women's participation in trade contributes to economic growth and sustainable development and take note of the WTO's work, alongside UNCTAD and ITC, on the topic (WTO, 2022b; 2024e). The WTO Secretariat subsequently expanded its work on gender mainstreaming, for example by mainstreaming gender into its Technical Assistance and Training plan (WTO, 2023b), aiming to provide trade and gender training to over 600 trade officials by 2025 (WTO, 2025d).

The IWG was also instrumental when the second Trump administration began attacking equality, inclusion and diversity policies, free trade, and multilateralism in early 2025. As we discuss further in chapter 6, the WTO Gender Hub's second World Trade Congress on Gender was an early political victim of the second Trump administration trade policies, when the WTO Secretariat cancelled the event. Nonetheless, the IWG continued its work regardless of the anti-gender politics pursued by the government of one of the most powerful WTO members. It developed a new work programme in June 2025 (WTO, 2025e), which, among other goals, set out concrete plans for mainstreaming gender across all WTO bodies to be achieved by the 14th WTO Ministerial Conference in March 2026 in Cameroon. The IWG also continued joint work with the IWG on MSMEs on promoting financial inclusion, access to finance and women's empowerment through digital trade (see, for instance, WTO, 2025f).

Outside of the WTO, the ITC continues to promote women's economic empowerment and women's entrepreneurship initiatives with a particular focus on digital trade, trade and finance, and trade facilitation, working together with governments from all around the world through its *SheTrades* programme (ITC, 2026). To mark the ten-year anniversary of *SheTrades*, it launched its online 'SheTrades@10' seminar series, educating women entrepreneurs on trade facilitation, digital trade and trade finance, with support from corporate sponsors such as UPS or Visa (see, for instance, ITC, 2025c).

A wide range of institutions have also participated in the policy discussions through which free trade feminism has been normalized and from which it has emerged as hegemonic. One example is the involvement of WTO Secretariat staff in producing policy and scholarly publications on gender and trade, including in an ILO publication, *Integrating Trade and Decent Work* (WTO, 2022a; der Boghossian, 2023a; 2023b; 2023c; 2023d; 2023e; ILO, 2023). The publications diffuse free trade feminist beliefs in the virtuous circle of trade expansion and gender equality and in the assumed positive links between women's economic empowerment, trade growth and poverty reduction across global governance and into the ILO's decent work agenda (WTO, 2022a, p 7; ILO, 2023, p 251). There is very little, if any, acknowledgement of the negative impacts of trade liberalization on wages or the conditions of work that feminists have consistently documented and critiqued, nor of the processes that we refer to as housewifization and trading on social reproduction.

Instead, the publications promote free trade feminism's particular understanding of 'negative gender social norms', such as discriminatory domestic laws and regulations, higher burdens of reproductive and care work, and gender-based violence, as being prime reasons for women's reduced ability to enjoy gains from trade (WTO, 2022a, p 8; ILO, 2023, p 251), typically citing the World Bank and WTO flagship report as evidence for the various claims (WTO, 2022a, pp 7–8; ILO, 2023, p 250).

Given the hegemonic status that free trade feminism has reached in trade governance and global governance today, it is therefore time to ask what its political project means for the entanglements of trade governance with gender-based and other forms of inequality and exclusion in the contemporary political economy.

Conclusion

Despite being largely driven by global policy elites, gender mainstreaming in trade was initially varied and contested, with emerging free trade feminist narratives and policy initiatives existing alongside gender mainstreaming approaches that aimed to address, at least in part, some of the structural features of global trade that we identified in Chapter 2. The Secretariats of the three main multilateral trade governance institutions, the WTO, ITC and UNCTAD, all played decisive roles at varying points in time in establishing free trade feminism as the hegemonic governance approach to gender and trade across the world today. As it turned out, their political capabilities to pursue their preferred mode of gender mainstreaming in trade were unmatched by the regional institutions, or by opponents from the ranks of WTO members or civil society.

While global trade policy elites devised and implemented free trade feminism, its political project is not specific to the global North, nor has it remained confined to trade governance alone. As we will further document in the next two chapters, governments and regional trade institutions of developed and developing countries alike drive gender mainstreaming agendas and free trade feminist discourses and initiatives within the WTO and in regional and national policies.

In order to further examine what free trade feminism means for gender-based and other forms of inequality in the global economy, the next two chapters delve into two trade sectors where free trade feminist policy initiatives are particularly active: food and agricultural trade and digital trade (see World Bank and WTO, 2020, p ix). While food and agriculture are some of the most long-standing controversial areas of global trade governance, free trade feminism largely overlooks these contestations, and posits the integration of women into global agricultural value chains as an obvious solution to the problems of *both* women's marginalization *and* of underdevelopment, food insecurity and (for some) climate change.

In contrast, digital trade is a relatively new, but increasingly important, aspect of trade governance. It also has potentially dramatic implications for gender relations, though trade governance bodies and free trade feminist policy elites tend to leave those unaddressed. Instead, they focus primarily on how digital inclusion can benefit women entrepreneurs. In exploring these two areas in detail, we both illuminate the limits of free trade feminism and, drawing on broader political economy literatures, outline how this approach risks reproducing key forms of gender and intersectional inequality and fuelling geographically specific and variegated crises of social reproduction.

4

Food Trade

Food trade has long been one of the most heavily contested aspects of global trade governance. In 1994, peasants in Chiapas, Mexico, engaged in an uprising sparked by fears that Mexico's participation in NAFTA would threaten the livelihoods of its small corn producers while also undermining food security and fuelling migration to the US (Gonzalez, 2006, p 345). In 2003, during the WTO's Cancún Ministerial Conference, South Korean farm union leader Lee Kyung Hae stabbed himself in protest over WTO agricultural negotiations (La Via Campesina, 2013; National Farmers Union, 2023). When negotiations collapsed in the WTO's July 2008 meeting (see Chapter 1), the Indian-led initiative for special food security safeguards under the WTO Agreement on Agriculture was widely seen as the reason, with the Cotton Initiative spear-headed by Benin, Burkina-Faso, Chad and Mali being the only other unresolved issue on the agenda (for overviews see Singh and Gupta, 2016; Scott, 2017).

While trade rules play an important role in governing the production and distribution of food globally, this is a complex governance landscape. On the one hand, rules pertaining to agricultural tariffs, state aid for farmers, food and agricultural production and safety standards, and emergency measures for food security are negotiated at the WTO. But the global governance of food is dispersed among a much broader range of (non-trade) institutions, including the FAO, the World Food Programme and a number of UN agencies (Margulis, 2023). These institutions have separate mandates and have traditionally been guided by different problematics – that is, how to promote and expand an open and liberal trading regime versus how to ensure food security and the sustainability of the global food system in the context of population growth and climate change (Clapp, 2017a).

However, in the past three decades, food governance has increasingly converged around the aims of what Jennifer Clapp (2017a) calls 'trade-ification'. Agriculture, which was largely excluded from the (masculinist and productivist) Bretton Woods trade institutions (see Chapter 2), became an issue for *trade governance* with the shift towards trading on social reproduction at the end of the 20th century. Clapp's work on trade-ification shows how the norm of agricultural trade liberalization has also come to be 'increasingly and consistently' linked to efforts to achieve food sustainability in global *food governance* (Clapp, 2017a, p 337). Similarly, Matias Margulis has documented how the international community has gradually come to see '*insufficient* international agricultural trade' as a cause of food crises and food insecurity (Margulis, 2014, p 333, emphasis in original).

Though the gendered implications of these trade-ification trends in global food governance are often overlooked, feminist scholars and activists have argued that these are crucial areas of concern in a world where the majority of the population is dependent on food trade for their subsistence. This is so because many women globally work in food production and food trading, because food production, purchase and preparation constitute forms of reproductive labour, and because food, alongside water and shelter, is a fundamental component of social reproduction (Mies and Shiva, 1993; Mies and Bennholdt-Thomsen, 1999; Doss et al, 2018; Lombardozzi, 2024; Mezzadri et al, 2024).

In this context, feminist and women's movements have long called on the WTO to halt further agricultural liberalization, noting how this form of trading on social reproduction has disproportionately negative impacts on the livelihoods and food security of peasants and small farmers, a large proportion of whom are women (Young and Hoppe, 2003, p 19; see also Mies and Shiva, 1993). A key concern relates to how agricultural trade liberalization undermines forms of subsistence production, which is housewifized in the sense of being devalued, considered to be unproductive, and associated with poverty and backwardness (Mies and Bennholdt-Thomsen, 1999, p 5; see also McMichael, 1997).

We argue in this chapter that free trade feminism instead perpetuates a productivist approach to food, in the sense that it is overwhelmingly focused on how to improve the productivity of women working in food and agriculture, which is fostered by commercialization and the integration of women into global or regional value chains. In so doing, free trade feminism promotes and legitimates heavily contested ideas regarding the commercialization of agriculture and agri-food value chains, including what these processes and relations mean for gender equality, food (in)security and the environment. Key policies deployed by trade governance institutions to achieve these goals include those aimed at the orientation of women's farming techniques and food provisioning towards high productivity goals and technology-intensive practices, value chain integration, trade facilitation, the expansion of digital trade, financial inclusion, and technical capacity building for women entrepreneurs and exporters.

In deploying these policies, free trade feminism mobilizes false dichotomies between capitalist/modern and pre-capitalist/traditional forms of agricultural labour, which, as we demonstrated in Chapter 2, date back to the colonial period (see also Ali and Stevano, 2022, p 71). Here, the various forms of informal,[1] casual, subsistence and/or reproductive labour involved in producing and trading food tend to be lumped together as un- or under-productive, housewifized, and seen as needing targeted interventions to foster gender equality and women's empowerment, as well as economic growth and development, food security, and environmental sustainability. This entirely disregards the numerous, long-standing controversies over agricultural trade that have taken place in and around the GATT/WTO. These include high profile struggles over food security and food safety within the WTO and other trade governance arenas, as well as struggles over the role of trade and trade governance institutions in promoting an industrial corporate-led global food system, despite its links with global poverty and environmental crises.

It is our contention that in working to integrate marginalized and often informal female farmers and food traders into agricultural value chains, free trade feminism is helping to create new profit-making frontiers for food corporations and investors in the global South in the context of a long-standing deadlock in agricultural negotiations at the WTO. This pushes forward and legitimizes trading on social reproduction while crowding out alternative visions for feminist food justice and a sustainable global food system that prioritizes the centrality of food for forms of life-making.

Trading on agriculture in the global South

The context for the emergence of the free trade feminist approach to gender and food is the incorporation of agriculture into the trade governance arena, which is part of the broader shift towards trading on social reproduction. As mentioned in Chapter 2, from the GATT Uruguay Round 1986–1994 onwards, global trade governance institutions, and notably the WTO, have regulated food and agricultural trade. Yet, insofar as trade rules and regulations have increasingly played a role in governing this important aspect of social reproduction, a considerable proportion of food and agricultural production remains on the outside of global trade, including various forms of subsistence casual, informal and small-scale production.

From the perspective of free trade feminism, these ways of producing and distributing food are un- or under-productive. Free trade feminist policy elites see women's concentration in these forms of labour as generating gender-based inequalities, while at the same time providing opportunities for policy interventions in the name of women's economic empowerment. In this section we show that free trade feminist perspectives on food trade are largely focused on promoting the commercialization of women's agricultural labour, including the commercialization of informal food production and trade. Despite some contestation around its effects, gender mainstreaming policy initiatives in food trade focus on driving forward the integration of forms of agricultural labour that are considered unproductive into food value chains.

The commercialization of agriculture in the global South

Free trade feminism takes as its starting point the idea that women make up a large proportion of the agricultural labour force (43 per cent globally, according to the World Bank and WTO [2020, p 58]), especially in developing countries. However, female farmers are less likely to produce cash crops than male farmers, leading to a gender gap in agricultural productivity of somewhere between 20 and 40 per cent. They are also less likely to engage in the production and marketing of agricultural products that are traded on international markets (World Bank and WTO, 2020, p 58; see also FAO, 2023, p 6). The reasons for this gap lie in the 'gender differences in equality of opportunities', including in access to land, agricultural inputs and market opportunities (2020, p 59). This reasoning thus broadly follows 'the neoliberal orthodoxy that agriculture [will] flourish through the promotion of free market principles, entrepreneurship and private land ownership' (Prügl et al, 2021, p 1421).

Free trade feminist policy interventions typically target subsistence and small-scale female farmers and informal women traders. Some also target women employed in food processing in the global South. Strikingly, across our research, we have not found any actors discussing global North countries when it comes to the gendered imbalances of food trade. The lack of a global perspective masks known problems with the market-based, trade-led food system across the global North and South, which include class-based, gendered and racialized inequalities in access to food, and in access to high nutritional value food (sometimes observed in the persistence of *both* hunger *and* obesity in the world); labour abuses in agricultural and food value chains; and the environmental impacts of commercial farming.

The rationale for commercializing Southern women's agricultural and food practices posits commercial (read: 'modern') in direct opposition to subsistence (read: 'traditional') agriculture. Replacing the latter with the former, it is believed, will increase productivity and competitiveness, which is seen as going hand in hand with women's empowerment and national development/poverty reduction. A UNECA strategy report (funded by the EU) epitomizes the free trade feminist view:

> While playing a key role in food production, female farmers confront various challenges that limit their productivity in the agricultural sector. These include, amongst others, limited access to finance, inputs, extension services and markets. Exploiting intra-African market opportunities through a shift from subsistence-oriented production

> systems provides significant empowerment opportunities, including for female small-scale producers and exporters to competitively participate in high-value regional agricultural value chains. (UNECA, 2021b, p 89)

As this quote shows, key to the free trade feminist perspective is the view that by moving into commercial agriculture, women can produce higher value crops and thus not only participate in trade, but also 'upgrade' into higher value sectors.

With certain variations, this view appears across the main trade governance institutions. The World Bank and WTO, for example, assert that '[t]he increasing commercialization of agriculture in rural areas of poor countries and the shift into agro-processing and higher-value crops is central to poverty reduction in many countries' (World Bank and WTO, 2020, p 115). The WTO Secretariat's analysis of TPRs identifies 'increasing productivity and production' as the key objectives in agricultural support measures for small-scale agricultural producers and women farmers (WTO, 2019c). The IWG on Trade and Gender also regularly identifies agricultural commercialization and export-promotion as key pillars of women's entrepreneurship initiatives (WTO, 2021b; 2024d). Its 2021 progress report specifically treats 'increasing agricultural productivity' and the expansion of 'agricultural value chains' as key to promoting 'women's social and economic empowerment' (WTO, 2021b, p 12). From this perspective, the productivity of women working in agriculture and of the agricultural sector as a whole are expected to rise in tandem. To achieve these gains, there is a need to further expand global trade, namely via the expansion of agricultural value chains. In the words of the World Bank and WTO, trade 'can help close the gender productivity gap' in agricultural development (2020, p 114).

Long-standing feminist research casts doubt over these free trade feminist assumptions. It shows that the impacts of the commercialization of agriculture on women and other social groups are highly context-dependent, with much depending on how the pace and nature of commercialization interact with the gendered nature of pre-existing land rights and agrarian production systems (for a recent review of this vast multidisciplinary literature, see Prügl et al, 2021). In cases where the commercialization of agriculture has advanced rapidly, the results have almost invariably been negative for women, notably where large-scale land transactions or land grabbing have been involved (Behrman et al, 2012; Daley and Pallas, 2014; Prügl et al, 2021). Feminists intervening in WTO agricultural debates of the early 2000s already warned about agricultural trade liberalization in the global South leading to land concentration and the 'expansion of [transnational corporation]-controlled commercial crop production' (Young and Hoppe, 2003, p 20). Typically, traditional small-scale farmers, processors and petty food traders, which are disproportionately women, are unable to compete with these actors (Baden, 1998; Joekes, 1999).

Sidestepping such critiques, many free trade feminist policy elites are optimistic about the opportunities provided by the commercialization of agriculture, which then allows for women's integration into value chains; that is, a form of slow-paced agricultural commercialization. They see value chains as directly or indirectly connecting women-owned and -run MSMEs and small-scale farmers to export markets (for example, World Bank and WTO, 2020, pp 124–135). Feminist research on agricultural commercialization however shows that value chain integration typically occurs in low value-added segments of chains, for example when individuals are integrated as agricultural workers, contract farmers and small-scale producers for export markets (Prügl et al, 2021a). It shows that each type of value chain integration differs in how it interacts with pre-existing labour and land relations in local communities, including the social relations of gender (Hall et al, 2017). In the past, agricultural value chain integration has often reached male farmers and farm workers, with women tending to be integrated in low-pay and seasonal work, if at all (Prügl et al, 2021). This has negatively impacted women's earnings, pushed them into informal labour (including in domestic work) and increased their unpaid labour (Okeyo, 2002; Tsikata and Yaro, 2014; Hajjar et al, 2019; Prügl et al, 2021). Such effects have often been compounded along intersectional dimensions of inequality, such as class and caste (Levien, 2017).

While free trade feminism does generally acknowledge the concentration of women at lower value-added segments of value chains, it is typically attributed to social and cultural barriers (including limited access to education) and the lack of targeted interventions (training, networks, and so on). The World Bank and the WTO (2020), for example, are committed to the idea that economic upgrading in value chains can bring about social upgrading in the form of improved working conditions across different groups of workers, including women. They posit that upgrading may lead to a higher demand for skilled workers, and make it more costly to 'artificially restrict the supply of skills in the economy' (2020, p 134), reiterating arguments about the pressures of competitiveness made by Becker (see Chapter 2).

UNCTAD and ECLAC reflect a greater recognition of the problems with agricultural commercialization from a gender perspective. However, as we discuss later, UNCTAD in particular simultaneously advances free trade feminist agendas on food trade. In its 2022 analytical and policy framework *Linking Trade and Gender towards Sustainable Development*, UNCTAD notes that women tend to be integrated into global agricultural chains as wage workers, rather than as traders in product markets in their own right. Citing World Bank (2016) research, UNCTAD (2022b, p 13) notes the limitations of free trade feminist approaches, recalling that in global South countries that have experienced value chain integration in non-traditional agricultural exports, 'gender segregation in employment is prevalent … resulting in the crowding of women into low-skilled positions and hence not fully supporting their empowerment'. This is because 'women are concentrated more in harvesting, slicing, grading and packaging, while men are more involved in operating machinery, truck driving or loading, and … also dominate supervisory roles'. UNCTAD (2022b, p 14) concludes that 'overall, women are more likely to be in part-time, seasonal and low-paid jobs in agri-food value chains, and their seasonal or daily wage labour on farms has proven critical to keeping production costs low and export demand high'. That is, they recognize that the precarious labour of women has underpinned success in agri-food value chains.

ECLAC (2019, p 52) also explicitly makes this point, highlighting how 'women have entered jobs in the most precarious or least value-added segments of global value chains. Low wages have been considered a "comparative advantage" for locating some value chain segments in Latin America and the Caribbean'. According to feminist and other critical scholarship, the integration, especially of informal economic actors, into value chains must involve targeted policy interventions to assure benefits and to prevent integration from reinforcing existing inequalities, or creating new forms of exploitation and oppression in the world economy (Chen, M., 2006; Barrientos et al, 2011; Meagher, 2013).

ECLAC shows some awareness of these arguments. A 2020 report provides a rich empirical discussion of employment creation for women following value chain integration in traditional and non-traditional agricultural sectors across Latin America, noting that women's employment in agriculture tends to be 'highly informal' (ECLAC, 2020, p 149). The report highlights the importance of diligent implementation of regulatory and private standards, including voluntary certification schemes such as fair trade or organic, but also of standards 'regulating and compensating for women's precarious working conditions in various export sectors, especially agriculture', in order to ensure that commercializing traditional and informal agriculture can contribute to closing gender inequality gaps (ECLAC, 2020, p 166). However, these regulatory and private standards are generally omitted from trade rules and regulations which instead rely on governments, corporations and standard-setting bodies to ensure that the benefits of trade are equally distributed.[2]

While recognizing that women face inequalities in the agricultural sector, free trade feminist policy initiatives focus primarily on the barriers that prevent women's market participation, rather than on the structural characteristics of agricultural value chains themselves. This is what drives free trade feminism toward gearing value chain integration initiatives specifically at women in agriculture, and promoting women's rights (usually by advocating for domestic laws and adherence to non-trade international treaties such as ILO agreements).

Implementing the free trade feminist consensus

Food trade is one area in which gender mainstreaming in trade governance is particularly active. The WTO's AfT review, for example, shows an overwhelming desire to support women in agriculture among WTO members. It confirms that '92% of developing countries identify [the] agriculture sector for future support for women's economic empowerment' (WTO, 2022c, p 130). To this end, national, regional and domestic policy makers promote access to high-tech farming methods, finance, trade facilitation and the expansion of digital trade.

This work is ongoing across the global economy and takes different shapes and forms. The Islamic Development Bank, for example, collaborates with the ITC and the Trade Facilitation Office of Canada on projects aiming to integrate Moroccan women-owned MSMEs into value chains in the processed foods sector. The expectation is that 'increasing the participation of women-owned businesses in trade by improving their competitiveness and strengthening their market linkages' will lead to 'higher incomes … and a better livelihood for the community in general' (ISDB, 2021). In its trade and gender training courses, UNCTAD focuses, among other things, on 'the gender impact of technological upgrading in agriculture' (WTO, 2021b, p 14). It also runs local 'farming-as-business workshops' through its entrepreneurship programme, Empretec. The successes of Empretec are reported in terms of women farmers' productivity increases, or alternatively, as increases in business turnover (UNCTAD, 2019b).

As we already saw in Chapter 3, trade policy elites actively promote financial inclusion as a central mechanism for helping women to overcome barriers to trade and market participation. This is also the case in food trade. For example, Canada operates a number of microfinance projects that aim to increase the use of financial services in agriculture in Haiti and the Democratic Republic of Congo. It reported to the WTO IWG that 'in Haiti, the agricultural loan product continues its success … reaching a cumulative total of 2,080 beneficiaries, of whom 83% women who work in the agricultural value chain' (WTO, 2024d, p 4). Australia runs an 'Investing in Women Initiative' that has enabled '7,000 women smallholder farmers to participate in markets and supply chains vital to food security' in Indonesia, the Philippines and Vietnam (WTO, 2021c). Chile and Colombia run financial inclusion initiatives such as Chile's Mujer Exporta programme or Colombia's Fondo para el Financiamiento del Sector Agropecuario (WTO, 2024d). In a review of agricultural value chain transformation in Southern Africa, UNECA (2022a, p 33, emphasis added) critiques that 'the financial incentives currently offered to support agricultural value chain development … are *insufficiently targeted* towards smallholder farmers, women, young people and other marginalized groups'.

While it is beyond the scope of our analysis to evaluate the impact of these initiatives, it is clear from research on 'poverty finance' (Rankin, 2013) that microfinance and financial inclusion initiatives, including the increasingly prolific expansion of digital financial inclusion initiatives, do not necessarily result in greater gender equality. The extensive feminist political economy literature on microfinance, financial inclusion and the financialization of development troubles the assumption that access to finance can address the structural inequalities that fuel gender-based inequalities in the global political economy. It also points to how inequalities may be reproduced, for example as loans support survival versus enterprise, credit comes at a high cost, debt collection practices are coercive, and managing and juggling the (often overlapping) repayments is a form of unpaid labour done in the service of capital (see, for instance, Roy, 2010; Karim, 2011; Zulfiqar, 2016; Natile, 2020; Guérin et al, 2023).

Instead of recognizing that such critiques have been widely made in the development policy space, free trade feminist policy elites promote success stories of commericalized or industrial export-driven food production as examples of women's empowerment in food trade. The promotional videos of ITC *SheTrades* mentioned in Chapter 3 are one example of this. Also, of the very few women's groups that have presented to the WTO IWG on Trade and Gender, two were groups that showcased industrial food production and commercial farming-for-export models. The Association of Lady Entrepreneurs of India presented three success stories of 'women's entrepreneurship and innovative technology for women-owned enterprises' that all operated in the biotech, processed foods and nutrition supplements sector (WTO, 2021d). Ecuadorian representatives gave a presentation about a group of indigenous women trained by a governmental women's empowerment programme to engage in sustainable cocoa farming and chocolate-making (WTO, 2021e). The decision to invite the Association of Lady Entrepreneurs of India to the WTO IWG is striking, given that India openly opposes the WTO gender mainstreaming agenda and is not an IWG member. Ecuador's presentation on the Waorani women to the IWG, on the other hand, does not contextualize its women's empowerment programme within the Ecuadorian state's long-standing and ongoing conflictual relationship with the Waorani people. Thus, instead of reflecting on the wider political contexts of its interventions (a point to which we will return later), free trade feminism promotes an unquestioned belief in the wonders that agricultural commercialization and value chain integration can do for women's empowerment as well as for national development.

What is never acknowledged within the free trade feminist paradigm is the way that the historical evolution of trade governance has shaped existing forms of agricultural production in the global South. As we outlined in Chapter 2, the remaking of farming in the global South to suit global market demand was a key feature of colonial trade relations, while the unilateral trade liberalization required under SAP conditionalities had devastating effects on agricultural producers and food security. As scholars of African studies have shown, for example, both processes have played their part in sealing Africa's structural subordination in the global trade regime, and in creating a diverse and extensive informal economy that is central to meeting the subsistence needs of much of the population (Ossome, 2015; Price, 2025).

Furthermore, free trade feminism ignores long-standing critiques of the industrialized, corporate-led global food system into which women are being integrated. With its undue optimism about the possibilities of agricultural commercialization, free trade feminism has forged a corporate-centric food trade agenda despite the fact that the corporate-led global food system is itself mired in the gendered inequalities of global food trade. It is to these gendered inequalities in global food trade that we now turn.

Food trade, 'informality' and the housewifization of labour

As we have seen, free trade feminism promotes tackling the un-/under-productivity of women's labour in agriculture, and the exclusion of subsistence-based, informal, causal and small-scale women food producers, workers and traders in the global South from the corporate-led global food system. Integrating them into this system is viewed as being positive for gender equality goals, economic growth and national development – and for some, food security and sustainability – and trade policy interventions have been developed accordingly.

UNECA (2022a, p v), for example, recognizes continued 'growth of informal markets' in Southern Africa, but maintains that value chain integration will lead to 'the formalization of many jobs in the informal sector', which it expects to benefit in particular those who are 'currently employed informally as cross-border traders'. Therefore, its training course on gender mainstreaming under the African Continental Free Trade Area (AfCFTA) focuses, among other topics, on 'women-owned business, small-scale and informal cross-borders traders' (UNECA, 2022b). Similarly, when promoting its gender and trade training courses in the WTO IWG, UNCTAD has drawn attention to its course on informal cross-border trade, which it notes is a priority area given the significance of informal cross-border trade for food security (WTO, 2021f). As we discussed before, financial inclusion initiatives fast-track agricultural commercialization of informal and small-scale actors in the global South.

In many instances, these different forms of labour relations in the food sector are all collapsed together and viewed as traditional and backward in relation to capitalist/modern/formal/commercial agriculture (Alessandrini et al, 2022). This fuels the housewifization of these various forms of labour, which, as we argued in Chapter 2, were not eliminated but rather reproduced through the expansion of capitalism globally. They remain critical to the production of life, as well as the accumulation of capital. Indeed, as feminist scholars have noted, the labour involved in food production in the global South takes on many forms, which often overlap, including formal, informal, casual and subsistence labour (Ali and Stevano, 2022, p 71). From our perspective, the existence of these forms of labour is not an anomaly in the world economy, but one of its structural features (see also Mezzadri, 2019). By presenting informal and other labour that is considered unproductive as an untapped terrain of economic opportunity, free trade feminism drives forward the housewifization of subsistence agriculture.

The many faces of 'informality'

Within food trade, as in many other sectors of gender mainstreaming, trade policy elites are working to integrate so-called 'informal' actors into more formal economic relations, including through agricultural value chains. This often entails a conflation of different types of informality. For instance, in its report on how best to support the integration of women in traditional and non-traditional agricultural sectors into value chains, ECLAC (2020) shows little awareness of the fact that informal economic actors are not a coherent cohort, and that different sets of informal economic actors face distinct risks of exploitation when interacting with more powerful economic agents. This is shaped by local contexts. While some informal actors may act as suppliers and contractors for formal firms, others take on informal modes of employment in formal enterprises. The latter constitute informal labour, while the former may be classified as entrepreneurship, which may be formal or informal.

As research has shown, informal firms in value chains can end up in dependent positions *vis-à-vis* formal, usually transnational, lead firms and operate on low margins, with the economic benefits mainly flowing to the lead firm (Pedersen and McCormick, 1999; Ranis and Stewart, 1999; UNIDO/GTZ, 2008). When it comes to informal entrepreneurs, a further differentiation ought to be made between those who have a measure of economic autonomy versus so-called 'survival entrepreneurs' (Meagher, 2013, p 16) who deploy coping strategies under conditions of extreme deprivation and poverty.

Other global South trade governance institutions show a more explicit acknowledgement that many women engaged in informal trade (including in agriculture, where women are over-represented), do so out of economic necessity rather than entrepreneurial ambition. As ECOWAS notes, women in the region 'operate at small scale and/or in an informal manner precisely because of the high transaction costs involved in trading formally' (ECOWAS, 2019, p 22). While there are formalization schemes in place, these often have 'limited uptake by women' due to their complexity and cost (2019, p 22). Similarly, UNECA recognizes that 'not all self-employed women in Africa are truly entrepreneurs' as many are 'necessity-driven' and engage in 'survival entrepreneurship' (UNECA, 2017, p 4).

Workers and survival entrepreneurs often circulate between formal and informal work, which is typically the result of their precarious economic positions, sub-contracting and casualization processes, and a generalized lack of social provisioning, labour representation and unionization (Harriss-White and Guptu, 2001; ILO, 2002; Devey et al, 2006; Altman, 2008; Valodia and Devey, 2010). Women in particular engage in household and reproductive labour alongside such juggling, which can reinforce various dimensions of inequality (Valodia, 2001; Bocquier, 2005) and leads to 'the burden of precarious employment falling hardest on women and youth' (Meagher, 2013, p 8). This is particularly a problem where informal women workers are integrated into value chains, which tends to lead to modes of incorporation that intensify poverty and exclusion (Carr and Chen, 2002; Oxfam International, 2004; du Toit and Neves, 2007).

In our research on gender mainstreaming in food trade, we have not come across any policy makers acknowledging that these complexities require attention. Typically, this is because the ideological commitment to trade productivism means that policy makers see these problems to be rooted within 'society', and not within 'the market', and/or because they believe that 'the market' provides solutions. Having recommended that 'strong linkages should be created between large commercial agro-manufacturing firms and smaller women-owned firms', UNECA (2021b, p 89), for instance, remarks that '[i]t will be necessary as part of this shift to address persistent gender stereotypes that keep women in low paid and less skilled work in certain nodes of the agricultural value chain'. Thus, for UNECA, what keeps women-owned firms at the bottom of value chains are societal stereotypes (which are not seen to lie within the purview of trade policy), not the economic power relations within value chains themselves (which are less easily dismissed as irrelevant to trade policy).

While free trade feminism may call on the state to compensate the 'losers' of agricultural value chain integration, this is also believed to occur naturally, through 'the market'. Thus, in a separate report, UNECA (2022a) notes how the introduction of supermarkets – a highly concentrated global sector dominated by a small number of monopolistic players (Josling, 2012) – can out-compete informal food producers and informal food markets in African countries. Yet, UNECA (2022a, p 21) is quick to point out that '[f]rom a consumer's perspective … that development is often positive, as people can obtain their food from supermarkets rather than from small local stores or markets'. In an advocacy document developed for Myanmar, UNCTAD (2023a) recommends integrating women farmers into *both* agricultural *and* tourism value chains, via access to technology and finance. Such so-called 'multifunctional agriculture' was a hallmark of gender mainstreaming in European agricultural policies in the 2000s, where the 'neo-liberal regulatory context encourage[d] a diversification of rural incomes through tourism, local crafts production, the development of on-farm enterprises and off-farm service jobs' (Prügl, 2004, p 360).

Both examples show how individual women are expected to manage the vulnerabilities arising from value chain integration. UNECA fails to consider that the vast majority of African consumers assure their subsistence through informal activities, raising questions about where the out-competed local shopkeeper will obtain the income that will allow for shopping in a transnational supermarket. UNCTAD fails to consider that running both an agricultural and a tourism enterprise at the same time increases burdens on women to deal with the precarities of both sectors. Further, Myanmar provides an example of a country where free trade feminism intervenes in a context of long-standing political conflict, although this is left unacknowledged in UNCTAD's report. However, where informal economic activity and informal cross-border trade are embedded in conflict zones and war economies, this can have an extremely wide range of governance implications for integrating informal actors into value chains (Titeca and De Herdt, 2010). These implications are highly context-dependent and can range from the undermining of political orders through smuggling and illegal activities, to the provision of hybrid governance systems, where informal actors fill gaps in social and community provisioning that are left by a collapsing state (Meagher, 2013). Yet, it remains the case that lead firms in food and agricultural value chains are integrating new forms of dependent, highly flexibilized and precarious labour into their operations, as a result, in part, of the free trade feminist agenda in women's empowerment in food trade.

Housewifizing subsistence labour

In lumping together the different forms of labour involved in food production and trade in the global South and positing them as un- or under-productive, free trade feminism is assessing the value of this labour from the perspective of what it means for the accumulation of capital and the trade-based expansion of the world market. From a feminist political economy perspective, it is necessary to start from a different premise, asking what this labour contributes to processes of social reproduction, including what it means from the perspective of subsistence. Maria Mies and Veronika Bennholdt-Thomsen developed what they called 'the subsistence perspective', which refers to a perspective that puts 'everything necessary to produce and maintain life on this planet at the centre of the economic and social activity' rather than 'the never-ending accumulation of dead money' (1999, p 5; see also Mies and Shiva, 1993). While their specific approach has been subject to various forms of criticism, the point that social and economic activity should work to support life, including nature, informs much feminist political economy analysis, including our own. This is not the case for free trade feminism, which housewifizes subsistence labour, essentially foreclosing questions of how food trade may or may not support life-making. We address the former point here, before turning to the latter in the final section of this chapter.

As stated earlier, free trade feminist approaches to food trade regularly promote the adoption of high-tech farming methods, such as those relying on seeds, fertilizers and machinery, and an industrial approach to agriculture (for example, UNCTAD, 2020; World Bank and WTO, 2020). In the process of doing so, they at times discredit traditional and subsistence farm work, particularly in relation to African agriculture. Citing FAO research, UNECA makes clear that African agriculture must '[shift] from subsistence-oriented production systems towards more market-oriented and inclusive paradigms' (UNECA, 2022a, p.2). This echoes the World Bank and WTO view that 'high-value, export-oriented agro-industries can bring better opportunities for women as farmers and workers than traditional agricultural work' (World Bank and WTO, 2020, p 115).

In one of the starkest formulations that suggests the continued endurance of modernization and anti-agrarian mindsets in development (see McMichael, 1997) and trade (see Mies and Bennholdt-Thomsen, 1999), UNCTAD goes as far as to frame subsistence farming as a barrier to women's empowerment. As its advocacy document on policy options to support women farmers explains, 'farmers' view of agriculture as a traditional activity rather than a business is an important *obstacle* to developing and modernizing the agricultural sector' (UNCTAD, 2021d, p 2, emphasis added).

This devalues the traditional knowledge held by women and others relative to masculinized 'scientific' knowledge (Allen and Sachs, 2007). At the same time, continuing with colonial-era patterns of extractivism, it posits nature as there to be exploited by global capital (Shiva, 2001; 2005). This is further fuelled by corporate land-grabs which critics argue are worsened by trade liberalization, and which 'deprive women of their land and livelihood resulting in widespread hunger that destroys communities and deepens women's misery' (ActionAid, 2018, p 18).

In a blog that simultaneously lumps together and housewifizes subsistence farming, small-scale farming and various forms of casual and informal labour, the African Development Bank Group asserts that female-dominated informal cross-border trade *and* small-scale *and* subsistence farming in sub-Saharan Africa constitute 'an untapped potential to feed, integrate and industrialise Africa' (Dosso, 2019; see also UNECA and ATPC, 2022). Free trade feminism thus drives forward longer-standing trends in development policy, which devalues the un- and under-paid work that women do while also harnessing the potential of small-scale, poor, marginalized and informal economic actors for economic and social progress (Prahalad and Hart, 2002; Guha-Khasnobis et al, 2006; World Bank, 2007; Yunus, 2010).

Yet, from our feminist political economy of trade perspective, the roots of gender inequality do not lie in the 'inefficient' use of the labour of women and other marginalized groups, but rather in the systemic devaluation of this labour which is not viewed as directly serving capital accumulation. As Diane Elson (1999, p 13) put it over a decade ago, in the context of debates over SAPs being imposed by international financial institutions, women are an 'over-utilized rather than an under-utilized' resource (see also Hoskyns and Rai, 2007). At the same time, the housewifization of labour operates as a strategy of capital accumulation. This occurs in part through the structural connection of this devalued labour to value chains in the ways outlined earlier. At the same time, unpaid and invisibilized reproductive labour also subsidizes the social reproduction of the 'productive household' (Mezzadri, 2016, p 1881).

When productive and reproductive labour are both taken into account, it becomes clear that commercializing women's agriculture often implies trade-offs between paid work and unpaid care work and leisure time. This can lead to a decline in the quality of care provided within households, families and communities (UNDP, 1999; Grown et al, 2000, p 1152; Çağatay, 2001). While some of the negative impacts of women's entry into commercialized, 'productive' labour relations on the provisioning of care and reproductive labour could be addressed via increased state support for public services such as healthcare, childcare and/or education, these are not systematically supported by free trade feminist interventions. Instead, agricultural governance norms that centre around commercialization and connections to global markets tend to go hand in hand with reduced public spending in reproductive services (Glipo, 2003). According to Joms Salvador of the GABRIELA Alliance of Filipino Women, these are simultaneously driven by the WTO's push for trade liberalization – including by, as we have shown, free trade feminism. She argues that 'the WTO's promotion of liberalization and deregulation have strengthened transnational corporations' control over vast lands and resources', which, combined with competitive pressures driving down wages and labour standards 'have further heightened women's vulnerability with the privatization of social services such as education and health' (cited in APWLD, 2017).

Instead of acknowledging such limitations, the free trade feminist paradigm puts a 'feminist face'[3] on the trade-ification of food and creates the 'woman sustainable food securer' and 'natural carer' for the environment as idealized subjects that justify continually expanding the trade-based, corporate-led global food system.

Free trade feminism, trade productivism and the trade-ification of food security and sustainability

Central to free trade feminist approaches to food security and food sustainability is trade productivism, that is to say the governance technique that governs trade *as if* it was separate from gender relations, reproductive labour, life-making and social reproduction processes, and that sees these spheres as 'trade-related' at best. As the previous discussion suggested, the vast majority of gender mainstreaming initiatives in food and agricultural trade are in fact *not* concerned with food security and food sustainability. This is because, within the ideological and institutional framework of trade productivism, agriculture and food are typically viewed from the perspective of productivity and economic growth, and not from the perspective of life-making (which includes the making of the environment). Accordingly, free trade feminist policy elites promote agricultural commercialization and the housewifization of agricultural labour through trade policy initiatives, but see food security and food sustainability as falling under 'social issues' (WTO, 2023c, p 9) or 'domestic policy purposes' (UNCTAD, 2022b, p 75).

At the same time, they tap into the trade-ification norm that has emerged in global governance over the past several decades and that treats trade in general, and free trade in particular, as key mechanisms for assuring that sufficient food is available across the world and that food production does not cause irreversible environmental damage (Clapp, 2017a; see also Watkins, 1996; Clapp and Murphy, 2013; Margulis, 2014). Relying on gendered stereotypes of women as successful food securers and as natural carers for the environment, free trade feminist interventions in food trade further legitimate and entrench trade-ification norms, by linking them to the causes of women's economic empowerment and gender equality.

The 'feminist face' of the trade-ification of food

As already noted, women's empowerment initiatives in food trade rarely pursue food security or food sustainability directly, instead pursuing the goals of commercialization, increased productivity, women's entrepreneurship, and so on. The 2019 WTO survey of women's empowerment policies shows that fewer than 16 of 111 members under review reported having food security and food aid provisions in their programming (WTO, 2019c). The IWG further notes that there exists only one legal provision that 'addresses food security for women' in any existing trade agreement (WTO, 2023c, p 22), namely Article 44 of the Association Agreement between the EU and Central America.[4] Where it is referenced in policy documents, it is typically depicted as an obstacle to women's empowerment that is separate to the global food trade system itself. For instance, UNECA explains how the lack of 'agroecological practices' among small-scale farmers 'exacerbates food insecurity and reduces the incomes of smallholder farmers and marginalized members of agricultural communities' (UNECA, 2022a, p 34). UNCTAD (2020b) sees water scarcity as an obstacle to increasing the productivity of commercial farming and as an obstacle to women's empowerment.[5]

While not directly targeting food security and food sustainability problems within their gender mainstreaming initiatives, free trade feminist policy elites nonetheless *believe* that agricultural commercialization and trade expansion *will* support the fight against hunger and the climate change response. Addressing the IWG in 2021, Australia, for example, highlights its efforts to support 'women smallholder farmers to participate in markets and supply chains vital to food security' (WTO, 2021c, p 4). UNECA cites FAO research showing that 'when access to land, credit and essential services is equalized between men and women, agricultural productivity can increase by between 20 and 30 per cent, with a positive impact on food security and well-being' (UNECA, 2022a, p 34). It further assumes that 'smallholder family-owned operations, which are often women-led' will increase their incomes and help meet 'food needs in a sustainable and environmentally friendly manner', so long as 'resilient and climate-smart agricultural practices' are adopted (UNECA, 2022a, p 34). APEC also held a workshop in 2023, explaining that 'farmers who are women play an important role in addressing food insecurity and climate change, given agriculture's impact on growth and sustainability' and calling for 'women's empowerment in climate-smart agriculture' (APEC, 2023). In its presentation to the WTO IWG, Ecuador referred to the Waorani women producing and exporting chocolate as an example of a success story of climate-smart agriculture.

These examples point to how the trade-ification of food security/sustainability is increasingly being fused with the norms of gender equality and women's empowerment. Agricultural trade liberalization became a dominant food security norm within the WTO system, the FAO and the World Food Summit in the wake of the Uruguay Round (Watkins, 1996). A 'free-trade-for-food-security perspective', which takes agricultural trade liberalization as a precondition for the eradication of hunger, was further consolidated across global food security institutions during the world food crises of the 2000s (Margulis, 2014). In this perspective, a market-oriented world trade system is essential for achieving food security (World Food Summit, 1996, cited in Watkins, 1996).

In terms of food sustainability, free trade was linked with environmental protection with the emergence of liberal environmentalism in the 1990s (Conca, 2000; Bernstein, 2001; Weber, 2001). Examples of this include EU agricultural policy reform (Prügl, 2004; 2010), NAFTA (Charnovitz, 1994) and the UN Rio Earth Summit 1992 (Clapp, 2017a). Under the environmental liberal vision for trade, continued trade expansion is seen as an essential tool for achieving sustainability and enhancing environmental protection. Accordingly, liberalized trade in agriculture is seen as an essential mechanism that can help shift the global food system onto a sustainable footing. This vision is also increasingly prominent in climate governance, given the centrality of the global food system in the response to climate change (Clapp, 2017a).

Gender equality and women's empowerment were connected to the food-trade nexus in some areas of governance prior to the rise of free trade feminism. For example, in the early 2000s, the German Green Party proposed women farmers' entrepreneurship as an associated norm of liberal environmentalism in European agriculture and trade politics (Prügl, 2004). The SDGs also bring together food security, food sustainability and free trade norms, which, in SDG 2 (Zero Hunger) are further connected to gender equality. The approach is rooted in gendered ideas about women's ability to be rational economic operators while *simultaneously* engaging in reproductive and care work for families, local communities and nature (Prügl and Joshi, 2021).

Elisabeth Prügl and Saba Joshi (2021) have shown that in the gendered discursive constructions of non-trade food governance institutions, such as the FAO, the World Bank and the UN Special Rapporteur on the Right to Food, women are framed as agricultural agents who can outperform men on two fronts simultaneously. Women farmers are believed to be able to surpass men in agricultural productivity (given access to the same productive assets as men) and in assuring that the nutritional needs of families and communities are met, especially in situations of food scarcity (Prügl and Joshi, 2021). The ideological construction of women as productive farmers celebrates women's ability to succeed as profit-oriented economic actors, while the construction of women as food and nature securers celebrates feminized rationalities, such as altruism, care and solidarity.

As feminist scholars have shown, these contradictory constructions of women as both rational self-optimizing market actors *and* sacrificial wives and mothers exist across other (non-trade-specific) articulations of the business case for gender equality (Roberts and Zulfiqar, 2019). Part of the reason for this contradictory framing is that insofar as women's rationality is presumed to make them successful in the sphere of the market, few concrete efforts are made to relieve their responsibility for the reproductive labour, including care work, performed in households and communities (Griffin, 2009; Chant, 2016). As Özlem Altan-Olcay argues, this contradiction emerges 'precisely because the discourses of individual responsibility do not work in real life' (2014, p 240).

Free trade feminism replicates this contradictory framing of women-as-productive-farmers and women-as-successful-food-securers. As shown earlier, it assumes that removing barriers to market participation will unleash women's untapped potential and enable them to empower themselves in the commercial production and trade of food, while also nourishing their families and communities. To substantiate this point, free trade feminism typically references evidence indicating that female-led households in the global South display less malnutrition and have higher education rates than male-led households. The evidence that free trade feminism brings is typically geographically specific and results from non-trade-specific research. It is nonetheless presented in language that suggests an established pattern of gendered behaviour that can be relied upon as a means of explaining how women can be empowered through trade. It also relies on heteronormative assumptions that implicitly assume women as a biological category, and as cis-gendered, heterosexual, and wanting to have (and being capable of having) children. This again is not unique to free trade feminism, but has long been a feature of gender and development interventions by institutions such as the World Bank (Griffin, 2009; Calkin, 2015).

One commonly evoked source is UNICEF's (2007) report, *State of the World's Children: Investing in Women's Rights to Advance the Rights of Both Women and Children*. The report cites research showing that in rural Bangladesh, '[c]hildren living in female-headed households consume a more diverse diet than those in male-headed households, especially micronutrient and protein rich foods that provide the necessary nutrients for the growth and mental development of young children' (UNICEF, 2007, p 29). Although the report is specific to Bangladesh and the underlying research did not interrogate the relationship between gendered food provisioning practices and Bangladesh's position in international food and agricultural trade, the World Bank and WTO flagship report on trade and gender evokes UNICEF (2007) as providing evidence that women are superior food securers to men. To further bolster this claim, the report cites additional non-trade-specific country studies from India and Nepal, indicating that there is less stunting among children and reduced child mortality in female-headed households compared to male-headed households (World Bank and WTO, 2020, p 61).

Occasionally, some voices cast doubt over the optimistic view that the commercialization of women's agricultural production will enhance food security. The 2017 Human Rights Impact Assessment of the AfCFTA, provided by UNECA and Friedrich-Ebert-Stiftung, for example, highlights 'the disparities between the needs of poor net food consumers for low food prices and the needs of producers for higher food prices', which can lead to opposing interests among local, food-insecure trade constituencies (UNECA and FES, 2017, p 88). It advocates for the need to take the food-insecure positions of women, cross-border traders and other vulnerable groups into consideration when designing and implementing trade policies. These detailed considerations, however, remain an outlier in gender mainstreaming in trade governance and find a paradoxical response in the free trade feminist view that commercializing agriculture is a means of mitigating the negative effects of the commercialized food system.

In its policy framework document, *Linking Trade and Gender towards Sustainable Development*, UNCTAD, for example, clearly expresses the free trade feminist position that trade-related risks to food security require *more* agricultural commercialization in the name of food security. The report recognizes the dilemmas emerging from trade liberalization on food prices, stating: 'The imports of cheap food following from trade liberalization can reduce the domestic price of agricultural produce and erode the already low earnings of subsistence farmers, a group dominated by women… This is a bigger issue for net food-importing countries and may result in food insecurity' (UNCTAD, 2022b, p 27). UNCTAD then explains: 'A viable solution would be to make small entrepreneurs in import-competing agricultural sectors more competitive through increased investment and technological upgrading' (UNCTAD, 2022b, p 27). Thus, for free trade feminism, deeper integration into global food trade circuits is the answer to food security problems arising from integration into these circuits.

Free trade feminism reinforces the feminist face of trade-ification by merging women-as-successful-food-securers with other stereotypes, such as the gendered notion that women and other minorities are naturally disposed to be good caretakers of the environment (Doss et al, 2018). UNECA (2021a), for example, explains:

> Given that women often play a key role in ensuring food security, are very adept at managing their operations and are repositories of indigenous knowledge regarding irrigation and crop storage, their empowerment as critical stakeholders in agricultural value chains will reflect the objectives [of accelerating agricultural growth in a sustainable manner to achieve food security in Africa] (African Union 2016).

Yet, as we explore in more detail later, free trade feminist agendas pay little to no attention to the ecological implications of their trade policy initiatives and recommendations.

At the same time, unlike in *non-trade* food governance settings (Prügl and Joshi, 2021), we have not come across trade policy makers that credibly promote expanding women's economic *and* social and political rights under their gendered discursive constructions of women as successful market participants and food securers.

Extending political rights?

As we have seen, free trade feminism is overwhelmingly concerned with women's economic rights and economic opportunities within the confines of the market economy and the sphere of production.[6] Grounded as it is in trade productivism, it typically sidelines the reproductive sphere entirely from its considerations of how women should be empowered in food and agricultural trade. The WTO AfT review (2022c), for example, presents 'the main constraints of women-owned SMEs to enter, establish or move up value chains in agri-food' as 'difficulties in accessing finance services, informal employment, lack of access to digital services' (WTO, 2022c, p 130). As stated earlier, where it recognizes women's reproductive labour, it sees it as a trade barrier. The World Bank and WTO report recommends increasing foreign competition in 'critical services' in order to empower women, and identifies finance, transport, logistics and wholesale services as critical (World Bank and WTO, 2020, pp 114–115). Yet, from a feminist perspective, service sectors such as health, education, utilities and social care are all critical dimensions of how women and other marginalized groups are situated within global food and agricultural markets, and supporting these sectors should be a minimum requirement for a feminist trade agenda.

Where free trade feminism advocates extending women's political rights, this is usually in reference to 'inclusive stakeholder consultation' (WTO, 2021g, p 5) or the acknowledgement that 'women should also be granted a voice in policy-making' (UNECA, 2022a, p 34). Unlike in the area of economic rights, there is no explicit reflection on what types of political rights and forms of participation would make this possible for women.

The scholarship on the role of social movements and civil society in trade politics gives reason for pessimism that calls for 'voice' and 'inclusion' will lead to a meaningful expansion of women's rights to political participation and self-determination in trade policy making. Indeed, only very rarely are civil society voices meaningfully included in trade governance. Typically, civil society is either invited into trade institutions, but without exerting significant influence (Dür and de Bièvre, 2007), or, where they are shown to have influenced trade governance, this is typically the case because they have adopted dominant policy approaches and ideologies (Del Felice, 2014; Hannah, 2016). Both practices undermine the ability of civil society groups to shape trade governance according to their political goals. Where civil society voices have been able to exert influence, this has been the result of extensive and well-funded transnational campaigning (von Bülow, 2010; Trommer, 2014). However, as we have already noted, this funding has been dwindling since the global financial crisis.

There is a further literature, which we will explore in greater detail in what follows, that cautions that there is no direct link between integration into value chains and broader economic rights for women. Specifically, it shows that where small-scale and informal actors are linked into formal, regional or transnational value chains, 'regulatory and material support from the state as a guarantor of economic rights' is required for empowerment to take hold, and to prevent the benefits of inclusive policies from disproportionately flowing to political lobbies, non-governmental organizations and more powerful businesses (Mosiane, 2011, p x; see also Watson, 2009). If meaningful resources for social, political and economic participation are not provided to informal and small-scale agents, there is a risk that international and corporate interests will benefit at the expense of local livelihoods, and that 'new costs on the poor' may ensue (Watson, 2009). As Kate Meagher (2013, p 24) warns, these may include new 'techniques of governance and subordination'.

In sum, in gender mainstreaming in food trade, it is less the case that gendered constructions of women as efficient farmers, food securers and guardians of nature gives rise to calls for their civic and political empowerment. It is more the case that these gendered constructions serve as justification for why commercializing women's farming and food trading activities in the global South are expected to lead to women's empowerment, poverty alleviation, as well as supporting national development, the fight against hunger and climate change adaptation. Its policy agenda risks intensifying the exploitation of women and other marginalized groups, given that free trade feminism expects women in the global South to achieve all of this based on access to a narrow set of productive assets alone. In so doing, it risks imposing new, and potentially unachievable, productive, reproductive and ecological responsibilities on women, while depleting the resources needed to accomplish these tasks.

Food, trade governance and trading on social reproduction

From the perspective of free trade feminism, the virtuous circle between trade liberalization, gender equality, women's empowerment, development, and food security and sustainability is common sense. However, these assumptions are in fact highly contested, as is the trade liberalization agenda to which free trade feminism lends legitimacy.

One important area of contestation revolves around the trade-ification of food security and sustainability (Clapp, 2017a; see also Watkins, 1996;

Margulis, 2014), to which free trade feminism has lent a 'feminist face'. In so doing, the free trade feminist vision for food trade aligns itself with long-standing efforts in global governance to promote free trade and market-oriented global food policies as preconditions for meeting global goals of development, food security, as well as sustainability and climate change goals. Seen from our feminist perspective, it aligns itself with forces seeking to further advance trading on social reproduction.

The argument that free trade promotes food security has a long history of being challenged as 'a recipe for social, economic and environmental dislocation' and 'a convenient smokescreen for the pursuit of vested interests' (Watkins, 1996, p 245). From our perspective, these are economic actors that create value directly from the life-making work of others through the mechanism of global trade. Trade scholars have identified these actors as residing within global net food-exporting countries, such as Canada, Australia and the US; within emerging agro-industrial powers from the global South, such as Brazil, Argentina, India, Thailand and Vietnam; and with large transnational corporations that dominate the global food system (Watkins, 1996; Margulis, 2014).

Despite having been included in the WTO regime, agricultural trade has remained a sector marked by relatively high trade barriers globally, compared to industrial or manufacturing sectors, showing that trading on social reproduction relies on the expansion of corporate and investor rights, whether through liberal or protectionist trade policies (see Chapter 2). On the one hand, OECD countries have traditionally used protectionist trade policies and domestic support systems to boost domestic agriculture and the WTO Agreement on Agriculture has allowed continuation of these practices (Gonzalez, 2002). Over the past two decades, a number of emerging economies, such as Argentina, Brazil, India and Vietnam, have also risen as 'agro-powers' and used WTO agricultural negotiations to expand their standing in world agricultural trade (Margulis, 2017). On the other hand, in line with the anti-agrarian bias inherent in modernization approaches to development (McMichael, 1997; Mies and Bennholdt-Thomsen, 1999), barriers to agricultural and food trade were dismantled in many developing countries either via SAPs or the Agreement on Agriculture (Bernstein, 1990; Watkins, 1996; Bello, 2008; Margulis, 2014). Many developing countries emerged from these processes as import-dependent for food. As UNCTAD (2022a, p 27) acknowledges, '[s]ince 1995, food imports per capita in net food-importing developing countries have increased by 300 per cent and, in low-income food-deficit countries, by over 500 per cent'.

In the context of import dependence for food security, many populations around the world have become vulnerable to fluctuations in global commodity prices when it comes to satisfying basic food needs, which are central to social reproduction. At the same time, a reliance on food imports may lead to dietary changes, including the introduction of ultra-processed foods, that have negative implications for health that are experienced unevenly (Lombardozzi, 2024; Stevano, 2025). Critics argue that this is in part a result of the emphasis that global North and global South governments have placed on cheap food imports as the main mechanism of food provisioning (Watkins, 1996).

In their rejection of the WTO 2017 Declaration, women's civil society groups and their allies pointed to negative experiences with trade policies that promote the 'influx of subsidised food and inputs and displaces local production' (Our World is Not For Sale, 2017). They also demanded that the WTO 'allow[s] for pro-poor public stockholding of food', which is one of the issues over which the Doha Development Round stumbled, as we saw at the start of this chapter (Our World is Not For Sale, 2017). These concerns go back much further, garnering resistance from peasants and small farmers across the world over what we would categorize as resistance to capital accumulation via trading on social reproduction. As Mies and Shiva see it (1993, p 231), '[t]he conflict is not between farmers of the North and those of the South, but between small farmers everywhere and multinationals'.

Yet, free trade feminism largely sidesteps these long-standing debates about food trade dependencies, food insecurity and agricultural liberalization. As we saw in Chapter 3, these controversies are one reason why WTO members such as South Africa take the stance that if gender equality is to be achieved via trade, there is a need to conclude the agricultural agenda of the Doha Development Round. Instead, free trade feminism formulates a market-based response to such structuralist critiques of the global trade regime that avoids liberalizing global agricultural trade in line with the demands made by developing countries in the WTO Doha Round, while simultaneously supporting the trade-ification of food, and the expansion of trading on social reproduction more broadly. It achieves all of this despite negotiating deadlocks on agriculture in the WTO.

Whether market efficiency could or should be the centrepiece of approaches to food sustainability and environmental protection more generally is a related long-standing debate in trade governance that free trade feminism leaves unacknowledged. As noted earlier, much feminist scholarship would instead start from the perspective of what is needed for subsistence, that is, from the perspective of social reproduction. Thus, for instance, the subsistence perspective 'insists on the priority of use-value production. It is based on the recognition that, on a limited planet, limitless growth of money and commodities can only be destructive. To avoid this we must strive for a cyclic economy. It cannot be based on global free trade and investment' (Mies and Bennholdt-Thomsen, 1999, p 58; see also Mies and Shiva, 1993). Others have approached the issue from the perspective of national food self-sufficiency. As Jennifer Clapp points out, this does not mean that no food is imported, but rather that a country 'has the capacity to produce food in sufficient quantities to meet its domestic needs' (2017b, 89).

Environmental, ecological and feminist scholarship has further challenged the notion that environmental sustainability can be reached within existing frameworks of trade governance. They have argued, for instance, that trade liberalization can intensify food insecurity and environmental degradation by dedicating agricultural land to production for export and promoting 'chemical-intensive, monocultural farming techniques that produce serious ecological harm' (Gonzalez, 2006, p 352). Commercializing agriculture for purposes of export and integrating it into food supply chains has been shown to have large environmental costs. These derive from the use of toxic chemicals, fresh water and soil depletion, deforestation, the reliance on transportation (including cooling) and communications infrastructures, and the high consumption and waste patterns associated with this model (Conca, 2000; Gonzalez, 2006).

These costs are unevenly carried across the globe. Carmen Gonzalez (2000, p 983) highlights 'the [global] North's resource-intensive, consumption-oriented lifestyle as the primary cause of global environmental degradation' and critiques how trade and environment initiatives in global trade governance obscure this reality by putting trust in techno-managerial solutions to environmental problems. She warns of so-called 'toxic colonialism' (2000, p 983), whereby imperial countries have tended to reap the benefits of economic expansion, while the associated environmental costs have tended to be borne by colonized peoples (2000, p 990). Within countries, they have also tended to be felt across intersecting lines of inequality (Gonzalez, 2000). Critics thus highlight the need to move away from the commodity-centric view of food and agricultural produce in trade debates and towards recognizing that agricultural activity provides essential ecological, livelihood and wellbeing functions (Rosset, 2006; Clapp, 2017a; 2017b).

In this context, it is important to recognize that the drive for ever increasing agricultural productivity in economic policy circles can reduce agricultural efficiency from an ecological point of view (Weis, 2010). To preserve the ecological functions of diversified agriculture, trade policy makers need to recognize that periods of redundancy are essential (Fuchs and Hoffmann, 2013). They also need to recognize that subsistence and poor farmers may well succeed in terms of food security and agricultural biodiversity *precisely because* they do not work on a market-oriented model of agriculture (Chappell et al, 2013; Graeub et al, 2015). The modes of commercialization driven by free trade feminism may well undermine the benefits that this approach expects to arise from commercializing subsistence agriculture in the global South.

Rather than acknowledging and engaging with these long-standing debates and critiques of the relationship between global food trade, food security and food sustainability, free trade feminism advances trading on social reproduction in the food trade sector under the banner of women's empowerment, pedalling gendered myths that women can succeed as productivity-maximizing economic agents, egalitarian food securers and guardians of nature, within the confines of the current global food and agricultural trade governance regime, all at the same time.

What is missing from free trade feminist visions for women's empowerment through food and agricultural trade is the recognition that the global industrial food system is in crisis, and that gendered inequalities are both constitutive of and intensified by this crisis. Scholars and international organizations have for some time urged a transformation of the global industrial food system, which has negative impacts on public health, environmental conditions, economic stability and social justice (Clapp and Moseley, 2020; Webb et al, 2020; Béné, 2022; Mezzadri et al, 2024).[7] All of these areas are key topics for feminists and have implications for productive economies as well as reproductive labour and the conditions under which social reproduction occurs around the world.

In failing to systematically engage with established critiques of the role of existing global trade relations in the global food system, free trade feminist agendas focused on food trade promote the reproduction of political economic forces that stand in the way of global food system transformation. These include not only the economic and political power of transnational food conglomerates to oppose food system reform (Bernstein, 2016; Clapp, 2023), but also the 'perceptions, beliefs and views of individual consumers, institutions, public and private policy-makers, investors, suppliers' (Béné, 2022, p 105881), which free trade feminism actively shapes in favour of the agro-industrial approach to global food provisioning. In doing so, free trade feminism casts urgently needed debates about feminist trade and feminist food justice – which, as we will see in the concluding chapter are alive and well – into the margins of global trade governance and policy making.

Conclusion

We have argued in this chapter that food trade is a feminist issue. However, in focusing primarily on how to commercialize agricultural production and render women's labour 'more productive', free trade feminism sidelines some of the most important questions about how the integration of food into trade governance impacts women, gender relations and relations of social reproduction more broadly.

As the WTO and other trade governance actors have converged with the FAO and other *non-trade* governance actors around the mutually reinforcing goals of trade liberalization and food security and sustainability, women's empowerment initiatives have emerged as drivers of this trade-ification of food governance. This is not a gender-neutral administrative shift, but entails the restructuring of social reproduction as it is structurally linked to trade. It has important implications for subsistence and other forms of informal, casual and/or reproductive labour that is housewifized and rebranded as an under-productive frontier that must be modernized though commercialization and value chain integration. In doing so, trade governance institutions bypass the critical concerns raised by feminist scholars and activists, choosing instead to mobilize colonial-era dichotomies that frame traditional, life-making agricultural practices as backward while positioning corporate-led, technology-intensive models as the sole path to empowerment and sustainability.

Ultimately, the promotion of a productivist approach to food trade serves to break the long-standing deadlock in agricultural negotiations by opening new profit-making frontiers in the global South. By framing women as both rational entrepreneurs and self-sacrificing providers, free trade feminism legitimizes a system that displaces small-scale farmers and undermines the very reproductive labour that sustains communities. To move towards genuine feminist food justice, we must look beyond categorical commitments to free trade or protectionism or narrow metrics of productivity and value-chain integration, and towards a trade system that prioritizes livelihoods and the centrality of life-making.

5

Digital Trade

Trade in the 21st century is fundamentally intertwined with advances in digital technology and digitization, as more and more goods and services are digitized (or partially digitized) and/or are being traded through digital means. While close to a third of the world's population remains offline, digitization of the world economy is changing forms of production and consumption and is dissolving traditional trade policy dichotomies such as goods versus services, or export versus import interests (Lodefalk, 2017). According to a report by the McKinsey Global Institute, '[v]irtually every type of cross-border transaction now has a digital component' (Manyika et al, 2016, p 3). In the foreword to the 2018 *World Trade Report*, then-WTO Director-General Azevêdo asserted that 'we are living through an era of unprecedented technological change', where innovations such as the Internet of Things, Artificial Intelligence (AI), 3D printing and blockchain 'have the potential to profoundly transform the way we trade, who trades and what is traded' (WTO, 2018b, p 3).

With digital trade, transnational data flows transmit streams of information that enable the transnational movement of goods, services, finance and people. Cross-border data flows are also emerging as a form of digital trade in their own right, with some seeing them as 'the lifeblood of digital trade' (OECD, 2019, cited in Ismail, 2020, p 3). According to McKinsey, such data flows now have a greater impact on global gross domestic product than trade in goods flows (Manyika et al, 2016).

Although there is some contestation, as we shall see, many trade policy makers are enthusiastic about these transformations. They believe that digital technologies can, among other things, lower trade costs, speed up trade and increase trade volumes, increase access to markets and finance, democratize production and expand GVCs (WTO, 2018b, pp 3, 46). This is believed to afford new opportunities to developing countries and MSMEs, and to foster sustainable development more broadly (Manyika et al, 2016).

In trade productivist fashion, gender considerations have been mostly absent from the international regulatory frameworks for digital trade that governments have developed over the past decades and that are instrumental to shaping the digital transformation of the global political economy. The WTO, for example, has two main areas of work on digital trade, neither of which explicitly addresses gender issues: the Work Programme on E-commerce, commenced in 1998, and the Joint Statement Initiative (JSI) on E-Commerce launched in 2017 – that is to say, in tandem with the WTO's gender mainstreaming agenda.

The Work Programme serves as a multilateral deliberative process in which WTO members discuss matters related to digitization and trade and has, until recently, been relatively dormant. Accompanying the establishment of the Work Programme was a provisional agreement known as the 'e-commerce moratorium', which is a commitment made by WTO members to refrain from imposing tariffs on electronic transmissions. The moratorium has been repeatedly extended, with some WTO members, including the US and the EU, pushing for it to be made permanent. The JSI is a plurilateral negotiating process through which a sub-set of WTO members are working towards a WTO agreement on e-commerce that is open to all WTO members, but only binding for signatories. At the 2026 WTO Ministerial Conference, a sub-group of 67 members announced their intention to apply a WTO Agreement on Electronic Commerce as an interim agreement, after they failed to convince the membership to include the text among WTO covered agreements (WTO, 2026c).[1] As one observer of WTO e-commerce talks remarked on the standing of gender equality and women's empowerment: 'it's nobody's focus. … The gender issues do not have a champion amongst the WTO Members participating in the e-commerce talks' (cited in Dommen, 2021; see also UNCTAD, 2023b).

Given slow progress in WTO negotiations, digital trade rules are predominantly advancing via FTAs and so-called 'megaregional' agreements, such as the Comprehensive and Progressive Agreement for Trans-Pacific Partnership (CPTPP), the United States-Mexico-Canada Agreement, dubbed 'NAFTA 2.0', or the Regional Comprehensive Economic Partnership (RCEP). There are also several digital economy agreements with a strong trade component, such as the Digital Economy Partnership Agreement or the Digital Protocol to the AfCFTA (Digital Trade Alliance, 2025). Only a handful of these include gender provisions (WTO, 2023c). This has met occasional criticism, for example when ECLAC asked for the WTO to mainstream gender into e-commerce negotiations in a presentation to the IWG on Trade and Gender (ECLAC, 2021).

Nonetheless, it remains the case that gender mainstreaming in digital trade, as in trade governance generally, leaves the existing regulatory and political frameworks for global trade intact and works to improve the position of individual women within existing global digital trade relations. It does this in large part by sidestepping debates about what digital trade rules and agreements should look like and instead focusing on how the expansion of e-commerce can lead to more 'inclusive' trade.

As we show in this chapter, free trade feminism aims to accomplish this by connecting women exporters and entrepreneurs to e-commerce platforms, via the promotion of the so-called 'digital inclusion' of women, women's digital entrepreneurship initiatives and digital financial inclusion. Though there is some discussion of how women consumers can benefit from the expansion of digital trade, policy interventions and resources are overwhelmingly focused on interventions designed to help women traders integrate digital technologies, including fintech and e-commerce platforms, into their business practices. There is little to no consideration of the demands of feminist digital justice groups, which call on economic forums and multilateral discussions of e-commerce to consider 'the manner in which relations of production and social reproduction are being restructured worldwide' in the context of digitization, and 'the ecological impacts of an unsustainable dominant digital paradigm' (Partenio and Weleilakeba, 2023, p 6).

As we elaborate in this chapter, the focus on digital inclusion depoliticizes digitization, which is a complex and highly contested ongoing transformation in the global economy, and takes a number of controversial debates regarding digital governance, and digital trade governance specifically, off the table. This perpetuates trade productivism by obscuring the gendered nature of this transformation, which includes, among other things, biased algorithms, data colonialism, the platformization of labour that further invisibilizes and extracts value from the labour of women and others and devastating ecological costs.

Furthermore, free trade feminism casts the potential of digital technologies to intensify double burdens – which we already saw in gendered constructions of women as successful food traders and food securers – in a positive light. It uses gendered constructions about women's presumed ability to succeed as *both* digital entrepreneurs and traders engaged in 'flexible' work *and* as carers for families and communities to justify its stance that digital inclusion can empower women while also contributing to economic growth and sustainable development.

From our perspective, this represents a new form of digitally enabled housewifization, which continues the devaluation of reproductive labour as a gendered structural feature of the global economy. As with earlier forms of housewifization, it also introduces new modes of exploitation, for instance by promoting digital trade programmes that connect digital 'mama-entrepreneurs' to large e-commerce platforms and the corporate actors that own them, and further promotes trading on social reproduction.

Overall, we suggest that free trade feminism supports the current approach to digital trade governance, which is narrowly driven by large trading nations and blocs, notably the US, China and the EU, and the interests of the large tech companies that influence their policies. By explicitly endorsing, and/or failing to question, the currently dominant approaches to digital trade, free trade feminism is helping to fuel corporate power and deepen existing inequalities between countries, between capital and labour, and along gendered lines. This also marginalizes feminist calls for the need to regulate the digital economy, and digital trade specifically, in the public interest.

Empowering women through e-commerce

Free trade feminist initiatives and discourses aiming to empower women through digital trade conceal the controversial politics of trade in the digital era under a narrow focus on e-commerce and e-commerce platforms (see also Gurumurthy and Chami, 2021; Scasserra, 2023). Women's empowerment initiatives in digital trade emphasize how digital technologies allow women and others considered to be marginalized in trade to find international customers and economic opportunities, typically via online commercial platforms such as Amazon, eBay, Etsy, Alibaba, Airbnb, Facebook and others (see, for instance, World Bank and WTO, 2020). In 2021, at the WTO IWG on Trade and Gender, Australia outlined three arguments underpinning free trade feminism's enthusiasm for women's empowerment via digital trade:

> a. Digital technologies (internet, digital platforms, mobile phones, and digital financial services) offer women opportunities to earn (additional) income, increase employment opportunities and access knowledge. b. Using technology, online platforms and e-commerce can be an easy and inexpensive way to enter foreign markets, expand women-owned businesses and promote women entrepreneurship c. The trust component of the e-commerce JSI (including online consumer protection, spam, etc.) will be particularly important for vulnerable groups by making the internet a safer and fairer place to do business in the future. (WTO, 2021c, p 2)

The COVID-19 pandemic is often cited as providing compelling evidence for how digitization enhances women's ability to participate in global trade. For example, Canada invited the IWG in 2020 to consider 'the impact of COVID-19 on women's participation in trade and the importance of digital trade/e-commerce to address issues and capture opportunities' (WTO, 2020b, p 2). Similarly, Australia concluded in the IWG in 2021 that the experience of the COVID-19 pandemic

> shows us the importance of the role of technology in helping to promote resilience and inclusive economic development: e-commerce

> can help women who own small and medium businesses to overcome key physical and economic challenges to their growth and support diversification … enable women traders and entrepreneurs to reach customers globally, as well as access government e-services, information, and … can help women traders overcome discriminatory socio-cultural norms, such as mobility constraints. (WTO, 2021g, p 4)

As the quote shows, women and MSMEs often appear as interchangeable within these accounts, or women-owned MSMEs are targeted directly. This conflation is typically based on the observation that the majority of women-owned companies are MSMEs (see, for example, ITC, 2020b; World Bank and WTO, 2020; OECD, 2021). It is further evidenced in the fact that the IWG on Trade and Gender and the IWG on MSMEs have begun producing joint documents, laying out shared policy agendas and programmes for solving the presumed mutual problems of digital exclusion that women and MSMEs face in the global economy (see, for instance, WTO, 2024c).

The gender work programmes at the multilateral, regional and state levels concentrate heavily on connecting women to e-commerce platforms, positioning it as the central challenge of the gender and digital trade agenda (see, for example, World Bank and WTO, 2020; UNCTAD, 2023b). The IWG's *Progress Report on WTO Members and Observers Technical Work on Women's Economic Empowerment*, for example, contains a section dedicated to e-commerce initiatives that support women entrepreneurs, while not saying much more about gender and digital trade outside of this context. In the report, the ITC, UNCTAD, the UN Economic and Social Commission for Asia and the Pacific, the Enhanced Integrated Framework, Australia, Ecuador, El Salvador, Japan and Turkey provide examples of active programmes in Africa, Central America, the Pacific and Southeast Asia that foster women's integration into e-commerce websites and platforms (WTO, 2021b). As we explain later on, these programmes typically deploy digital skills and literacy training, digital entrepreneurship training and digital financial inclusion to accomplish this goal (WTO, 2021b).

The common interchangeable use of the terms 'e-commerce', 'e-commerce platforms' and 'digital trade' in gender mainstreaming in trade governance however misrepresents what is at stake in digital trade. While the muddling of the terminologies of 'e-commerce' and 'digital trade' is common across trade governance generally (Gao, 2018; Ismail, 2020), digital trade governance does not facilitate the transnational sales of goods and services alone. It also facilitates the digitization of the global economy by governing the transnational flow of data, which is a central component of governing a global digital economy.

Data are the raw materials of the digital economy and are monetized into extremely profitable revenue streams (Srnicek, 2017). These financial gains are largely captured by a small number of oligopolistic firms and their investors. Microsoft, Apple, Amazon, Google, Facebook, Tencent and Alibaba – typically referred to as the 'Super 7' platforms – account for two-thirds of the total market value of the world's top 70 platforms (WTO, 2020c, section 3.4). The gendered implications of this concentration of power can neither be discerned nor redressed by a focus on the benefits of access to e-commerce platforms. This leads feminist and women's groups to accuse trade governance institutions of 'fail[ing] to grasp the interconnected and far-reaching nature of the digital economy into so many facets of our lives' (Wolfenden, 2023, p 62).

To understand how free trade feminism's fixation on e-commerce platforms is both politically plausible within trade governance and depoliticizing at the same time, we need to briefly review how the governance of e-commerce/digital trade has evolved in the era of digitization.

The evolution of digital trade governance

When the WTO started its e-commerce work programme in 1998, the term e-commerce was used to refer to those commodities that, due to technological innovation, could be traded in the form of an electronic transaction, rather than having to be shipped as physical merchandise. Key examples include books, films or music, which are today frequently streamed across borders (showing how digitization blurs the distinction between trade in goods and trade in services). As the example of the JSI on E-Commerce shows, the WTO has stuck with the 'increasingly anachronistic' terminology of e-commerce (Burri and Chander, 2023, p 99), even when it refers to broader matters of digital trade. In the 2010s, however, active campaigns driven largely by the rapidly globalizing American tech sector shifted aspects of internet governance *in general* into the trade governance arena and pushed for binding rules within the international trade regime that would support the 'facilitation' rather than the 'restriction' of digital trade (Kelsey, 2018; Azmeh et al, 2020, p 672; Azmeh, 2024a, p 383).[2]

Today, digital trade is commonly understood in global economic governance to refer to 'all trade that is digitally ordered and/or digitally delivered' (OECD et al, 2019). This definition set by the OECD, the WTO and the IMF encompasses: e-commerce; e-commerce platforms and the apps associated with the gig economy providing for ordering, transactions, payments and logistics; digitally enabled goods and services; cloud computing; and AI (Azmeh et al, 2020, p 672; Jones, 2023). It includes any situation where there is 'collection and transfer of data inherent to the provision of … goods and services, which may flow across multiple state borders' irrespective of whether there is a monetary charge on the consumer – for example, when participating in an online meeting or watching an ostensibly 'free' video (Burri and Chander, 2023, p 99). Because digital trade is today understood to include the regulation of data flows across borders, digital trade rules in multilateral, regional and bilateral trade agreements go beyond traditional questions of goods and services crossing borders, and govern transnational aspects of the digital economy generally speaking. Digital trade is thus a much wider phenomenon than e-commerce platforms, with more wide-reaching implications, including for the links between digital trade and gender relations, though these have gone relatively unexplored in the academic and policy literature.

As a starting point, to tease out these links it is important to recognize that data-related provisions anchored in trade agreements are central to the ability of big tech companies to monetize data across the global political economy. Existing trade treaties typically balance provisions that enable the digital economy with provisions that may restrict transnational data flows in the name of the state's regulatory autonomy (with the US generally tending to strive for less restrictive stances in its trade deals than China or the EU) (Burri and Chander, 2023; Burri and Kugler, 2024).

Data-related provisions in FTAs posit the freedom of cross-border data flows and ban or limit data localization measures and the forced disclosure of source code. Data localization requires 'data [to] be stored and/or processed within the domestic territory' of a particular country (OECD, 2023, p 5). Countries such as the US, those in the EU, and tech-heavy nations like Singapore, along with tech companies, argue that data localization prevents the internet from operating seamlessly, as intended. Source code disclosure requires software developers to transfer or provide access to source code and algorithms to governments (Dorobantu et al, 2021). As Mira Burri and Kholofelo Kugler (2024, p 398) explain, 'there is a critical interdependence between cross-border data flows and digital growth and innovation in all sectors of the economy and for future-oriented technologies – for instance, in the development of artificial intelligence', because AI hinges on data inputs (see also Chander, 2021).

To retain regulatory autonomy, different trade agreements contain different sets of exemptions, carve outs and provisions that allow for review and regulation in the exercise of public authority or to safeguard other public interests, such as in public health, safety, environmental protection or stability of the financial system (Burri and Kugler, 2024). Trade-related provisions typically also facilitate paperless trading, electronic signatures and electronic contracts, electronic invoicing and payments, and include online consumer protection and related concerns. As we explore in more detail across this chapter, how digital trade agreements strike the balance of facilitating and regulating the digital transformation of the global economy is problematic from our feminist perspective, and has proven controversial in the global politics surrounding digital trade (see also Azmeh et al, 2020; Burri and Chander, 2023, p 99; Jones, 2023).

Digital trade, the big equalizer?

By claiming that 'technology is an equalizer tool', as the Trade Experettes (2023) did in the IWG, proponents of free trade feminism sidestep critical debates over data governance. Such a framing risks exacerbating gendered and intersectional inequalities by reducing digital trade to a matter of platform access alone. Many policy makers promoting women's empowerment through integration into e-commerce platforms assert that digital trade has anti-discriminatory effects. The removal of face-to-face interaction, the concealment of gender markers in electronic transactions and algorithm-driven decision-making are typically cited as reasons for this (see World Bank and WTO, 2020, p 137; OECD, 2021, p 35). Consumer protection and internet safety rules in trade agreements, such as in the WTO JSI and the WTO Agreement on Electronic Commerce (which focus primarily on commercial trust and consumer protection and *not* content-related issues) are also thought to improve the safety of doing business online, especially for the most vulnerable groups.

New technologies, however, often reproduce rather than counteract social norms and material inequalities. For instance, the idea that concealing markers of gender difference will lead to more gender equitable outcomes only makes sense if such forms of direct discrimination are the main problem women face. These discriminations certainly do exist, and in contextually specific ways. The erasure of embodied markers of difference, however, does not erase the fact that women – and women of different classes, racial and ethnic groups, ability, sexuality, as well as gender-non-comforming groups and others – do not come to the digital marketplace as formally equal, but as embedded in broader social structures of inequality (see also Roberts, 2015a; Natile, 2020).

At the same time, as a long line of feminist scholars of technology have argued, algorithms are designed in ways that *build biases in*. Ruha Benjamin (2019), for instance, uses the term 'the New Jim Code' to explain how new technologies that are perceived to be more objective or progressive than previous (often face-to-face) systems reproduce existing racial and intersectional inequalities. They do this, for instance, by building in the biases of racist, sexist and classist societies in facial recognition technology. This may include culturally specific ideologies about what constitutes beauty, or what constitutes a man or a woman – or a person at all. Safiya Noble's (2018) *Algorithms of Oppression* offers numerous examples of what she calls 'technological redlining', whereby digital platforms and algorithms use data to profile and discriminate against specific groups. In the US context, these are most often people of colour and women.

Part of the problem is that the search engines and platforms that serve as entry points to digital commerce are not public or 'neutral', but are private, profit-driven infrastructures. They also tend to be configured by men, who dominate the masculinized tech sector, and from whose perspective much technology is designed.[3] Driven by the need to generate relative profit, platforms promote engagement and sensationalism, which feminists have argued amplifies gendered violence and harassment online, leaving women, particularly women of colour, and those who identify as LGBTQIA+, more vulnerable to abuse (Jane, 2017). As a study of online marketplaces in Pakistan showed, even where digital platforms have reduced traditional economic biases (for instance, in terms of prices for male and female buyers), they also facilitated harassment, as female buyers were more likely to receive unsolicited communications from male sellers (Asad et al, 2025). Digital trade rules that mandate the non-disclosure of source code and related algorithms prevent the public from identifying, challenging and dismantling these structural biases.

What is more, e-commerce platforms exploit user interactions, which are forms of unpaid labour, to generate revenue for platform operators and investors. In promoting e-commerce platforms as tools that help women to connect to new customers and/or economic opportunities beyond borders, free trade feminism fuels a new form of digital housewifization (Fuchs, 2014), a point to which we return later. The extraction and commodification of personal data serves as the backbone of accumulation, as user behaviours are tracked, predicted and manipulated to optimize advertising revenues and market control. As digital technology providers then monetize these data into profit, users are not just benefactors of new economic opportunities, but are also producers and commodities in the e-commerce platform business model, while their labour is both uncompensated and alienating (Fuchs, 2014).

Women and marginalized groups are often subject to more invasive monitoring and data exploitation in this process. For example, platforms track and commodify women's bodies and intimate aspects of their lives, such as reproductive health data through period-tracking apps and other forms of so-called 'FemTech'. While these apps may have some health benefits for women, they also raise concerns about privacy rights and bodily autonomy, as well as the reproduction of cis-heteronormativity (Ford et al, 2021; Amelang, 2022).

Feminist and other critical research has also revealed that digital platforms rely on invisibilized and un-/under-paid gendered labour, such as emotional labour, content moderation and caregiving roles facilitated through platforms. For instance, Kylie Jarrett (2016) argues that digital labour often mirrors domestic and emotional labour, and is disproportionately performed by women. The gig economy heavily relies on the precarious labour of women in roles like cleaning, caregiving and customer service (for instance via platforms like TaskRabbit or Care.com), while devaluing these forms of work. Yet liberalized digital trade regimes make it increasingly difficult to regulate technological ecosystems in the interests of labour (Digital Trade Alliance, 2024, p 2).

E-commerce platform providers thus combine data extraction, network effects and rent-seeking to consolidate power and dominate markets (Srnicek, 2017; Zuboff, 2019; Christophers, 2020). At the same time, as we will further argue later, platforms undermine worker rights, fuel new forms of precarious labour through gig work and appropriate unpaid labour. Feminist activists have argued that platformization 'transforms production, distribution and social reproduction in ways that reinforce the concentration of economic and social power in the hands of corporations and countries of the Global North' (Partenio and Weleilakeba, 2022, p 6).

It is occasionally recognized within free trade feminism that new forms of harassment may arise in online spaces and that digital business models may not be regulated by labour laws (OECD, 2021, pp 34–35; see also UNCTAD, 2023b). In some cases, the market power of digital technology providers is acknowledged as a problem. UNCTAD's 'gender and development' approach to e-commerce, for instance, notes that:

> The dominance of global platforms, their control of data, and their capacity to create and capture the resulting value tend to accentuate concentration and consolidation rather than reduce inequalities between and within countries. Global platforms can enter markets and expand rapidly as they are backed by large levels of funding, with the risk of a 'winner takes all' model (UNCTAD, 2019; International Development Research Centre, 2018; Rani and Singh, 2019). (UNCTAD, 2023b, p 17)

Unlike in UNCTAD's 2019 *Digital Economy Report* cited in this quote (which is *not* a gender-specific report), in the 2023 gender-focused report, the acknowledgement of the power of platforms is not followed up with any discussion of how digital trade governance propels the power of global platforms to dominate the digital transformation. It goes without saying that there is also no analysis of the gender dimensions thereof. Instead, women are encouraged to engage themselves in monetizing online interactions as 'business opportunities arise in a space where consumers spend time to get entertained or seek information' (UNCTAD, 2023b, p 18).

Overall, free trade feminism remains silent on the fact that digital trade rules that constrain governmental ability to regulate the digital economy – such as those mandating the free flow of data, or banning data localization and disclosure of source code – prevent the public from identifying, challenging and dismantling structural biases that are integrated into code and into the techniques developed to monetize the growing pervasiveness of data in the world economy.

Hence, the idea that digital trade is predominantly – and unproblematically – about integration into e-commerce platforms operates as a form of trade productivism, in the sense that it frames digital trade as a simple, powerful and gender-neutral logistical tool for transnational exchange. As we saw, free trade feminism does not join wider feminist demands for addressing gendered inequalities directly in spheres where digital trade is governed.

Similarly to how free trade feminism operates in food trade, it promotes digital trade agendas that integrate women into pre-existing global chains of production and reproduction, in spite of their wider gendered aspects. As we discuss later, free trade feminism recognizes that women face a disadvantage when it comes to digitization of the world economy, but they frame this disadvantage as emanating from gendered discriminations in law and society, which leave women lacking in access to technology and digital infrastructures, and lacking in digital skills and finance. This framing, and the conflation of integration into e-commerce platforms with digital trade, further work to conceal the wider gendered aspects of digital trade.

Notably, free trade feminism disregards the role played by digital trade governance in promoting the emergence of a highly monopolistic digital economy globally, which is rooted in the unequal trade relations set out in Chapter 2. Thereby, it risks reproducing, rather than undermining, divisions rooted in class, race, gender, place and more, and perpetuating old and new inequalities and exclusions in the global political economy.

From our perspective, free trade feminism promotes and actively participates in a corporate-centric agenda for digital trade by integrating small-scale economic operators (including agricultural producers) into the digital economy in the name of women's economic empowerment. Just like in food trade, it mobilizes gendered constructions to promote its vision for women's economic empowerment via digital trade. The idea of the digital mama entrepreneur in particular serves policy agendas that further promote the devaluation and exploitation of women's work and reproductive labour in the service of digital capitalism. Meanwhile, free trade feminism marginalizes environmental critiques and visions for digital democracy, digital commons and feminist digital justice. It is to these critiques that we now turn.

Closing the gender digital divide

Closing the gender digital divide is free trade feminism's preferred strategy for connecting women entrepreneurs, women-owned MSMEs and women exporters to e-commerce networks and platforms, which is assumed to lead to economic growth and development. Policy makers driving gender mainstreaming in digital trade recognize that women often face differential access to digital technologies when compared to men and implement digital inclusion initiatives in order to close the 'gender digital divide' (see, for instance, UNCTAD, 2023b).

The phrase 'digital divide' describes the divide between developed and developing countries in terms of access to technologies and the quality of the infrastructure and of the legal framework for the digital economy (WTO, 2018b; UNCTAD, 2023b). It is also used to refer to divides within countries, typically between large and small firms, between men and women, or other marginalized groups, such as indigenous peoples. In the context of rapid digitization of the global economy, the digital divide has also been widening, with only 27 per cent of populations in Least Developed Countries (LDCs) using the internet, in contrast with 63 per cent of the world population (UN, 2023; Burri, 2024).

Free trade feminist policy elites not only see closing the digital divide as providing access to economic opportunities, but also as compensating for the potential negative impacts of digitization, for example if automation causes more routine jobs, which are often performed by women, to become obsolete. It is argued that women will be able to respond to new labour market opportunities if they have better education, in particular in engineering, information technology and STEM subjects, and digital literacy (World Bank and WTO, 2020, p 145; OECD, 2021, pp 34–35). The main problems that women face when it comes to benefiting from the digital economy are thought to be lack of access to ICT, education and digital skills, and finance and capital (UNCTAD, 2023b, p 19), as well as gender stereotypes and time poverty resulting from domestic and care work (UNCTAD, 2023b, p 20).

Closing the gender digital divide is pursued in the deliberative fora of the gender and trade agenda, via government programmes/development aid that target women domestically, and, to a lesser degree, via FTAs with relevant provisions in either gender or digital trade chapters.[4] In terms of multilateral institutions, ITC *SheTrades*, for example, has a strong digital element, being primarily organized around a website dedicated to helping women entrepreneurs (see Chapter 3). Their *SheTrades Academy* tries to improve women's digital literacy by providing a virtual learning space with close to 200 training videos for women entrepreneurs or business owners. The *SheTrades Invest* platform uses digital technology to connect investors and women exporters. *SheTrades* also engages in several interventions on the ground that aim to help women sell their products on digital platforms such as Etsy, eBay and Amazon Handmade, and connects exporters to companies such as DHL, eBay, Etsy, Payoneer and PayPal, which provide technical training and offer preferential rates.

UNCTAD also has numerous interventions focused on e-commerce entrepreneurs. This includes the *eTrade for Women* initiative (funded by Germany, Sweden, Switzerland and the Netherlands) which supports, largely via training programmes, female entrepreneurs in developing countries working in the digital economy. It further advocates for the need to bring the voices of women entrepreneurs into policy processes at the local, regional and global levels.[5] UNCTAD also has partnerships with transnational logistics corporations such as DHL (UNCTAD, 2022c), and advocates for more public–private partnerships in e-commerce (UNCTAD, 2023b, p 1).

As we also saw in Chapter 4, gender mainstreaming in trade is often connected to financial inclusion initiatives. In digital trade, free trade feminists believe that mobile money, digital platforms that connect start-ups and providers of financial services and investment though crowdfunding and other platforms will enable women to succeed in the digital economy. Emerging technologies such as blockchain will also benefit women exporters (World Bank and WTO, 2020, p 140).

Governments promote women's digital inclusion domestically and via AfT. Spain, for example, reports 'allocat[ing] up to €51 million over the next three years to boost female digital entrepreneurship, through the Digital Entrepreneurs Programme … to support and promote, through financing, female digital entrepreneurship projects and reduce the existing gender gap in this area' (WTO, 2024d, p 12). Chinese Taipei runs '[d]igital marketing courses (in collaboration with Facebook and Google) and mentorship for women entrepreneurs' as part of its domestic women's entrepreneurship programme (WTO, 2021b, p 5), while Korea provides an 'online package to support women-led MSMEs and increase their exports', including 'training on topics such as e-commerce' (WTO, 2021b, p 5). The US launched its *Strategy on Global Women's Economic Security* in 2023, which is centred on increasing the availability of financial products and services for women and women entrepreneurs – this includes insurance, micro enterprise credit and agricultural credit – fostering access to property and land, promoting climate finance that increases gender equality, and encouraging the use of digital finance (WTO, 2024d, p 20). Japan targets low-income women in Vietnam for digital financial inclusion (WTO, 2021b, p 12), while Australia's *E-commerce Aid for Trade Fund* 'provides gender-sensitive assistance to the Cambodian Government to implement national e-commerce regulation and develop its positions in the WTO E-Commerce JSI' (WTO, 2021c, p 4).

Trade policy makers thus aim to improve the connectivity of individual women to the digitizing world economy, assuming that this will benefit women while also fostering economic growth and development. UNCTAD (2023b, p 6), for example, argues that in order for e-commerce to support the achievement of the SDGs, existing disparities must be overcome by 'addressing gender discrimination in society and in the economy, and more specifically gender digital divides'. Elsewhere, it explains, '[t]he boom in e-commerce has also raised new hope that digitalization can drive inclusive transformation and growth by having more women involved' (UNCTAD, 2022d, p 8) and cites estimates that women's participation in e-commerce can generate US$14.5 billion in Africa and US$280 billion in Southeast Asia (IFC, cited in UNCTAD, 2022d, p 8).

The World Economic Forum explains why it believes that inclusion will tilt the debate about inequality, globalization and the global trade regime. It says:

> Globalization got a bad rap, in part because, by sweeping aside barriers to the movement of capital, labour and goods, it was perceived to have favoured large corporate interests over all others. With the unfolding of the e-commerce revolution, however, a fairer and more inclusive balance is reshaping the global business environment to provide more room and opportunity for small businesses, especially those headed by women. … Cross-border e-commerce … can help change the two-decade narrative about opportunity, inclusion, fairness and balance in the global economy. (WEF, 2020)

As we explained earlier, however, digital trade is, in no small measure, about the transnational circulation of data, which underlies the ability of large corporations and investors to capitalize on the digital economy at scale. Who benefits in what measure from digital trade is thus not only a problem of access to technology, but also a problem of having, or lacking, the economic, political and social capital to shape the digital transformation of the global political economy to one's advantage. Although this perspective has been taken by a number of developing countries in WTO talks on e-commerce and by women's groups and civil society organizations, it does not find resonance within gender mainstreaming in digital trade.

Debating the 'digital divide'

In their statement to the WTO Ministerial Conference in 2017, the African Group – a WTO negotiating coalition made up of African WTO members and observers – attacked 'the propaganda that new e-commerce rules will be good for developing countries' (WTO, 2017c). They argued that 'multinational corporations, who have become global digital leaders, and have decimated smaller companies' have been the big winners from 'digital industrial policies, such as subsidies, R&D subsidies, development of, and access to, and ownership of technologies, economies of scale, government-sponsored infrastructure, tax benefits, etc.', putting them at an advantage vis-à-vis their own domestic companies (WTO, 2017c, p 3). They highlighted their continuous critiques of 'hard rules', including free data flows, bans on data localization and source code disclosure, the e-commerce moratorium, 'barring forced technology transfer, etc' (WTO, 2017c, p 3).

The e-commerce moratorium has become one particular area of contention in the digital trade/development debate. As technology continues to evolve, trade policy elites lack clarity about what the future of production and trade will look like, and therefore, around the classification of goods and services. This prompts debate on the question of which goods and services fall under the moratorium, and whether it should be maintained. Under a wide definition of digital trade as entailing all digitally ordered and delivered goods and services a permanent moratorium on customs duties for e-commerce 'would imply that effectively the countries are agreeing on reducing tariffs to zero on almost all of their non-agricultural manufactured products' (UNCTAD, 2017b, p 15). The loss of revenue is especially pertinent for developing countries and LDCs who, according to an oft-cited study, could stand to lose up to US$8 billion compared to US$212 million for developed countries (Banga, 2019, p 19). This loss of revenue could have potentially devastating implications on the ability for developing countries, in particular, to fund public services, among other things.

India and South Africa have similarly articulated arguments that are rooted in the view that global trade is structurally disadvantageous to the global South. In a 2020 WTO communication, they pointed out that three members – the US, China and the EU – account for 80 per cent of cross-border e-commerce globally, meaning that the benefits of the digital economy are highly concentrated (WTO, 2020c). While free trade feminists and other proponents expect that digital inclusion of (women-owned) MSMEs will lead to a rebalancing of digital trade, India and South Africa explained that this division has remained relatively unchanged for the past several decades (WTO, 2020c). They also pointed to UNCTAD's research, specifically its 2019 *Digital Economy Report*, which shows that the US and East Asia account for 90 per cent of the market capitalization value of the 70 largest digital platforms. In contrast, Africa and Latin America together make up 1 per cent.

They further saw the focus on MSMEs as a smokescreen that masks the intention to create new multilateral rules that entrench existing inequalities between countries, and argued instead for the completion of the Doha Development Round (WTO, 2020c). This demand stood in contrast with the text of Article 20 of the WTO JSI on E-Commerce, which frames development as supporting developing countries and LDCs to 'effectively participate and tap into growth opportunities in electronic commerce and the digital economy' (that is, via digital infrastructure and support for MSMEs) and support for capacity building in these countries (WTO, 2024f, p 18).

Developmentalist positions expressed within the WTO mirror academic and civil society critiques that the appropriation of data for value that underlies the digital business model amounts to a form of North–South resource appropriation, or what some are calling 'data colonialism' (Couldry and Mejias, 2019). This is because developing countries and LDCs become mere exporters of raw data, while the value is captured by corporations controlling data infrastructures (Civil Society Declaration, 2021, pp 5–6; Callo-Müller and Kugler, 2023; Burri, 2024). Data colonialism not only reduces resources available for countries in the global South to pursue industrial or other forms of development, but also their ability to use local data to design public policies or improve the quality of public services (though data may also be mis-used by governments), which has implications for social reproduction.[6] Echoing previous battles over IPRs, some have also argued that digitalization makes it increasingly difficult for indigenous people to retain control and sovereignty of their knowledge (Wolfenden, 2023, p 64).

Free trade feminist efforts to close the digital divide circumvent these long-standing debates about the digital transformation of the global economy and present an alternative approach to trade and development, in particular by aligning themselves with the MSME empowerment agenda. In its efforts to do so, free trade feminism mobilizes gendered constructions of women in ways that resonate with gendered constructions of women in food trade governance outlined in Chapter 4.

Housewifization and trading on social reproduction in the digital era

When it comes to digital trade, free trade feminism is focused on how closing the digital divide and bringing more women into e-commerce – especially as entrepreneurs and owners of MSMEs – will lead to women's economic empowerment, while also stimulating economic growth and development *within* the existing global trade paradigm. In this section, we discuss how free trade feminism casts the potential of digital technologies to intensify double burdens in a positive light. To this end, it relies on gendered constructions about women's assumed ability to succeed as *both* digital entrepreneurs and traders engaged in 'flexible' work *and* as carers for families and communities. From our perspective, this represents a new form of digitally enabled housewifization, which continues the devaluation of reproductive labour as a gendered structural feature of the global economy. It also introduces new modes of exploitation, for instance by promoting digital trade programmes that connect so-called 'mama entrepreneurs' to large e-commerce platforms and the corporate actors that own them.

Digital trade and mama entrepreneurs

When it comes to justifying the belief that access to technology can empower women and lead to economic growth and development, free trade feminism creates a gendered construction of the digital mama entrepreneur, revealing how forms of housewifization are unfolding in the digital era. We borrow this expression from the Russian Federation's *Mama-Entrepreneur* programme, presented to the IWG in a communication in 2024 (WTO, 2024g). *Mama-Entrepreneur* is an entrepreneurship training programme that is 'designed specifically for women on maternity leave and those with under-age children to help them start their own business and effectively combine caretaking for the family and professional self-realization' (WTO, 2024g, p 3).

Among the actors engaged in gender mainstreaming in digital trade, the belief that digital technologies usefully enable women entrepreneurs to simultaneously engage in productive and reproductive labour is common, and by no means unique to the Russian Federation. All multilateral trade institutions argue that digital entrepreneurship affords women flexibility and helps them to balance the time constraints arising from juggling paid work and childcare/family responsibilities (ITC, 2020b, p 35; World Bank and WTO, 2020, pp 10, 144; OECD, 2021, p 35; UNCTAD, 2022d, p 8). Since 2019, UNCTAD's *eTrade for Women* programme has for example been nominating eTrade for Women Advocates. These are female digital entrepreneurs and e-traders from global South countries that are tasked with helping to 'shape policies to promote gender equality in the digital age', which UNCTAD explains will 'revitalis[e] efforts for a gender-inclusive digital space' (UNCTAD, 2024). As we set out earlier, this may be an uphill struggle for individual women operating MSMEs in value chains operated by digital business models.

In celebrating the mama entrepreneur, free trade feminism again taps into and reproduces longer standing, patriarchal framings of women as primary carers in the domestic sphere, while also being 'productive' in a capitalist sense (Littler, 2017). These framings also underpin the idealized 'entrepreneurial woman' that feminists have identified in microfinance programmes and other development interventions in the global South (Rankin, 2001; Guérin et al, 2023).

Digital platforms are typically seen as making reproductive labour more efficient, while digital literacy is identified as the primary obstacle standing in women's ways when it comes to succeeding in entrepreneurship and performing household tasks simultaneously – or what previous generations of feminists referred to as the 'double burden'. The ITC, for instance, points to US-based research 'show[ing] that online shopping can decrease the total time spent on unpaid household tasks, freeing up time for women to spend on other activities such as paid work or entrepreneurship' (ITC, 2020b, p 35). In its WTO communication, the Russian Federation explains that 'e-commerce empowers women entrepreneurs to navigate work-life balance more effectively and overcome social biases and/or personal self-doubt that may have hindered their participation in international (or even domestic) trade' (WTO, 2024g, p 2).

As these examples show, under the 'flexibilized' labour regime that characterizes much work in the digital economy, the boundaries between production and social reproduction are becoming increasingly blurry. At the same time, it reinscribes and rewards patterns of work that assume that the worker is always available. This intensifies the exploitation of (re)productive labour. Belén Valencia Castro and Alejandra Santillana Ortiz have drawn a vivid picture of how

> [t]he permanent connection to the internet means that women multitask between product delivery and care work, for instance, while driving around the city, checking their children's homework, cooking, explaining how to use the washing machine, accepting a new order, etc., as they are exposed to multiple processes of precariousness, of life, time, and work. (Castro and Ortiz, 2023, p 25)

Women in the global South are often on the frontlines of this kind of exploitative platform labour while lacking access to its benefits. Civil society groups DAWN and IT for Change have raised these points in relation to digital trade expansion. They argue that:

> algorithmic mediation of the on-demand service work market by digital platforms perpetuates and reproduces traditional forms of gendered exclusion … reward[ing] and incentiviz[ing] workers who operate on a 'male breadwinner' logic, meaning they are willing to work very long hours. … Similarly, research on online crowd work in the global South suggests that the hegemonic discourse of empowering flexi-work masks the emergence of a new gender compact between the patriarchal household and the capitalist market where there is a heightened labour squeeze. … Flexi-work is thus a misleading label for the precarious, atomized, and alienating gigs of the platform economy. (DAWN and IT for Change, 2023a, p 6; see also Gurumurthy and Chami, 2021)

Domestic labour and care work are not re-valued under the 'flexibilization' view, but are primarily discussed in instrumentalist terms. This is also evident where reproductive labour is seen as an obstacle to paid work in the digital economy. Seen through the lens of free trade feminism, reproductive labour is a *problem*. This is because, as UNCTAD explains, '[t]he burden of domestic chores and care work that women globally shoulder limits the time they can devote to paid activities, including e-commerce, and their ability to quickly respond to orders' (APEC and USAID, 2020, cited in UNCTAD, 2023b, p 15).

Women's protection from gender-based violence or other harms is another motivating factor for promoting digital entrepreneurship in trade governance. The World Bank and WTO in particular argue that the ability to work or study from home that digital technologies afford reduces safety concerns associated with travelling to work or educational settings (World Bank and WTO, 2020, pp 10, 141). We have already noted that online spaces are far from safe for women or other marginalized groups, and this is a point that certain institutions recognize (see, for instance, UNCTAD, 2023b). Nonetheless, women's safety from violence is raised here as an argument in favour of digitally empowered work from home, regardless of what this implies for women's autonomy and freedom of movement outside of the household. This may also work to further the expansion of home-based work, which feminists have long argued enables capitalist relations of exploitation to reach into the household and which compounds the problems related to 'flexi labour' (Mies, 1982; 1998 [1986]; Delaney, 2004).

From our perspective, free trade feminism presents the digitization of the global economy as enabling women to better manage, rather than to escape, the modes of exploitation that result from housewifization. It is our contention that the links between women's integration into e-commerce platforms and digital trade and their empowerment (economic or otherwise) require much more critical interrogation as digitization of the world economy progresses.

Seen through our feminist lens, dominant approaches to digital trade governance put reproductive labour in the service of capital rather than the service of life. This happens not only under the marketization of reproductive labour, but also in the ways in which digital trade rules limit the ability of governments to collect fiscal revenue.

Digital trade and variegated crises of social reproduction

The trade policy elites enacting free trade feminism in the digital arena argue that as more and more services are provided digitally, including in health, education and social care, women's access to these services will improve (World Bank and WTO, 2020, pp 10, 162; OECD, 2021, pp 34–35). They point to presumed benefits of digital service provision to women not only in terms of combining productive and reproductive labour, but also via new job opportunities in these feminized sectors. They also assume that women are less likely to face discrimination in these sectors (World Bank and WTO, 2020, p 20). The digital provision of education services is further useful for helping women to start and grow businesses.

There are important questions to be raised about the ways in which digital platforms have inserted themselves into crises of social reproduction that are unfolding in variegated ways across the world, and for which platforms promise a 'fix' (Dowling, 2022). Rather than seeing digital reproductive services in a positive light, we see women's economic empowerment agendas in digital trade as fuelling trading on social reproduction. Free trade feminist approaches to empowering women in digital trade supports the broader commodification and privatization of social reproduction, as well as its digitalization and platformization, with little consideration for what this means for the workers (who may be working under precarious employment conditions associated with the gig economy) and/or the users of these services (who, if they can afford it, are increasingly assigned personal responsibility for accessing and successfully using these services).

As the feminist digital activist group IT for Change argues:

> Ed-tech and digital health sectors are booming with investments, especially from Big Tech companies. In emerging e-commerce and services trade agreements, education and health are cast as marketable commodities and not as public goods that the state is delivering to the most marginalized citizen. Under these conditions, digitalization will result in a de facto marketization of [public] services … directly disenfranchising the most marginalized women. (Gurumurthy and Chami, 2021, p 5)

These problems are compounded by the gendered dimensions of the e-commerce moratorium debate, mentioned earlier. Key to these debates are (currently open) questions of how the e-commerce moratorium will impact on public finances. While the multilateral e-commerce moratorium was not renewed at the 2026 WTO Ministerial Conference, the WTO Agreement on Electronic Commerce and standard mega-regional agreements and trade deals by countries such as the US or the EU make the e-commerce moratorium permanent, which is also the preferred position of corporate lobby groups (ICC, 2025). From our feminist perspective, a much broader analysis of the impacts of the moratorium is needed to understand, for instance, how the loss of government revenue through a reduction of tariffs may have a negative impact on public services, especially during times of fiscal contraction (Elson et al, 2007b). Given that women disproportionately rely on public services and are more likely to be employed in the public sector, this then has gendered impacts as well as impacts on other forms of inequality.

For its part, UNCTAD (2023b) notes that the e-commerce moratorium *may* have gendered effects if it means that countries must resort to other means of generating revenue, which might include consumption taxes or cuts to public services, both of which are gendered. However, it does not take a position on the moratorium, or even advocate conducting research on the gendered effects of the moratorium specifically. In this context, it is interesting to note that while certain divisions within UNCTAD are highly critical of the e-commerce moratorium, this is not necessarily the case in UNCTAD's gender work.

Other actors argue that the e-commerce moratorium is empowering for women and that revoking it would be contrary to gender equality goals. In a presentation made to the IWG, the Trade Experettes (2023), for example, warned that the e-commerce moratorium 'is part of business-as-usual for women-owned SMEs, so there's lack of awareness of what will happen if it is scrapped'. They expressed concern that the costs of importing digitally delivered services will rise and producers and exporters will become less competitive, losing market-share. What this means for gender equality beyond its impacts on individual exporters was not a driving concern.

From our perspective, it is equally important to understand how the moratorium, and digital trade rules more broadly, disproportionately benefit the large firms that currently dominate these markets, especially the Super 7 platforms. That is, while the elimination of tariffs on digital trade may indeed benefit individual female exporters, it is even more beneficial to those firms that have already monopolized these markets, and which stand to further profit from the expansion of e-commerce that takes place on their platforms.

At the same time, digital trade rules may facilitate the ability for large tech firms to engage in tax avoidance in other ways. For instance, digital trade agreements that prohibit countries from requiring a company to have a local presence may result in a loss of tax revenue. Trade rules that prohibit data localization requirements (as in the United States-Mexico-Canada Agreement, CPTPP and RCEP trade agreements) also make it harder for governments to tax the revenue generated from that data. Big tech firms, backed by the US, have also increasingly sought to use the long-standing principle of 'non-discrimination' that is built into much trade law to challenge the imposition of digital services taxes that disproportionately impact US firms (as the industry titans). This is evidenced in a recent legal challenge to a Canadian initiative to implement a 3 per cent tax on the revenues of certain large digital service providers (Digital Trade Alliance, 2024).

Many of these firms have also been accused of aggressive tax avoidance, with ActionAid International arguing 20 developing countries could have lost out on as much as US$2.8 billion in tax revenue from Facebook, Alphabet and Microsoft due to 'unfair global tax rules'. They argue 'US$2.8 billion could pay for 729,010 nurses, 770,649 midwives or 879,899 primary school teachers each year in 20 countries across Africa, Asia and South America' with obvious implications for gender equality and social reproduction more broadly (ActionAid, 2020). In this context, some women's rights groups and their allies have started to campaign against public–private initiatives aimed at 'upskilling' women and girls to work in the digital economy, which they believe are designed to legitimize trade rules that will ultimately undermine women's human rights while increasing the power and profits of big tech (IT for Change, 2022).[7]

Within the free trade feminist paradigm, however, rendering digital trade more gender inclusive is seen as being the task of women entrepreneurs, who may also be mama entrepreneurs. Similar to dynamics we identified in

Chapter 4, free trade feminism in digital trade connects with existing efforts in global governance to link the pursuits of digital technology, sustainable development and women's empowerment, and fuses these with an assumed need for continued digital trade expansion. It is to this that we turn next.

Who free trade feminism empowers in the digital economy

In this section we argue that rather than interrogating the power relations that are shaping the digitization of the global economy, free trade feminism combines digital trade expansion with pre-existing global governance norms that claim that digitization of the global economy, gender equality and sustainable development advance together. In doing so, free trade feminism dissociates itself from digital governance approaches that have aimed to integrate the political and social dimensions of women's empowerment. Instead, free trade feminism helps legitimize forms of digital trade governance that not only reproduce inequalities between and within countries, but also the ongoing extension of corporate power globally.

Free trade feminist agendas in digital trade are embedded in a longer history of governing the intersections of digital technology, development and gender equality. Like in food trade and in development policy, there exist long-standing feminist interventions that have advocated forms of women's empowerment that are not exclusively individualist but also structural in orientation. In 2003, the UN kicked off a four-year World Summit on the Information Society (WSIS) which was intended to develop a policy framework that would allow employing Information and Communication Technology, as it was then called, as a tool for development (Kleinwächter, 2004). Within this process, the WSIS Gender Caucus, alongside other civil society participants, 'advocated for gender equality as a fundamental principle for action and decision-making' (Dumas, 2008, p 496). This was pertinent because related UN processes, such as the Working Group on Internet Governance, had been narrowly focused on technical standardization and resource allocation, while not addressing 'gender, voice, inclusiveness, and other issues rooted in unequal access to [technology] and to the decision-making process including governance' (Dumas, 2008, p 496).

There is some institutional memory of these processes within institutions driving the gender and trade agenda. UNCTAD, for example, recalls that the 'WSIS gender track' was 'meant to ensure that the information society facilitates women's empowerment and their full participation *based on equality in all spheres of society and in all decision-making processes*' (UNCTAD, 2023b, p 6, emphasis added). Nonetheless, as we have seen, free trade feminism advances much narrower women's economic empowerment programmes centred on digital inclusion.

In doing so, free trade feminism is part of a trend of focusing on digital divides, which came to dominate global policy efforts of mobilizing digital and information technology for development and inclusion following the adoption of the SDGs. In 2015, that is to say on the eve of the emergence of gender mainstreaming in trade governance, the UN General Assembly called for a 'close alignment' between the WSIS and the SDG process, which was put into practice. Target 5.8 of SDG 5, for example, asks for 'enhanc[ing] the use of enabling technology, in particular information and communications technology, to promote the empowerment of women'. Since then, information technologies have generally come to be seen within the international community as helping to 'accelerate progress towards every single one of the 17 … SDGs' (ITU, 2021).

Feminists have criticized these simplistic assumptions and have identified a 'pressing need for international development policy makers and practitioners to focus beyond the statistics about women's ownership of mobiles, and even beyond the statistics on women going online' (O'Donnell and Sweetman, 2018, p 217). They have argued that '[f]or women to thrive in the male-dominated [information technology] space, they need to shift the status quo by participating in [technology] development' (Shava, 2021, p 17906) and that 'feminist – and intersectional – power analysis of the political, social and economic systems within which these technologies sit' are needed (O'Donnell and Sweetman, 2018, p 217).

Instead, free trade feminism asserts that women's economic empowerment in digital trade can contribute to the attainment of SDGs 5 as well as 8 (Decent Work and Economic Growth), 9 (Industry, Innovation, and Infrastructure) and 17 (Partnerships for the Goals), *inter alia* by increasing productivity, decent jobs, entrepreneurship, formalization, value chain integration, access to finance and increased exports (see, for instance, UNCTAD, 2023b, p 6). Free trade feminism also occasionally presents digital inclusion as a quick win not only for marginalized groups, but also for environmental sustainability. In its IWG presentation on the agricultural export successes of the Waorani women, mentioned in the previous chapter, Ecuador highlighted the role played by its *E-Commerce National Strategy* in 'women's economic empowerment in the Ecuadorian Amazon region while preserving their ecosystems and indigenous culture' (WTO, 2021e, p 1).

It is our contention that while it may indeed empower some women to participate in the digital economy, free trade feminism simultaneously tacitly endorses, and thus helps to reproduce, the power of big tech companies and a handful of influential trading nations to shape digital governance agendas. The political economy of the digital trade governance framework, which, as indicated earlier, combines multilateral and bilateral trade agreements, is largely being driven by the Super 7 and a handful of governments – first and foremost the US and China, and to a lesser extent the EU (for detailed accounts see Gao, 2018; Meltzer, 2019; Azmeh et al, 2020; Abendin and Duan, 2021; Jones, 2023; Burri, 2023; 2024; Callo-Müller and Kugler, 2023).

As we pointed out earlier, the development of digital trade rules has neither been straightforward nor has it taken place in a consolidated or centralized manner. Policy priorities and digital trade paradigms have shifted over time, ranging from libertarian approaches that aim to maximize the freedom of transnational data, to approaches facilitating active state regulation of data flows, whether around national security, internet safety, stability of the financial system or more. The former has been associated with the US' initial approach to digital trade governance (though it veered away from some aspects of digital trade libertarianism in the later years of the Joe Biden administration), while the latter approach has been most commonly associated with China.

Within the WTO, critiques of the JSI negotiating process echo long-standing critiques of GATT/WTO institutional practices that marginalized the voice of developing countries and sidelined their concerns in negotiations – once referred to as 'green room tactics' (see, for instance, Jawara and Kwa, 2004). Because the JSI is a plurilateral process, consensus of all WTO members is not required for the text to be adopted, which removes the veto power that each and every WTO member holds under consensus decision-making. While many developed and 'middle-income' countries support JSIs, they have been criticized by others for violating the principles of the WTO and threatening the multilateral system (Azmeh, 2024a, p 377; see also Kelsey, 2022; Azmeh, 2024b). This has relevance beyond digital trade since plurilateral negotiations also prevent so-called 'issue linkages' or 'cross-sectoral trade offs', which may allow for greater bargains around diverging interests among different WTO members.

India, South Africa and Namibia outlined their criticism of JSI in 2021 by stating that the process allows members to bypass Doha Development Agenda issues such as agriculture and to disregard existing mandates arrived at through consensus (WTO, 2021h). JSIs are also weakening pre-existing groupings within the WTO, including the African Group, which was highly active in e-commerce but has recently been paralyzed in certain areas, partly because of disagreements over JSIs (Azmeh, 2024a, p 388). According to Shamel Azmeh:

> While developing countries have always faced constraints on their ability to negotiate in the multilateral trading system, the informal convenor-led nature of the JSIs alongside the absence of institutional sources of power for developing countries, such as regional coalitions, renders the participation of many developing countries largely meaningless in terms of shaping the outcomes of these negotiations. On the other hand, developing countries who have joined the JSIs

> risk legitimizing a process which could ultimately diminish the power of developing countries in the multilateral trade regime. (Azmeh, 2024a, p 392)

India and South Africa in particular have emphasized the need for digital sovereignty, which asks for the autonomy of an organization, country or person over personal data (see, for instance, Kugler, 2025).

On the opposite side of the balance of power are the US and China. The US has been propelled by its oligopolistic tech sector to play a leading role in digital trade governance. In 2024, six of the top ten internet-based companies with the highest revenue globally were based in the US. Meta (which owns Facebook), Amazon.com and Alphabet Inc (which owns Google) were among the top 20 top spenders on lobbying the US government. These firms have played a central role in shaping the US position on digital trade which was, until recently, couched in a language that pits freedom and choice against barriers, discrimination and coercion (Kelsey, 2018, p 278).

The set of principles informing the US approach to e-commerce negotiations, called the Digital2Dozen, mirrored a list of demands published by tech industry groups (Kelsey, 2018, p 278). These principles informed the approach to digital trade developed in CPTPP. Despite US withdrawal from CPTPP under the first Trump presidency in 2017 and the involvement of a number of developing countries, the agreement limited the future regulation of digital trade and did not include development flexibilities (Kelsey, 2018, p 280). These same principles informed the concerted effort made by the US, along with Japan and the EU in 2016, to establish formal negotiations on digital trade in the WTO, and have framed subsequent trade negotiations, including those not involving the US. This shows how the digital landscape that free trade feminism sees as opening the space for women and developing countries to compete in the global market has been shaped by powerful governments and their tech companies in ways that support the interests of the latter.

Apart from the US, the other main actor shaping the digital trade agenda is China. In its engagements with the WTO, China has taken a more cautious approach than the US, proposing a narrower role for the WTO in governing digital trade. China has focused on clarifying and improving the application of existing rules rather than creating new ones, and separating discussions from tariff negotiations (Gao, 2018, p 314). China has aimed to support the development and globalization of its national digital firms and to maintain what has been called 'the great firewall of China' that restricts the access of other (especially US-based) firms (Azmeh et al, 2020, pp 680–681). While China has been able resist some assertions of US power in the digital trade realm, and to develop and project its own digital capabilities, this strategy is not available to other nations whose digital markets have already been largely integrated into US-led value chains (Korjan, 2023, p 67) or who are integrating into China-led chains.

Here too corporations play a crucial role in driving the digital trade agenda. The CEO of e-commerce platform Alibaba, Jack Ma, has been particularly influential. At the World Economic Forum in 2015, Ma suggested that Alibaba could build a platform to enable small businesses to trade globally. He called this platform first the 'e-WTO' and then the 'Electronic World Trade Platform' (eWTP). This initiative, which was welcomed by a number of G20 groupings, is a private-sector-led platform to collectively forge the rules governing e-commerce in ways that create a supporting business environment and more inclusive trade that better serves MSMEs (Gao, 2018, pp 308–310). The eWTP shares with free trade feminism a belief in the power of digital technology 'to empower SMEs, to support participation by women and youth, and to facilitate global consumption'.[8] Ma has also shown support for the business case for gender equality more generally, saying that female executives are Alibaba's 'secret sauce' and lauding the economic benefits of gender diversity in the company.[9]

Based in Hangzhou, Zhegiang province, China – the same city as Alibaba's worldwide headquarters – the eWTP has been involved in the creation of ecommerce hubs (which are central to the Digital Silk Road initiative) and digital free trade zones, including in Malaysia and Thailand, which facilitate cross-border e-commerce between these countries and China and beyond (Hardaker, 2025). It also offers financial services, including supply chain finance.[10] In 2019, Ma participated on a World Economic Forum panel on 'E-commerce 2030: enabling an inclusive future for e-commerce', alongside then WTO Director-General Azevêdo, World Economic Forum President Borge Brende and then UNCTAD Secretary-General Mukhisa Kituyi. He told the audience that 'many don't believe in [globalization] because it is not inclusive. … In the last 20 years, globalization was controlled by 60,000 companies worldwide, imagine if we could expand that to 60 million businesses' (cited in Johnston, 2020). While initiatives such as the eWTP may indeed enable MSMEs to export more, it also crucially strengthens the infrastructural power of Alibaba as a digital platform (Hardaker, 2025).

Within the FTA network, there are several templates emerging on cross-border data governance that align with the differential preferences and domestic political economy logics of the US and China, as well as the EU and increasingly, India. The so-called CPTPP model ensures free flow of data, bans data localization and allows for limited national data protection. The EU has created a model that is heavier on regulation, including references to digital sovereignty, the 'right to regulate' and a 'conditional data flow regime', whereby freedom of data applies so long as the EU's General Data Protection Regulation is adhered to (Burri,

2013; 2024). China also applies conditions to the free flow of data, which allow for far wider restrictions deemed necessary by the state.

What is more, the previously mentioned occasional optimism that the digital transformation of the global economy is positive from an environmental perspective is increasingly being called into question, as the environmental costs of digital trade are being more widely debated. Research on the environmental impacts of digital trade is only emerging, and, in line with the ongoing so-called 'climatization of global politics' (Aykut and Maertens, 2022), is focused heavily on the problem of climate change, to the exclusion of (equally pressing and related) questions of biodiversity loss, resource depletion and pollution.

This literature typically focuses on questions of energy needs of different types of trading activity – analogue or digital – and finds that while carbon footprints may diminish as certain forms of trade are shifted into digital spheres, it is also the case that digitization expands market activity overall, leading to further energy needs and environmental impacts (Borchert, 2025). The digital infrastructure is also 'increasingly energy-hungry, resource-intensive, and geopolitically entangled' (TaPP, 2025, p 3; see also Freitag et al, 2021). Data centres, which are particularly important to AI development, are more energy-intensive than many countries. Some scholars warn that by 2033, the world may face a 'digital data doomsday', when the energy requirements of the digital economy outstrip total supply of electricity (Castro et al, 2024). The monopoly position of big tech corporations is again problematic in tackling these issues. As Emily Jones and Christopher Adam (2023, p 1) argue, 'confronting market power will be central to realizing the social benefits of digitalization and supporting the green transition'. Based on our research, we are pessimistic that such confronting of market power will emanate from the gender and trade agenda in global trade governance.

As feminist digital justice activists write, '[t]he internet's affordances of horizontal peer-to-peer networking and decentralized communication have been seen as holding the key to new forms of emancipatory individuation, trans-local solidarity-building, and the rise of democratic cultures that transcend the watertight boundaries between the public and private spheres, overcoming traditional patriarchal controls on women's political participation' (DAWN and IT for Change, 2023a, p 4). However, 'the subsumption of the digital revolution into the logic of capital accumulation has thwarted this dream' (2023, p 4).

Conclusion

In this chapter we have shown that free trade feminism narrowly promotes digital literacy and the digital inclusion of women at a time when digitization is dramatically reshaping the social relations of production, social reproduction and trade. It focuses on individual women's opportunities to access markets, especially via e-commerce platforms. This is seen as the great leveller, while structural obstacles that limit women's ability to engage in paid labour, education or entrepreneurship are generally not considered in trade. Reproductive labour is housewifized, devalued and presented as an obstacle that needs to be overcome at the level of the individual. Digital trading on social reproduction is presented as an opportunity for women, and the restrictions that privatized essential services and reduced public revenues place on the ability of governments to support social reproduction are ignored.

Free trade feminism also overlooks the problems that come from integration into a digital economy that a small number of oligopolistic corporations and their state backers dominate. While different power blocs contest digital trade rules, free trade feminism has been surprisingly silent on these debates, which are deeply rooted in different conceptualizations of how the digital economy should be regulated, and in whose interests. Despite the various social, political, economic and ecological crises that this development engenders, governments and global and regional trade institutions lend legitimacy to narratives of women's empowerment via digital inclusion.

Free trade feminism does not recognize or mobilize a long history of feminist praxis that focuses on how to use the potential of digital technology to transform gender relations and other relations of inequality, including in the relationship with nature (Haraway, 1991). In our concluding chapter, we reflect on the feminist alternatives to free trade feminism that derive from our analysis, and draw particular attention to alternative approaches for feminist food trade and feminist digital trade that are already being formulated in various corners of global governance.

6

Conclusion: Beyond Free Trade Feminism

In March 2025, participants planning to attend the WTO's second World Trade Congress on Gender received notice that the three-day event, planned for June 2025, was cancelled. It was eventually replaced with a smaller scale gathering in July 2025. No official reason was given for the cancellation, although WTO budget constraints, which led to a shortening of the WTO Public Forum scheduled for September 2025, likely played a role. The news came within weeks of Donald Trump's second administration announcing that the US was pausing its WTO budgetary contributions, pending its review of US membership of all international institutions and treaties (US Mission Geneva, 2025). During this time, reports also emerged that officials in Geneva-based international organizations and non-governmental organizations had received a questionnaire from the US government, inquiring, *inter alia*, about their equality and diversity programmes, including the rights of transgender and gender-non-conforming persons within their organizations (Bussard, 2025). The US government's international actions appeared to be in line with a series of domestic executive orders that mandated the elimination of so-called 'illegal' diversity, equity, inclusion and accessibility mandates, policies, programs, preferences and activities in the departments and agencies connected to the federal government, and to the identification and abolishment of such 'illegal' practices in the private sector.

Meanwhile, the Trump administration had begun rolling out the trade component of its 'America First' doctrine, which is characterized by a focus on championing domestic, and largely male-dominated, industries and jobs, reducing trade deficits, and a confrontational approach to international trade relations centred around trade wars. While Trump's America First trade agenda began during his first term in office, it has taken a much more dramatic turn with Trump 2.0, as both targeted and blanket tariffs have been announced, delayed, raised, lowered, imposed and rescinded at staggering pace. This approach reached fever pitch on 2 April 2025, which Trump called 'Liberation Day', when he stood in front of TV cameras with a chart that he claimed showed tariff rates being imposed on US goods, to which he planned to respond with 'reciprocal tariffs' of historically high rates, including a 54 per cent tariff on China. He later backtracked on many of these threats, (Minsberg, 2025) and many imposed tariffs are being challenged through the US legal system at the time of writing (Zirpoli, 2026; Williams, 2026). On occasion, women's reproductive health has been drawn into the Trump administration's trade conversations with other nations, as happened when the US State Department used a pending special tariff arrangement for the UK to exert pressure on domestic UK legal cases and debates around safe access zones at abortion clinics.

According to Trump's rhetoric, a desire to shift the structural position of US industries in the world economy motivates his administration's trade policy approach. The administration aims to accomplish this by creating trade barriers and other incentives that would motivate large corporations to re-shore their value chains to the US and by attacking the trading practices of other countries perceived to be barriers to US exports. The Trump administration has also abandoned the liberal commitment to treating trade policy strictly in isolation from other policy domains. It has instead deployed tariff wars with a declared intention of curbing illegal immigration, solving the opioid epidemic and annexing territory, for instance in regard to Canada and Greenland. In 2026, the Trump administration also subordinated trade policy concerns to its military prerogatives. This is evident in the ongoing US-Israel conflict with Iran, where the closure of the Strait of Hormuz – a key global maritime shipping route for oil, gas and fertilizer – creates a global energy, transportation and supply chain shock with anticipated negative impacts on global food security, commodity markets, value chains and already restrained capacity of developing countries to service public debt obligations (UNCTAD, 2026).

Trump's trade policy approach has historical parallels in the Republican Party's trade policies of the late 19th and early 20th century, when Republicans used tariffs and other measures to coercively exert economic and political control and expand American imperialism (Palen, 2025). As such, it is part of the declining hegemony of the neoliberal 'free trade' policy consensus.

But what does this shifting landscape mean for free trade feminism? Does the rise of right-wing, anti-gender and anti-free trade movements in the US and beyond signal that free trade feminism has reached its limit? Should we be concerned if it has? Is it better to have a business case for gender equality than no case for gender equality? What alternatives to the business case are out there?

These are the questions that we tackle in this concluding chapter. We begin with a discussion of how free trade feminism finds expression in US legislators' and commentators' opposition to Trump's trade policies, continuing free trade feminism's trajectory as the globally dominant policy paradigm for tackling gender and trade questions. We explain why free trade feminism fails to pose desirable alternatives to either neoliberal or geopolitical trade, as it reproduces the complex structural inequalities of global trade that we have discussed across previous chapters. We then point to a multiplicity of existing alternatives to free trade feminism that offer promising ways of thinking about how trade can be radically restructured to privilege life-making above profit and to challenge intersecting forms of inequality globally. While some of these emerge from institutions discussed in this book, including ECLAC, UNCTAD, and the broader UN system, we also pay more attention here to how civil society actors are responding to the gender and trade agenda, and what they believe needs to be done differently.

In doing so, we aim to show that another world is indeed possible. The question is not one of free trade or protectionism as we currently know them, which, to paraphrase Karl Marx and Friedrich Engels (1888), both move entirely within the bounds of global capitalism. It is instead to conceive of ways of connecting bottom-up movements, many of which emanate from and are focused on the sphere of social reproduction, with the aim of advancing alternative visions that release us from the ever-encroaching capitalist relations of extraction and accumulation and the interconnected crises – economic, social, political, environmental and geopolitical – to which they give rise. Free trade feminism, in its current form, is not up to this task. Rather, as we have argued here, its agenda works to extend, legitimize and depoliticize existing global trade relations during a period of flux and to marginalize alternative visions. While there are spaces within this broad and ever-evolving project that may help feed into more transformative feminist visions, there is a need to look beyond free trade feminism.

Challenging America First

Critical trade scholars have long argued that trade policy making is predominantly done by a closed group of (usually male) experts who tend to share an orthodox understanding of how trade works (Hannah, 2016; Eagleton-Pearce, 2017; Hannah et al, 2022). To some extent, this orthodoxy has been upended by Trump. Eschewing the technical language of trade experts, Trump has rooted his trade policy in a populist rhetoric that appeals to his 'Make America Great Again' base. Trump and key supporters of his vision argue that free trade has worked against the interests of American workers by allowing the offshoring of production and ultimately the destruction of the industrial base of the American economy, which now relies on imports from abroad in ways that fuel disadvantageous trade deficits (Lighthizer, 2020). At the same time, Trump has attempted to leverage trade policy to increase the economic and political power of US big tech firms, including in the ways outlined in Chapter 5. Trump's trade policy thus seeks to enhance the power of American capital, while couching this in a rhetoric of serving the American (male) worker.

While the media and academics have had much to say about the problematic and contradictory aspects of Trump's trade policy, very little has thus far been said about its gender dimensions. The main challenge that has emerged focuses on the unequal impacts of tariffs, which economists have argued disproportionately impacts women. The term 'pink tariffs' has been used by economists to describe the disproportionate tariffs that tend to be placed on certain goods (mainly garments) consumed by women versus men. Shortly after 'Liberation Day', Democratic representatives Lizzie Fletcher of Texas and Brittany Pettersen of Colorado introduced legislation aimed at compelling the Treasury to conduct a study of 'pink tariffs' and their effects which they called the 'Pink Tariffs Study Act'. Drawing attention to the everyday effects of tariffs on all consumers, and especially on women, Congresswoman Fletcher argued: 'Now, as President Trump has imposed tariffs and started a trade war with our trading partners, it is even more important that we understand how higher tariffs will raise costs for everyone, and women in particular' (quoted in Sairam, 2025).

The proposed legislation raised the profile of 'pink tariffs', which then became the focus of several articles published across different media (Agarwal, 2025; Demopoulos, 2025; Brown, 2025). Similar attention has also been paid to the gendered effects of the so-called 'war on Barbie' which refers to the effects that tariffs on China are projected to have on the cost of toys such as Barbie, which is made by Mattel, primarily in China. The media has also paid some attention to the challenges that the tariffs will present for women-owned businesses and entrepreneurs as the increased costs and supply chain disruptions are especially difficult for small businesses to bear (Lesavage, 2025). Conversely, some reporting suggests that women-led businesses are outperforming the broader market (Hinchliffe and Ajemian, 2025). There has further been a small number of articles focused on how reciprocal tariffs will have disproportionate impacts on women in the global South, as those countries facing the highest tariffs are also major exporters of labour-intensive apparel and textiles to the US – industries that largely employ women (Argawal, 2025).

Given that both neoliberal and geopolitical trade negatively affect women working in these industries, what would seem to be needed is a radical transformation of the global trading system. However, this is not what the existing commentary on gender and Trump's trade agenda suggests. Instead, the problem has been articulated in the language of free trade feminism, focusing on 'barriers' that prevent the market from operating as it should, 'naturally' eradicating discrimination against women. Thus, for instance, one commentator explains that gender disparities in trade policy need to be addressed through the inclusion of gendered language that 'recognise[s] women – as business owners, traders, exporters, importers, consumers and workers – face unique challenges and barriers that impact them differently' and through 'women-specific trade solutions around access to finance, trade networks, markets, ease of trade and fair pricing for exports' (Argawal, 2025). Congresswoman Fletcher's website quotes a professor at Texas A&M as saying that while Trump's tariffs could narrow the gender gap by increasing tariffs on men's clothes, '[m]y policy preference would have been to lower tariffs for both men's and women's clothing'. While not focused on Trump *per se*, the World Bank and WTO (2020, p 82), among others, have also argued that trade liberalization is needed to reduce 'pink tariffs' that discriminate against women.

As we have argued throughout, the focus on this narrow range of issues prevents us from seeing how trade policy has much wider implications for gender relations, both within the US and globally. The focus on 'pink tariffs', for instance, precludes a broader understanding of how consumption (beyond just apparel) is gendered, and falls unevenly on the poorest consumers. At the same time, there is a need to consider how and why the cost of tariffs, as taxes on imports, are then passed on to consumers, which reflects the power of large retailers. When the US consumer protection group *Public Citizen* explained to the US House Committee on Ways and Means in May 2026 how and why the Trump administration's trade policies serve the interests of corporations and investors over those of workers and demanded trade policies that support the public good, they overlooked the gendered nature of existing imbalances (see Public Citizen, 2026). Equally, there are gender implications for how the revenue raised by tariffs is used: will it go to fund public services or childcare (as Trump suggested at one point in his campaign), or will it be used to pay for tax cuts for the rich, increased military expenditure, or other regressive measures?

Additional questions arise around how and why the America First vision seeks to protect primarily masculinized, male-dominated and often extractive industries such as steel, aluminium, auto, copper, lumber, oil and big tech while feminized and female-dominated industries (including textiles) and services sectors are not seen to be in need of protection. While 'Make America Great Again' looks back with nostalgia to a time when domestic manufacturing was strong, this era of trade productivism (as outlined in Chapter 2) was rooted in a male-breadwinner gender order that is also viewed nostalgically, for instance with the rise of 'trad wives'. This type of trade was also dependent on highly uneven global trade relations. While the consequences of the US (and other countries) unilaterally abandoning long-standing commitments to trade liberalization for countries in the global South is not yet clear, it will likely hurt those in the most marginalized positions and with the fewest labour protections, including women workers in global supply chains, the most. The same is true for the socio-economic consequences of the closure of the Strait of Hormuz, which we are only beginning to see unfold at the time of writing in May 2026.

In focusing primarily on how to best enable women to benefit from liberalized trade, free trade feminism is not well equipped to engage with these and other important questions. They do little more than scratch at the surface of the gendered relations of trade. Feminist and women's groups have also been surprisingly silent on these issues, likely because many of them are not well prepared to engage in activism related to gender and trade. This is a tragic missed opportunity as this period of flux offers a potential opening for feminist praxis. Rather than doubling down on free trade feminism, there is a need to look for alternative radical, transformative, feminist visions of trade. It is to these that we now turn.

Alternative feminist visions in existing institutions

As we have noted throughout, free trade feminism is neither coherent nor uncontested within different institutional spaces and there are many examples where leading trade governance institutions go beyond the limits of this approach. From our perspective, this is particularly evident when the relationship between trade and social reproduction is recognized, and the latter supported and/or prioritized above the goals of economic growth and sustainable development, narrowly understood (see also Hannah et al, 2022).

Some of the most notable examples in this regard come from Latin America. As we have shown, in many instances, ECLAC stands out as exceptional among institutions, eschewing the commitment to trade liberalization and the business case for gender equality made by many others. From its inception in the 1940s, ECLAC has been informed by structuralist and neostructuralist traditions of thought that see trade governance as perpetuating a core–periphery model that structurally disadvantages the developing world. In the 1990s it began advocating 'productive transformation with equity', which attempted to tether a neoliberal growth model to social justice aims. It has long maintained a relatively more holistic view of development than other trade governance institutions, including a focus on intersectional forms of inequality and environmental concerns. The Regional Gender Agenda – a product of the Regional Conference on Women in Latin America and the Caribbean – put care at the forefront of the agenda. While the 2010 Brasilia Consensus recognized care as a public responsibility and human right, the 2016 Montevideo Strategy explicitly recognized 'the sexual division of labour and the unfair social organization of care' as one of several overlapping structures of inequality that needed to be addressed. The COVID-19 pandemic further propelled discussions of the 'care crisis', culminating in the 2022 *The Care Society* report, mentioned in chapter 3. The report entails a radical paradigm shift that recognizes the interrelations between production and social reproduction. It argues for the need to reorient the aims of economic policy making to supporting the care society.

Though it does not say much about trade specifically, *The Care Society* report does suggest that this can be done by restructuring trade policy in order to support those sectors that 'can provide a major boost to economic, social and environmental sustainability, create quality jobs, incorporate innovation and technological advances, and diversify exports' (ECLAC, 2022, p 137). This includes industries such as the health manufacturing industry (including pharmaceuticals) which works to improve people's living conditions and health and creates quality jobs for women and men (ECLAC, 2022, p 137). ECLAC has also articulated an explicit critique of the normative idea that free trade is beneficial from a gender equality perspective, arguing that ideas of 'static comparative advantage' have led to an extractivist model of development in Latin America, based on the exploitation of natural resources and intensive low-skilled and/or low-wage labour, including the labour of women whose low pay generates a comparative advantage. It advocates a regional trade strategy aimed at creating good quality jobs in industries that have broader social benefits.

There is much promise in ECLAC's approach, which marries the long-standing critique of historically inequitable trade relations to the care crisis unfolding across the region. However, it is not yet clear what this means for trade rules and policies in the region. For one, many of the gender and trade-related programmes advanced by ECLAC remain focused on promoting women's entrepreneurship while care concerns run alongside but are not yet fully integrated into trade policy making. At the same time, it is unclear how a regional trade strategy that remains wedded to capitalist models of accumulation will avoid the 'race to the bottom'. The establishment of systems of international and enforceable labour rights and protections, such as those being advocated by the ILO, will be central to this vision, as will long-term fiscal commitments to prioritize care in a challenging macroeconomic environment.

Another promising example is the linking of trade to social reproduction in the gender chapter of the free trade agreement between Chile and Argentina, which is arguably the most advanced gender chapter from a feminist perspective (for further discussion, see Hannah et al, 2022). This chapter does not just stress the need to extend employment opportunities to women, but notes the requirement for decent quality work and acknowledges the importance of developing care policies and programmes that will reconcile 'working life with parental co-responsibility' (Article 15.3.4). However, these commitments are largely unenforceable and do not have a bearing on trade liberalization commitments made in other parts of the agreement, externalizing care from the core concerns of trade policy making.

One of the central findings to emerge from our research is that UNCTAD, one of the first movers on gender mainstreaming in trade, has increasingly come to reflect a narrow view of how trade is gendered and what is to be done. However, as we traced in chapter 3, there is also a long history of gender and trade research and policy at this institution. As one prominent feminist economist who has long worked on these issues said to us, UNCTAD used to be the only place in the UN system where you could talk about capitalism. While there does not seem to be much talk of capitalism in its gender and trade division now, there are also numerous examples, some of which we have highlighted here, that show where UNCTAD goes beyond the confines of free trade feminism. Of particular interest is UNCTAD's *Gender and Trade Toolbox* which is one of the most comprehensive impact assessment frameworks developed to date for analysing the gender-based impacts of trade across multiple spheres of life. As noted in Chapter 3, the *Toolbox* begins from the premise that trade liberalization can have either positive or negative impacts on women and gender inequalities, and it presents a methodology for assessing the context-specific impacts of trade agreements on a case-by-case basis. While it is mainly focused on how trade agreements impact women's work in the productive sphere, it also asks what measures are in place to assess and address the impacts of trade and 'accompanying measures' on public services, as well as unpaid labour and care work.

The *Toolbox* is limited in its scope, focusing, for instance, mainly on the export sector while the impact of trade agreements on services, IPRs, investment protection, digital trade, and so on, are not included (for more see Hannah et al, 2018, pp 34–36). It also sees trade as separate but related to relations of social reproduction. This leads to the advocacy of measures that aim to mitigate the negative impacts of, rather than to transform, global trade. Nonetheless, the *Toolbox* has the potential to be used by feminist advocates seeking to advance gender equality within the existing trade policy making paradigm – though it is not one that has been widely used or discussed in the policy documents and settings we surveyed.

Despite our deep reservations about free trade feminism, we acknowledge that the fact that trade governance institutions, including those that were formerly dismissive of gender concerns such as the WTO, now include domestic labour and care work in documents and discussions shows the great strides that feminists and gender advocates have made in drawing attention to this invisibilized work in recent decades. Here, advancements that have come from outside of the trade policy realm have made their way into gender discussions on trade. As we have noted in several places throughout, the UN's SDGs, especially SDG 5, are a central reference point for many of those seeking to explain why trade governance institutions have a responsibility to address gender inequality in their work. Within this broader framework, target 5.4 identifies the need to 'Recognize and value unpaid care and domestic work through the provision of public services, infrastructure and social protection policies and the promotion of shared responsibility within the household and the family as nationally appropriate'. While free trade feminism has tended to overlook this part of SDG 5, preferring to focus on its references to women's economic empowerment, other international organizations have continued to develop frameworks to advance these aims. For instance, drawing on research by feminist economists, civil society organizations such as Oxfam, and institutions such as the ILO and OECD, the UN has developed a '5R framework' for supporting paid and unpaid care, which calls for Recognizing, Reducing, Redistributing, Rewarding and Representing care (UN Women, 2022). 'Recognition' involves acknowledging the value and extent of unpaid care work, often through time-use surveys and its integration into national statistics. 'Reduction' aims to decrease the sheer amount of time required for care tasks through investments in infrastructure (like clean water and energy) and time- and labour-saving technologies. 'Redistribution' seeks to achieve a more equitable sharing of care responsibilities, that is, between women and men within households (for instance, through paternity leave), between families and the state/community (for instance, through public childcare services), and between labour and capital via 'family friendly' policies. 'Reward' is about decent work for all care workers across the formal and informal economy while 'Representation' is connected to formalization drives, collective bargaining and equal treatment.

This framework goes well beyond much free trade feminism, which tends to treat care as an obstacle to productive employment. It also goes some way in challenging the trend towards trading on social reproduction that has been advancing over the past three decades. Yet, it is still not clear how care can be recognized, redistributed and rewarded within existing market frameworks. As we have been arguing, gender-based inequalities do not simply exist alongside, but are rather constitutive to how the global economy has developed over time. Addressing them, including via this very different treatment of care, requires more fundamental shifts in economic policy. It requires talking about and, crucially, challenging capitalism.

If we hope to fully comprehend and comprehensively address gendered and other inequalities within global trade and the global economy more widely, we also have to seek greater democracy. As we have argued elsewhere (Hannah et al, 2021a), the views of people affected by trade should be incorporated in trade policy making, which involves greater funding for civil society organizations that represent the most impacted. This must include opportunities for the participation and representation of a diversity of women, non-gender-conforming people and other marginalized groups, because how trade policy measures affect people's daily lives varies across the global economy and universal trade policy paradigms, such as those represented by 'free trade' or 'protectionism', are unable to reflect the local specificities and complexities of organizing trade in ways that support social reproduction.

One positive outcome of the emergence of gender mainstreaming in trade governance has been the creation of the Gender and Trade Coalition, which, as we set out in Chapter 3, was founded in response to the 2017 WTO Declaration. The Gender and Trade Coalition brings together civil society groups and activists from all around the world to discuss the implications of global trade relations for gendered inequalities, as well as ways and means for feminist responses. While it is impossible to comprehensively review the work of the coalition here, we return to our empirical focus on food trade and digital trade in order to show that a wide range of approaches and initiatives already exist and constitute the foundations of a nascent and urgently necessary global feminist trade movement.

Feminist food trade

All over the world, there is an abundance of local, national, regional and global activism that works to promote and put in place alternatives to the corporate-driven global food system. Whether under the banner of the subsistence economy, food justice, food sovereignty, food solidarity or organic, local or slow food, social movements are working towards agri-food alternatives. Women play central roles in advancing the agri-food alternatives movement and its institutions, although it remains the case that gendered power relations often go unchallenged within both movement organization and the production and distribution of food under the various alternative agri-food models (Allen and Sachs, 2007). As Patricia Allen and Carolyn Sachs point out: 'there is a curious absence of feminism per se in women's efforts to create change in the agrifood system' (Allen and Sachs, 2007, pp 13–14). There is arguably equally a curious absence of systematic engagement with the role played by unequal global trade relations in producing and reproducing the global food system.

Nonetheless, a number of agri-food alternative movements exist that combine feminist practice with agricultural and food-related campaigning in trade governance. One example is provided by La Via Campesina, a movement founded in 1993 'bringing together millions of peasants, landless workers, indigenous people, pastoralists, fishers, migrant farmworkers, small and medium-size farmers, rural women, and peasant youth from around the world' (La Via Campesina, 2025). Often credited with coining the concept of food sovereignty, La Via Campesina has also increasingly turned its attention to gendered exploitations and violence within the food system and food cultures, thanks to bottom-up feminist campaigning within the movement (Calvário and Desmarais, 2023). In its 2021 *Manifesto for the Planet*, La Via Campesina declares:

> Social peace, social justice, gender justice and solidarity economies are essential pre-conditions for realizing food sovereignty. … [Food sovereignty] calls for a society that rejects discrimination in all forms – caste, class, racial and gender – and urges people to fight patriarchy and parochialism. … Peasant women and other oppressed gender minorities must find equal space in the leadership of our movement at all levels. … Food sovereignty offers a manifesto for the future, a feminist vision that embraces diversity. It is an idea that unites humanity and puts us at the service of Mother Earth that feeds and nourishes us. (La Via Campesina, 2021)

The Manifesto also offers an alternative vision for global trade relations. La Via Campesina (2021) calls for 'strong local communities and defends their right to produce and consume before trading the surplus' and for 'an international trade order based on cooperation and compassion as against competition and coercion'. While the Manifesto is not more specific, La Via Campesina has opposed agricultural trade reforms anchored in the WTO Agreement on Agriculture and in FTAs over a 30-year period of trade campaigning (La Via Campesina, 2024; see also Martínez-Torres and Rosset, 2010). It 'opposes all free trade agreements that jeopardize a country's food sovereignty, undermine the autonomy and self-sufficiency of local economies, and have adverse effects on the lives, living conditions and wages of all workers, including migrant workers and women'. La Via Campesina has pointed to the failure of the global trade regime to address food security issues but also to the ways in which intellectual property, investment and other provisions anchored in trade agreements work to 'expand market access for Global North Corporations, and the agribusinesses based in other export-oriented countries' (La Via Campesina, 2024). It also sees the global trade regime as standing in the way of 'a meaningful transition to peasant agroecology, and the defense of land, water, and forests' (La Via Campesina, 2024).

From our feminist political economy perspective, La Via Campesina's call for 'an International Trade Framework founded on principles of solidarity, social justice, internationalism, and food sovereignty' (La Via Campesina, 2024) is welcome. As a point of reference in existing global governance arrangements, La Via Campesina highlights the *UN Declaration on the Rights of Peasants and Other People Working in Rural Areas*. Adopted in 2018, this resolution of the Human Rights Council of the UN General Assembly specifies the rights of peasants and persons working in rural areas as they result from existing international law securing human, environmental and labour rights, and asks states and non-state actors, including transnational corporations, to centre the rights of peasants in all of their operations.

A number of activists and organizations affiliated with the Gender and Trade Coalition have also presented reflections and policy papers that are relevant for feminist food trade. Although their paper series 'Feminist Trade Explainer' focuses on climate change, rather than on food and agriculture *per se*, it contains a section titled 'How Have Trade and Climate Governance Impacted Food Production?' (GTC, 2024). The trade explainer highlights the role that global trade relations have played in bringing about both the economic vulnerabilities of small-scale and subsistence farmers and the continuous increase in fossil fuel emissions. It highlights in particular the pressures on small-scale and subsistence farmers that are arising in the global South, but also elsewhere, from a combination of exploitation in corporate food and agricultural value chains, the advancement of climate change and the lack of appropriate policy responses. While its five strategic policy proposals formulated from a feminist trade perspective are targeted at trade and climate change, proposals 1–4 also apply to the relationship between trade and food insecurity. They are: (1) abandon trade liberalization as a blanket policy goal; (2) revise relevant trade rules and agreements, including the WTO's Agreement on Agriculture, to allow developing countries to provide subsidies to their agriculture and fisheries sectors; (3) invest in public services; and (4) waive IPR restrictions, including the commitments under the TRIPs Agreement and bilateral and regional trade agreements on climate-related technology (GTC, 2024) – and, we might add, IPR commitments more generally that prevent farmers from farming autonomously around the world.

Overall, a systematic engagement with the role of trade in gendered food relations tackles how existing food and agricultural trade arrangements empower food corporations and investors to consider food, first and foremost, as a domain of capital accumulation.

In its *Feminist Trade Explainer*, the Gender and Trade Coalition points out that 'the intrinsic importance of access to nutritious, affordable food has been overridden by the desire to accumulate wealth: trade in food was worth $1.7 trillion as of 2021, yet 783 million people are food insecure worldwide' (GTC, 2025). As we compose our concluding chapter, global food insecurity is on the rise as a result of various global conflicts, including practices such as the return of forced starvation as a means of warfare (BDS, 2023), and the knock-on effects of the closure of the Strait of Hormuz (Chu, 2026). It is safe to assume that trade governance institutions will insist that tackling such problems is outside of their mandates. Nonetheless, it remains the case that monopolizing food production and distribution within the hands of a small number of powerful global actors, whether state or non-state, works in favour of using food distribution as a means to political ends.

Feminist digital trade

There is also a considerable amount of feminist activism that focuses on what is required to develop a more just and equitable digital economy that does not operate in the service of capital. While we agree with free trade feminism's assessment that there is a need to address the digital divide and gender inequalities in the digital economy, there is also a need to move beyond a narrow imaginary of inclusion as connectivity, of digital trade as e-commerce, and of MSME activity as development. As DAWN and IT for Change have argued, what is needed is a transformative reimagining of what it means to participate in the 'digitalizing socio-economic order' and to create a digital commons that prioritizes the public good above private profit (DAWN and IT for Change, 2023a, p 5). The Gender and Trade Coalition makes a similar point, arguing that '[t]rue equality … requires a shift from the traditional narrow focus on digital divides to the broader concept of digital inclusion, which encompasses the intangible elements of connectivity, civic participation, trust, privacy and safety' (GTC, 2021).

As Caroline Bassett and colleagues write in *Furious: Technological Feminism and Digital Futures*, the digital is 'a space of antagonism within which it is possible to rethink critical and political positions, including feminism' (2020, p xi). Indeed, feminist scholars and activists have long engaged with technology, producing new ways of thinking about both feminism and the digital economy. Donna Haraway's *Cyborg Manifesto* (1991) is central here, as it developed a powerful critique of gender essentialism that continues to inform much feminist, queer and transgender political economy. Her point is not that technology is inherently patriarchal or oppressive, but that it is a human creation that has the potential for enabling domination as well as liberation if freed from its patriarchal and militant roots. These insights for how to build feminist and decolonial alternatives in the digital era have been further developed by numerous scholars (see, for instance, Arora, 2019; Bassett et al, 2020; Costanza-Chock, 2020; D'Ignazio and Klein, 2023).

We are especially inspired by the Southern feminist approach to digital justice that has been outlined by the Working Group on Feminist Digital Justice, co-convened by DAWN and IT for Change. They are among the few to explicitly consider the role of trade rules in creating forms of digital inequality as well as alternatives to the dominant paradigm outlined in Chapter 5. They argue that while '[t]he narratives of techno optimism are strongly felt in economic forums and multilateral discussions of e-commerce', transformations associated with the digital economy are fundamentally about 'the manner in which relations of production and social reproduction are being restructured worldwide', and 'about assessing the ecological impacts of an unsustainable dominant digital paradigm' (Partenio and Weleilakeba, 2023, p 6). Their digital justice manifesto is summarized in Box 6.1.

Box 6.1: The Declaration of Feminist Digital Justice

'Rejecting the enclosure and manipulation of network-data technologies as infrastructures of domination, we call for a feminist reclamation of the digital paradigm through the following core principles' (p. 3):

1. A Feminist Digital Economy
   1.1. An AI economy organized along democratic and distributive integrity
   1.2. Alternative platform models for regenerative appropriation
   1.3. Platformization rooted in care and mutuality
2. A Digital Society Based on Reciprocity and Solidarity
   2.1. Communicative sociality devoid of commodification
   2.2. An inclusive public sphere for our posthuman condition
   2.3. Freedom from the network-data panopticon
   2.4. Democratic and community-controlled network infrastructure
3. A Digital State Grounded in a Feminist Social Contract
   3.1. Public digital infrastructures for gender-responsive services
   3.2. Gender-aware design for transformed governance systems
   3.3. Digital welfare systems that guarantee substantive citizenship
   3.4. Feminist body politics in digital health programs
   3.5. Access to social care as a fundamental right
4. A Feminist Paradigm for Digital Governance
   4.1. Data sovereignty as a constituent of the right to development
   4.2. Big Data as a societal commons
   4.3. A feminist digital constitutionalism
   4.4. Feminist digital justice as a transversal policy axis

Source: DAWN and IT for Change, 2023b, pp 4–8.

For the Gender and Trade Coalition, digital inclusion goes beyond inclusion into the existing digital structures to involve a 'gender-transformative global digital paradigm that addresses inequalities in digital infrastructure and know-how that prevent developing countries from advancing into the higher value segments of the global digital economy, and creates a fair and just digital marketplace for all women MSMEs'. Rather than simply involving 'capacity building', this equally requires 'challenging the status quo of unequal digital trade rules that entrench the concentration of data resources and digital intelligence in the hands of a few transnational digital corporations and powerful countries in the global economy' (GTC, 2021).

Engaging with and developing feminist visions of digital economic governance requires going beyond the trade arena. Instead of further extending trade governance into more and more aspects of everyday life, we share the view expressed by some civil society actors that trade rules are not the best means of regulating the digital economy, as long as they are designed to support profit over the interests of labour, social reproduction and/or environmental protection. While some feminist activists have pointed to the UN's Global Digital Compact (GDC) (see Box 6.2), adopted in 2024, as an important alternative governance platform (see for instance, Korjan, 2023), the GDC lacks strong enforcement mechanisms and sufficiently strong language around states' obligations under international human rights law.

Box 6.2: Objectives of the UN Global Digital Compact

1. Close all digital divides and accelerate progress across the Sustainable Development Goals
2. Expand inclusion in and benefits from the digital economy for all
3. Foster an inclusive, open, safe and secure digital space that respects, protects and promotes human rights
4. Advance responsible, equitable and interoperable data governance approaches
5. Enhance international governance of artificial intelligence for the benefit of humanity

Source: UN, 2024.

It is argued that the GDC lacks ambition regarding the establishment of a digital data commons, and was designed without adequately considering the intersectional feminist principles presented by various civil society organizations during consultations. Nonetheless, activists, including those associated with IT for Change, have argued that while 'we renew our struggles for emancipatory digital futures', a coordinated strategy is needed to follow through on the mandate provided by the GDC (Gurumurthy and Chami, 2024). Part of this involves the need to press for further financing for digital infrastructure, including the creation of digital public goods. This should not take the form of private or blended finance, but should take the form of official development assistance that is owed to the global South as a debt, and/or raised through a Digital Development Tax imposed on big tech. Among other things, there is also a need to further illuminate 'the connections between international economic law regimes and digital injustice' (Gurumuthy and Chami, 2024).

Forging transformational feminist trade agendas

In 2025, the Gender and Trade Coalition published its *Feminist Trade Agenda* which sets out the Coalition's strategies in working towards 'the intertwined goals of trade and gender justice' and envisioning feminist alternative trade systems (GTC, 2025). As a cursory look at the Gender and Trade Coalition website shows, there are many other topics that activists in the global feminist trade movement explore and campaign on, including themes such as post-conflict recovery, migration, climate change, public health and more. Research that moves beyond the limits of free trade feminism is an integral part of this task.

In this book, we have presented a feminist political economy analysis of trade, which underscores how gendered and trade inequalities have been historically entangled and reproduced over time – including through ongoing processes of housewifization, the ideology of trade productivism, and the trading of more and more aspects of social reproduction. From our perspective, it is crucial to understand trade as a human activity that is embedded in social relations, including the relations of gender. We are not alone in our concern. Indeed, as outlined in Chapter 1, there are many scholarly perspectives on trade and gender inequalities, emanating from a wide range of academic traditions and disciplines. Many of these approaches will also contribute to supporting transformative feminist trade agendas, from the global to the local.

Such works may also explore the many aspects of free trade feminism that we have left un-explored in this book. We have studied free trade feminism as a policy paradigm in global governance, but have not assessed the application and impacts of free trade feminist policy programmes in countries all around the world. While we have reason to doubt that these programmes will overthrow the gendered social relations of trade, there are many open questions about who these programmes benefit, how, and what could be done to improve them, or reform them into more meaningful programmes for social change. There are also many sectors and their associated value chains that we have left un- or under-addressed, from manufacturing and industry to care chains and those sectors that governments rarely negotiate on, but that are nonetheless foundational to the globally integrated economy, such as waste trade and the global trade in sex work. What is more, we have only been able to identify that governance agendas around global trade, gender equality, global finance, environment and digital economy are merging – and that they do so in ways that pin development on economic growth and the further empowerment of corporations and investors. These processes of 'de-siloing' global governance around essentially liberal economic prerogatives ask for future scholarly explorations, particularly in an era when many have pronounced the death of neoliberalism, or even 'the end of capitalism' (World Economic Forum, 2012).

To address trade and gender justice, scholars need to produce knowledge that supports emancipatory trade campaigning and policy development. We hope that our book can help galvanize such future works.

APPENDIX

List of Interviews

Feminist activist	
FA1	May 2019
FA2	May 2019
FA3	June 2019
FA4	July 2019
FA5	January 2020
FA6	January 2020
Trade unionist	
TU1	July 2019
International organization or government employee	
IO1	December 2019
IO2	December 2019
IO3	December 2019
IO4	June 2020

Notes

Chapter 1

1 As the WTO's annual flagship conference, the Public Forum gathers around 2,000 participants at its Geneva headquarters, including representatives from international organizations, national governments, business associations, trade unions, academic institutions, civil society groups and media outlets (Pouliot and Thérien, 2018). Its goal is to 'exchange views on trade and suggest ways to improve the multilateral system' (WTO, 2025a).

2 Interview with feminist activist (FA5), January 2020.

3 According to one activist, it was the WTO's newfound interest in gender and trade in the mid-2010s that opened 'a new battlefront' for feminist activism in trade and led to the creation of a new coalition of women's groups and allied non-governmental organizations called the Gender and Trade Coalition. Anonymous interview with feminist activist (FA6), January 2020.

4 This contrasts with understanding gender analytically, as a set of structural power relations that shape the economy (see also Griffin, 2010).

5 The World Bank and WTO (2020, p 24), for example, focus on 'three key aspects of the relationship between gender equality and trade: the economic opportunities that women have through participation in the economy (employment, entrepreneurship), the generation and accumulation of income (capital, assets, wages), and consumption and related decisions affecting individual and household well-being'. The ITC (2015, p 4) states that '[a] woman is economically empowered when she has the ability to succeed and advance economically and the power to make and act on economic decisions'. Elsewhere it notes that gender equality and women's economic empowerment are both 'preconditions for sustainable development and economic growth' (ITC, 2020a, p x).

Chapter 2

1 See, for instance, the preface to the 2014 edition of Mies, M. (1998 [1986]) *Patriarchy and Accumulation on a World Scale* published by Zed Books.

2 On the colonial divisions of labour, see Watson (2017).

3 Neoclassical trade economics has of course come a long way since the days of its founding fathers. Nonetheless, the Ricardian model and Heckscher-Ohlin, Stolper-Samuelson theorems continue to provide justification for contemporary political positions in favour of the infallibility of free trade (see also Krugman, 1987).

4 In our reading, the fact that GATT negotiations excluded agriculture and textiles, two sectors that are of particular interest to both formerly colonized countries and to reproductive labour and social reproduction processes, is not coincidental. It is rather an expression of the masculinist/productivist focus of the GATT governance regime, that is infused with Western ideas of economic values and progress.

[5] A search of the GATT digital archives (Stanford University, 2024) using the search terms 'women/women', 'gender', 'female/feminine/feminist', for example, gives no results for the Bretton Woods decades. It only gives one result overall, despite the fact that GATT operated until 1994.
[6] Listians supported protectionism based on the theories of German-American political economist Friedrich List. For a review of their positions in trade debates see Palen (2024).
[7] The triangular trade was notoriously fundamental to imperial Britain building its hegemonic standing in the global textiles trade.
[8] Some of these actors would not have considered themselves to be feminists *per se*.
[9] This differs from our use of the term. As set out in Chapter 1, we use free trade feminism to refer to a 21st-century trade governance paradigm that aims to unleash an assumed mutually beneficial cycle of trade liberalization and gender equality.
[10] She also advanced a gender analysis of trade, writing, among other things, about how working-class women employed in the American manufacturing sector suffered the costs of protectionist policies (Palen, 2024).
[11] Broadly speaking, free trade was practised by Britain from 1846, in the European network for reciprocal trade agreements that sprung from the 1860 Cobden-Chevalier Treaty, and by the 1861–1865 Confederate States of America (Palen, 2013). France, Germany, Russia, Japan, the US and the Ottoman Empire applied protective tariff regimes and provided state support for domestic corporations (Palen, 2024).
[12] In principle, goods are liberalized by what they are (determined by tariff classifications). Both goods and services are also liberalized by where they originate (determined by rules of origin).
[13] On the gender impacts of SAPs more broadly, see, for instance, Elson (1987; 1994).

Chapter 3

[1] The policy trend is evident in buzzwords such as 'inclusive trade', 'inclusive growth', 'inclusive finance', 'inclusive development', and so on. While the meaning of inclusive trade is not entirely clear, it broadly refers to trade governance agendas that aim 'to create better outcomes for more people as a result of trade, and in the process ideally ensure that the benefits of trade are widely shared' (Goff, 2021, p 273).
[2] The US refused to sign the Declaration under the first Trump administration, but signed in 2021 following the inauguration of Joe Biden. It also joined the WTO IWG on Trade and Gender (Migdon, 2021).
[3] The WTO Chairs Programme operates in developing country members and provides research and knowledge transfer support for appointed Chairs over a four-year period (WTO, 2026a).
[4] The programme for the 2023 Youth Trade Summit on Gender is available online at https://www.wto.org/english/tratop_e/womenandtrade_e/women_1311202309_e/women_1311202309_e.htm. The WTO Conference Services YouTube channel is available at https://www.youtube.com/@WTOConferenceServices.
[5] This was the title of a plenary session for the 2022 World Trade Congress on Gender. The conference programme is no longer available online.
[6] Previous IWGs have been convened around themes such as investment, government procurement, competition policy, technology transfer, and trade, debt and finance.

Chapter 4

1 The definition of 'informal' labour is contested in the literature, but is often taken to refer to 'income generating activities that operate outside the regulatory framework of the state' (Castells and Portes, 1989, cited in Meagher, 2013, p 2).

2 For a critique of voluntary certification schemes and standards, see, for instance, Das (2011), LeBaron (2021) and LeBaron et al (2022).

3 This term takes inspiration from Prügl (2017) who writes about 'neoliberalism with a feminist face' in an influential article about the World Bank's gender interventions.

4 Article 44 of the Association Agreement between the EU and Central America focuses on public health cooperation. The agreement identifies women as a vulnerable group and connects their wellbeing to food and nutritional security.

5 ECLAC (2019, p 174) shows better recognition of the intersections of gender relations, economy and environment when explaining how women resort 'to a variety of survival or adaptation strategies that are influenced by their caretaking responsibilities and their limited economic autonomy' in order to cope with the effects of climate change on agriculture. ECLAC cites FAO/CCAFS data showing that these strategies often include women reducing their food consumption or consuming less nutritious foods. The report asserts that '[f]ood insecurity and undernutrition lead to an increase in disease and other deficiencies and this, in turn, gives rise not only to health risks but also to a greater demand on the time of the women who serve as unpaid caregivers' (ECLAC, 2019, p 174). Yet, the ECLAC report deals with food exclusively under its climate change chapter, and not under its trade chapter. Separating the analysis implies that the full environmental implications of recommending commercializing agriculture and food trade as women empowerment strategies are not teased out by ECLAC. This is an important omission, as ECLAC does recommend commercializing women's agriculture and food trade practices.

6 This is consistent in other areas of gender and trade governance beyond food, social and political rights are rarely the focus, and are often presumed to follow on naturally from women's economic empowerment.

7 The negative impacts of the global industrial food system include the persistence of both undernourishment and of obesity in the world (FAO et al, 2020), the contributions made by the global industrial food system to carbon emissions, soil depletion, deforestation, biodiversity loss and water depletion (Gonzalez, 2006; Ranganathan et al, 2016; Clapp, 2017a), the price volatility of the highly financialized and concentrated global industrial food production network (Clapp, 2023), and the poor labour conditions in much of global agriculture, which include the various dimensions of informality and precarity outlined above, as well as the fact that 'agriculture and agri-food industry are indeed the economic sector with the world highest prevalence of forced and child labour' (Béné, 2022, p 105881). It is not clear how linking informal and subsistence women farmers and food traders in the global South into the formal, industrial food system will undermine the latter's negative tendencies, unless such integration is actively linked into ongoing global efforts towards global food system transformation.

Chapter 5

1 The members are: Argentina; Australia; Bahrain, Benin; Brunei Darussalam; Burkina Faso; Cabo Verde; Canada; China; Costa Rica; EU; The Gambia; Georgia; Hong Kong, China; Iceland; Israel; Japan; Kazakhstan; Kuwait; Kyrgyz Republic; Laos; Liechtenstein; Malaysia; Mauritius; Moldova; Mongolia; Montenegro; New Zealand; North Macedonia; Norway; Oman; Peru; Philippines; Qatar; Singapore; South Korea; Switzerland; Ukraine; the United Arab Emirates; and the UK.

2 Within trade governance and scholarship, debates tend to focus on 'facilitative' versus 'restrictive' digital trade regulatory measures. The former includes measures such as regulation regarding e-documents and signatures, consumer protections, liability protections for intermediaries, privacy and data protection rules, and cybersecurity. Restrictive measures might involve measures restricting domain names, bans on online sales, and rules regulating the cross-border flow of data (Baker and Le, 2023). The aim of many trade governance institutions, including the WTO, is to create binding rules that facilitate digital trade and prevent governments from being able to enact what they understand to be overly restrictive regulatory measures.

3 For instance, at the time of writing, all of the top ten internet-based companies were being led by men. It is also an industry well-known for its 'bro culture' that emphasizes competitiveness and risk-taking and often excludes women, racialized minorities and other groups under-represented within the sector.

4 Closing the gender digital divide is the focus of a small number of select FTAs, particularly those with gender chapters. There are also some provisions promoting capacity-building for women formal and informal traders and digital skills for women entrepreneurs, for example in the Protocol on Trade and Service of the AfCFTA or the Chile-Ecuador Economic Complementarity Agreement No. 75 (WTO, 2023c).

5 UNCTAD (nd) *eTrade for Women*. Available at: https://unctad.org/topic/ecommerce-and-digital-economy/etrade-for-women

6 See, for instance, the opposition to digital trade rules expressed by the Trade Justice Movement (available at https://www.tjm.org.uk/trade-issues/digital-trade-e-commerce).

7 In this instance, the groups IT for Change, Public Services International (Asia & Pacific) and Third World Network, along with other women's rights organizations, labour unions and allies, jointly opposed the Indo-Pacific Economic Framework for Prosperity Upskilling Initiative. This initiative was introduced by the US Department of Commerce in September 2022 to empower women and girls in line with goals of the Indo-Pacific Economic Framework for Prosperity (IPEF). It aims to provide '7 million or more digital-based training and education opportunities to women and girls in the emerging economies and middle-income partners of the IPEF', including in Brunei, Fiji, India, Indonesia, Malaysia, the Philippines, Thailand and Vietnam. See https://ipefupskillinginitiative.org/

8 Electronic World Trade Platform (nd). Available at https://www.ewtp.org/

9 Ma's framing of the business case for gender equality draws on heteronormative and gender stereotypes that essentialize women, as he claims that gender diversity is important since '[m]en think about themselves more; women think about others more. … Women think about taking care of their parents, their children' (cited in Kokalitcheva, 2015).

10 Electronic World Trade Platform (nd). Available at: https://www.ewtp.org/

References

Abbott, K. (2003) 'Development policy in the new millennium and the Doha "Development Round"', *Public Law and Legal Theory Papers*, Working Paper 25. Available at: https://law.bepress.com/nwwps-plltp/art25

Abendin, S. and Duan, P. (2021) 'Global e-commerce talks at the WTO: Positions on selected issues of the United States, European Union, China, and Japan', *World Trade Review*, 20(5), pp 707–724.

Acharya, R., Alamo, O.F., Al-Battashi, S.M.T., der Boghossian, A., Ghei, N., Herrera, T.P., et al (2019) 'Trade and women: Opportunities for women in the framework of the World Trade Organization', *Journal of International Economic Law*, 22(3), pp 323–354.

ActionAid (2018) 'From rhetoric to rights: Towards gender-just trade', 4 October. Available at: https://www.actionaid.org.uk/publications/from-rhetoric-to-rights-towards-gender-just-trade

ActionAid (2020) '$2.8bn "tax gap" exposed by ActionAid research reveals tip of the iceberg of "Big Tech's big tax bill" in the global south', 26 October. Available at: https://actionaid.org/news/2020/28bn-tax-gap-exposed-actionaid-research-reveals-tip-iceberg-big-techs-big-tax-bill-global

Addams, J. (1915) 'Women and internationalism', in J. Addams, E. Balch and A. Hamilton (eds) *Women at the Hague*. Macmillan, pp 124–141.

Agarwal, P. (2025) *'Pink tariffs' worse for women: Are Trump's new tariffs gender-biased?*, ODI Global, 10 April. Available at: https://odi.org/en/insights/pink-tariffs-worse-for-women-are-trumps-new-tariffs-gender-biased/

Alessandrini, D. (2022) 'Global value chains, development and the *long duree* of trade and investment law', *Leiden Journal of International Law*, 35(3), pp 619–640.

Alessandrini, D., Cortes-Nieto, J.d.P., Eslava, L. and Yilmaz Vastardis, A. (2022) 'The dream of formality: Racialization otherwise and international economic law', *Journal of International Economic Law*, 25(2), pp 207–223.

Ali, R. and Stevano, S. (2022) 'Work in agro-industry and the social reproduction of labour in Mozambique: Contradictions in the current accumulation system', *Review of African Political Economy*, 49(171), pp 67–86.

Allen, P. and Sachs, C. (2007) 'Women and food chains: The gendered politics of food', *The International Journal of Sociology of Agriculture and Food*, 15(1), pp 1–23.

Altan-Olcay, Ö. (2014) 'Entrepreneurial subjectivities and gendered complexities: Neoliberal citizenship in Turkey', *Feminist Economics*, 20(4), pp 235–259.

Altan-Olcay, Ö. (2020) 'Politics of engagement: Gender expertise and international governance', *Development and Change*, 51(5), pp 1271–1295.

Altman, M. (2008) 'Formal-informal economy linkages', Human Sciences Research Council. Available at: https://www.gtac.gov.za/wp-content/uploads/2022/02/Formal-Informal-Economy-Linkages.pdf

Amelang, K. (2022) '(Not) safe to use: Insecurities in everyday data practices with period-tracking apps', in A. Hepp, J. Jarke and L. Kramp (eds) *New Perspectives in Critical Data Studies: The Ambivalences of Data Power*. Springer International Publishing, pp 291–321.

Amin, S. (1974) 'Accumulation and development: A theoretical model', *Review of African Political Economy*, 1(1), pp 9–26.

Antunes de Oliveira, F. and Kvangraven, I.H. (2023) 'Back to Dakar: Decolonizing international political economy through dependency theory', *Review of International Political Economy*, 30(5), pp 1676–1700.

APEC (2019) *The La Serena Roadmap for Women and Inclusive Growth (2019–30)*. Available at https://www.apec.org/meeting-papers/annual-ministerial-meetings/2019/2019_amm/annex-a

APEC (2023) *Proposals: APEC Workshop on Empowering Women in Remote Areas through Climate-Smart Agriculture for Sustainability and Inclusivity*. Available at: https://aimp2.apec.org/sites/PDB/Lists/Proposals/DispForm.aspx?ID=3501

APWLD (2017) 'Press Release: Women's Rights Groups call on Governments to Reject the WTO Declaration on "Women's Economic Empowerment"', Asia Pacific Forum on Women, Law and Development. Available at: https://apwld.org/press-release-164-womens-rights-groups-call-on-governments-to-reject-the-wto-declaration-on-womens-economic-empowerment/

Armah, B. (1995a) 'The demographics of trade-affected services and manufacturing workers (1987–1990): A comparative analysis', *The Review of Black Political Economy*, 23(4), pp 43–67.

Armah, B. (1995b) 'Trade affected workers in the service sector: 1987 and 1990', *American Journal of Economics and Sociology*, 54(2), pp 163–181.

Arora, P. (2019) *The Next Billion Users: Digital Life beyond the West*. Harvard University Press.

Arun, S. (2017) '119 nations back move to remove barriers limiting women's participation in trade', *The Hindu*, 14 December. Available at: https://www.thehindu.com/business/Economy/119-nations-back-move-to-remove-barriers-limiting-womens-participation-in-trade/article21581261.ece

Asad, S.A., Ahmad, H.F. and Majid, H. (2025) 'Price and prejudice: Gender discrimination in online marketplaces', *Journal of Development Economics*, 177, Article 103540.

Avant, D., Finnemore, M. and Sell, S. (2010) *Who Governs the Globe?* Cambridge University Press.

Aykut, S.C. and Maertens, L. (2022) 'The climatization of global politics: Introduction to the special issue', in S.C. Aykut and L. Maertens (eds) *The Climatization of Global Politics*. Springer International Publishing, pp 1–18.

Azmeh, S. (2024a) 'Developing countries and joint statement initiatives at the WTO: Damned if you join, damned if you don't?', *Development and Change*, 55(3), pp 375–397.

Azmeh, S. (2024b) '"Saving the WTO": Middle power insiders and joint statement initiatives at the World Trade Organisation', *New Political Economy*, 29(1), pp 60–74.

Azmeh, S., Foster, C. and Echavarri, J. (2020) 'The international trade regime and the quest for free digital trade', *International Studies Review*, 22(3), pp 671–692.

Baden, S. (1998) *Gender Issues in Agricultural Liberalisation*. Institute for Sustainable Development.

Bahri, A. (2019) 'Measuring the gender-responsiveness of free trade agreements: Using a self-evaluation maturity framework', *Global Trade & Customs Journal*, 14(11/12), pp 517–527.

Bahri, A. (2020) 'Women at the frontline of COVID-19: Can gender mainstreaming in free trade agreements help?', *Journal of International Economic Law*, 23(3), pp 563–582.

Bahri, A. (2025) *Trade Agreements and Women: Transcending Barriers*. Oxford University Press.

Bahri, A. and Boklan, D. (2022) 'Not just sea turtles, let's protect women too: Invoking public morality exception or negotiating a new gender exception in trade agreements?', *European Journal of International Law*, 33(1), pp 237–269.

Bahri, A. and Amaral, R. (2024) 'Gender equality provisions in trade and investment agreements: Are they widening the negotiation capacity gap?', *World Trade Review*, 23(1), pp 47–71.

Bahri, A., López, D. and Remy, J.Y. (2023) *Trade Policy and Gender Equality*. Cambridge University Press.

Baker, B.K. (2016) 'Trans-Pacific Partnership provisions in intellectual property, transparency and investment chapters threaten access to medicines in the US and elsewhere', *PLoS Medicine*, 13(3), e1001970

Baker, P.R. and Le, L. (2023) 'Promoting sustainable development through digital trade and digital trade policies', *ARTNeT Working Paper Series*, No. 229, ESCAP.

Bakker, I. (2003) 'Neoliberal governance and the reprivatization of social reproduction', in I. Bakker and S. Gill (eds) *Power, Production, and Social Reproduction*. Palgrave Macmillan, pp 66–82.

Bakker, I. (2007) 'Social reproduction and the constitution of a gendered political economy', *New Political Economy*, 12(4), pp 541–556.

Bakker, I. and Gill, S. (2019) 'Rethinking power, production, and social reproduction: Toward variegated social reproduction', *Capital & Class*, 43(4), pp 503–523.

Baldwin, R. (1995) 'The effect of trade and foreign direct investment on employment and relative wages', *NBER Working Paper*, No. 5037, National Bureau of Economic Research.

Baldwin, R. (2014) 'WTO 2.0: Governance of 21st century trade', *The Review of International Organizations*, 9(2), pp 261–283.

Baldwin, R. (2020) 'The greater trade collapse of 2020: Learnings from the 2008–09 great trade collapse', *VoxEU.org Column*. Available at: https://voxeu.org/article/greater-trade-collapse-2020

Bandele, O. (2016) 'An equal seat at the table: Gendering trade negotiations', *International Trade Working Paper*, 2016/14, Commonwealth Secretariat.

Banga, R. (2019) 'Growing trade in electronic transmissions: Implications for the South'. Research Paper No. 29 UNCTAD/SER.RP/2019/1/Rev.1. United Nations Conference on Trade and Development.

Barrientos, S., Gereffi, G. and Rossi, A. (2011) 'Economic and social upgrading in global production networks: A new paradigm for a changing world', *International Labour Review*, 150(3–4), pp 319–340.

Barry, B. (1971) *Le royaume du Waalo, 1659–1859*. Mimeo.

Bassett, C., Kember, S. and O'Riordan, K. (2020) *Furious: Technological Feminism and Digital Futures*. Pluto Press.

BDS (2023) 'Act now against these companies profiting from the genocide of the Palestinian people'. Available at: https://bdsmovement.net/Act-Now-Against-These-Companies-Profiting-From-Genocide

Becker, G. (1971) *The Economics of Discrimination*, 2nd edn. University of Chicago Press.

Bedford, K. (2005) 'Loving to straighten out development: Sexuality and "ethnodevelopment" in the World Bank's Ecuadorian lending', *Feminist Legal Studies*, 13(2), pp 295–322.

Bedford, K. (2009) *Developing Partnerships: Gender, Sexuality, and the Reformed World Bank*. University of Minnesota Press.

Behrman, J., Meinzen-Dick, R. and Quisumbing, A. (2012) 'The gender implications of large-scale land deals', *Journal of Peasant Studies*, 39(1), pp 49–79.

Bello, W. (2008) 'How to manufacture a global food crisis', *Development*, 51(4), pp 450–455.

Béné, C. (2022) 'Why the great food transformation may not happen: A deep-dive into our food systems' political economy, controversies and politics of evidence', *World Development*, 154, Article 105881.

Benería, L. (1999) 'Globalization, gender and the Davos Man', *Feminist Economics*, 5(3), pp 61–83.

Benjamin, R. (2019) *Race after Technology: Abolitionist Tools for the New Jim Code*. Polity Press.

Benz, S.F. (1985) 'Trade liberalization and the global service economy', *Journal of World Trade Law*, 19(2), pp 95–120.

Bergeron, S. (2003) 'The post-Washington Consensus and economic representations of women in development at the World Bank', *International Feminist Journal of Politics*, 5(3), pp 397–419.

Berik, G. (2017) 'Beyond the rhetoric of gender equality at the World Bank and the IMF', *Canadian Journal of Development Studies*, 38(4), pp 564–569.

Berik, G., van der Meulen Rodgers, Y. and Zveglich, J.E. (2004) 'International trade and gender wage discrimination: Evidence from East Asia', *Review of Development Economics*, 8(2), pp 237–254.

Bernhofen, D.M., El-Sahli, Z. and Kneller, R. (2016) 'Estimating the effects of the container revolution on world trade', *Journal of International Economics*, 98, pp 36–50.

Bernstein, H. (1990) 'Agricultural "modernisation" and the era of structural adjustment: Observations on sub-Saharan Africa', *The Journal of Peasant Studies*, 18(1), pp 3–35.

Bernstein, H. (2016) 'Agrarian political economy and modern world capitalism: The contributions of food regime analysis', *The Journal of Peasant Studies*, 43(3), pp 611–647.

Bernstein, S. (2001) *The Compromise of Liberal Environmentalism*. Columbia University Press.

Bernstein, S. (2002) 'Liberal environmentalism and global environmental governance', *Global Environmental Politics*, 2(3), pp 1–16.

Bhala, R. and Wood, C. (2018) 'Two dimensional hard-soft law theory and the advancement of women's and LGBTQ rights through free trade agreements', *Georgia Journal of International and Comparative Law*, 47, pp 299–366.

Bhambra, G.K. (2020) 'Colonial global economy: Towards a theoretical reorientation of political economy', *Review of International Political Economy*, 28(2), pp 307–322.

Bhattacharya, T. (ed) (2017) *Social Reproduction Theory: Remapping Class, Recentering Oppression*. Pluto Press.

Bhattacharyya, G. (2018) *Rethinking Racial Capitalism: Questions of Reproduction and Survival*. Rowman & Littlefield.

Blackmon, P. (2021) 'The Lagarde effect: Assessing policy change under the first female managing director of the International Monetary Fund (IMF)', *Global Society*, 35(2), pp 171–190.

Bocquier, P. (2005) 'Informal sector versus informal contracts in Nairobi, Kenya', *DIAL Working Paper*, 10.

Borchert, I. (2025) 'Digital trade and its impacts', in *TaPP Insight: The Environmental Effects of Digital Trade*. Available at: https://tappnetwork.org/resource/tapp-insight-the-environmental-effects-of-digital-trade/

Boserup, E. (1970) *Woman's Role in Economic Development*. George Allen & Unwin.

Brodsky, A., Lim, J. and Caporal, J. (2021) *The WTO Informal Working Group on Trade and Gender: What It Is, What It Should Consider, and What It Could Be*. Center for Strategic and International Studies. Available at: https://www.csis.org/analysis/wto-informal-working-group-trade-and-gender-what-it-what-it-should-consider-and-what-it

Broeze, F. (ed) (2017) *The Globalisation of the Oceans: Containerisation from the 1950s to the Present*. Liverpool University Press.

Brown, S (2025) *Pink Tariff? Black Women Hit Hardest by Trump's Trade Moves*, Post News Group, 9 April. Available at: https://www.postnewsgroup.com/pink-tariff-black-women-hit-hardest-by-trumps-trade-moves/

Burbidge, J.B. (1979) 'The international dimension', in A.S. Eichner (ed) *A Guide to Post-Keynesian Economics*. Routledge, pp 139–150.

Burri, M. (2013) 'Should there be new multilateral rules for digital trade?' *Think piece for the E15 Expert Group on Trade and Innovation, Geneva*. International Centre for Trade and Sustainable Development.

Burri, M. (2023) 'A WTO agreement on electronic commerce: An inquiry into its legal substance and viability', *Georgetown Journal of International Law*, 53(4), pp 565–625.

Burri, M. (2024) 'Inequalities in digital trade and digital trade regulation', in E. Askin and H. Stoll (eds) *Contested Equality*. Edward Elgar, pp 203–220.

Burri, M. and Chander, A. (2023) 'What are digital trade and digital trade law?', *American Journal of International Law*, 117, pp 99–103.

Burri, M. and Kugler, K. (2024) 'Regulatory autonomy in digital trade agreements', *Journal of International Economic Law*, 27(3), pp 397–423.

Bussard, S. (2025) 'Surreal questionnaire stuns international Geneva'. Available at: https://genevasolutions.news/global-news/surreal-us-questionnaire-stuns-international-geneva

Busse, M. and Spielmann, C. (2006) 'Gender inequality and trade', *Review of International Economics*, 14(3), pp 362–379.

Çağatay, N. (1994) 'Themes in Marxian and post-Keynesian theories of international trade: A consideration with respect to new trade theory', in M. Glick (ed) *Competition, Technology and Money: Classical and Post-Keynesian Perspectives*. Edward Elgar, pp 237–250.

Çağatay, N. (2001) *Trade, Gender and Poverty*. United Nations Development Programme.

Çağatay, N. (2005) *Gender Inequalities and International Trade: A Theoretical Reconsideration*, Serie Seminarios y Talleres N.136. Centro Interdisciplinario de Estudios sobre el Desarrollo.

Caglar, G. (2013) 'Gender mainstreaming', *Politics & Gender*, 9(3), pp 336–344.

Calkin, S. (2015) '"Tapping" women for post-crisis capitalism: Evidence from the 2012 World Development Report', *International Feminist Journal of Politics*, 17(4), pp 611–629.

Calkin, S. (2018) 'The World Bank and the challenge of "the business case" for feminist IPE', in J. Elias and A. Roberts (eds) *Handbook on the International Political Economy of Gender*. Edward Elgar, pp 311–322.

Callo-Müller, M.V. and Kugler, K. (2023) 'Digital trade, development, and inequality', *American Journal of International Law Unbound*, 117, pp 116–121.

Calvário, R. and Desmarais, A.A. (2023) 'The feminist dimensions of food sovereignty: Insights from La Via Campesina's politics', *The Journal of Peasant Studies*, 50(2), pp 640–664.

Cantillon, S., Mackett, O. and Stevano, S. (2023) *Feminist Political Economy: A Global Perspective*. Agenda Publishing.

Carey, H. (1859) *Principles of Social Science*, Vol. 3. J.B. Lippincott and Company.

Carney, M. (2026) 'Special address by Mark Carney, prime minister of Canada', *World Economic Forum*. Available at: https://www.weforum.org/stories/2026/01/davos-2026-special-address-by-mark-carney-prime-minister-of-canada/

Carr, M. and Chen, M. (2002) 'Globalization and the informal economy: How global trade and investment impact on the working poor', *Working Paper on the Informal Economy,* 2002/1, International Labour Office.

Castells, M. and Portes, A. (1989) 'World underneath: The origins, dynamics, and effects of the informal economy', in A. Portes, M. Castells and L. Benton (eds) *The Informal Economy*. Johns Hopkins University Press, pp 1–40.

Castro, B.V. and Ortiz, A.S. (2023) 'Neoliberal Ecuador: The precariousness and exploitation of platform workers', *DAWN Informs*, December, pp 23–26.

Castro, V., Georgiou, M., Jackson, T., Hodgkinson, I.R., Jackson, L. and Lockwood, S. (2024) 'Digital data demand and renewable energy limits: Forecasting the impacts on global electricity supply and sustainability', *Energy Policy*, 195, Article 114404.

Chamarbagwala, R. (2006) 'Economic liberalization and wage inequality in India', *World Development*, 34(12), pp 1997–2015.

Chander, A. (2021) 'AI and trade', in M. Burri (ed) *Big Data and Global Trade Law*. Cambridge University Press, pp 115–127.

Chant, S. (2016) 'Women, girls, and world poverty: Empowerment, equality or essentialism?', *International Development Planning Review*, 38(1), pp 1–24.

Chant, S. and Sweetman, C. (2012) 'Fixing women or fixing the world? "Smart economics", efficiency approaches, and gender equality in development', *Gender & Development*, 20(3), pp 517–529.

Chappell, M., Wittman, H., Bacon, C., Ferguson, B., García Barrios, L., García Barrios, R. et al (2013) 'Food sovereignty: an alternative paradigm for poverty reduction and biodiversity conservation in Latin America', *F1000Research*, 2:235.

Charnovitz, S. (1994) 'Free trade, fair trade, green trade: Defogging the debate, symposium greening the GATT: Setting the agenda', *Cornell International Law Journal*, 27(3), pp 459–526.

Charusheela, S. and Zein-Elabdin, E. (2003) 'Feminism, postcolonial thought, and economics', in M.A. Ferber and J.A. Nelson (eds) *Feminist Economics Today: Beyond Economic Man*. University of Chicago Press, pp 175–192.

Chase-Dunn, C.K., Álvarez, A. and Liao, Y. (2023) 'Waves of structural deglobalization: A world-systems perspective', *Social Sciences*, 12(5), Article 301.

Chen, A. (2006) 'A reflection on the South-South coalition in the last half century from the perspective of international economic lawmaking: From Bandung, Doha and Cancun to Hong Kong', *The Journal of World Investment & Trade*, 7(2), pp vii–232.

Chen, M.A. (2006) 'Rethinking the informal economy: Linkages with the formal economy and the formal regulatory environment', in B. Guha-Khasanobis, R. Kanbur and E. Ostrom (eds) *Linking the Formal and Informal Economy: Concepts and Policies*. Oxford University Press, pp 75–92.

Choudhury, B. (2012) *Public Services and International Trade Liberalization: Human Rights and Gender Implications*. Cambridge University Press.

Christophers, B. (2020) *Rentier Capitalism*. Verso.

Chu, B. (2026) 'How the Hormuz closure could affect food, medicines and smartphones', *BBC News*, 27 March. Available at: https://www.bbc.co.uk/news/articles/c4gjxv5g19no

Civil Society Declaration (2021) *Civil Society Declaration for the Fifteenth Session of the United Nations Conference on Trade and Development*. United Nations Conference on Trade and Development.

Clapp, J. (2006) 'WTO agriculture negotiations: Implications for the Global South', *Third World Quarterly*, 27(4), pp 563–577.

Clapp, J. (2017a) 'The trade-ification of the food sustainability agenda', *The Journal of Peasant Studies*, 44(2), pp 335–353.

Clapp, J. (2017b) 'Food self-sufficiency: Making sense of it, and when it makes sense', *Food Policy*, 66, pp 88–96.

Clapp, J. (2023) 'Concentration and crises: Exploring the deep roots of vulnerability in the global industrial food system', *The Journal of Peasant Studies*, 50(1), pp 1–25.

Clapp, J. and Murphy, S. (2013) 'The G20 and food security: A mismatch in global governance?', *Global Policy*, 4(2), pp 129–138.

Clapp, J. and Moseley, W.G. (2020) 'This food crisis is different: COVID-19 and the fragility of the neoliberal food security order', *The Journal of Peasant Studies*, 47(7), pp 1393–1417.

Coburn, E. (2019) 'Trickle-down gender at the International Monetary Fund: The contradictions of "femina economica" in global capitalist governance', *International Feminist Journal of Politics*, 21(5), pp 768–788.

Conca, K. (2000) 'The WTO and the undermining of global environmental governance', *Review of International Political Economy*, 7(3), pp 487–496.

Condon, B.J. (2018) 'Captain America and the tarnishing of the crown: The feud between the WTO appellate body and the USA', *Journal of World Trade*, 52(4), pp 535–556.

Connors, J., Gwartney, J.D. and Montesinos, H.M. (2020) 'The transportation-communication revolution: 50 years of dramatic change in economic development', *Cato Journal*, 40(1), pp 153–198.

Costanza-Chock, S. (2020) *Design Justice: Community-Led Practices to Build the Worlds We Need.* MIT press.

Couldry, N. and Mejias, U. (2019) 'Data colonialism: Rethinking big data's relation to the contemporary subject', *Television and New Media*, 20(4), pp 336–349.

Daley, E. and Pallas, S. (2014) 'Women and land deals in Africa and Asia: Weighing the implications and changing the game', *Feminist Economics*, 20(1), pp 178–201.

Dalla Costa, M. and James, S. (1972) *The Power of Women and the Subversion of Community*. Falling Wall Press.

Danby, C. (2004) 'Toward a gendered post Keynesianism: Subjectivity and time in a nonmodernist framework', *Feminist Economics*, 10(3), pp 55–75.

Das, R. (2011) 'Gender in practices of fair trade and decent work', *Gender, Technology and Development*, 15(1), pp 101–125.

Davis, A. (1983) *Women, Race and Class.* Vintage Books.

DAWN (2023) 'Towards feminist digital justice', *DAWN Informs*, December. Development Alternatives with Women for a New Era. Available at: https://www.dawnfeminist.org/wp-content/uploads/2023/12/DI-on-FDJ-2023.pdf

DAWN and IT for Change (2023a) 'Toward a feminist digital justice vision: Issue mapping of critical considerations', Feminist Digital Justice Working Group. Available at: https://www.dawnfeminist.org/wp-content/uploads/2023/08/FDJ-Background-paper.pdf

DAWN and IT for Change (2023b) 'The declaration of feminist digital justice'. Available at: https://www.dawnfeminist.org/wp-content/uploads/2023/05/FDJ-declaration_EN.pdf

Delaney, A. (2004) 'Global trade and home work: Closing the divide', *Gender & Development*, 12(2), pp 22–28.

Del Felice, C. (2014) 'Power in discursive practices: The case of the STOP EPAs campaign', *European Journal of International Relations*, 20(1), pp 145–167.

Demopoulos, A. (2025) '"Financial Microaggressions": Why 'pink tariffs' hurt women more than men', *The Guardian*, 17 March. Available at: https://www.theguardian.com/us-news/2025/mar/17/pink-tariff-tax-women-clothes

der Boghossian, A. (2023a) 'Enhancing and strengthening economic opportunities for women through gender-responsive trade policies', *Staff Working Paper*, World Trade Organization.

der Boghossian, A. (2023b) 'The blended approach to gender-responsive trade policy making', *Staff Working Paper*, World Trade Organization.

der Boghossian, A. (2023c) 'Gender-responsive WTO: Making trade rules and policies work for women', in A. Bahri, D. López and J.Y. Remy (eds) *Handbook on Trade Policy and Gender Equality*. Cambridge University Press, pp 21–43.

der Boghossian, A. (2023d) 'Gender social norms: New trade barriers addressed through trade policy', in J. Chaisse and C. Rodríguez-Chiffelle (eds) *The Elgar Companion to the World Trade Organization*. Edward Elgar, pp 416–434.

der Boghossian, A. (2023e) 'Trade and gender: Addressing barriers to women's decent work through trade policies', in *Integrating Trade and Decent Work, Vol 2: The Potential of Trade and Investment Policies to Address Labour Market Issues in Supply Chains*. International Labour Organisation, pp 249–286.

Desai, M. (2002) 'Transnational solidarity: Women's agency, structural adjustment, and globalization', in N.A. Naples and M. Desai (eds) *Women's Activism and Globalization: Linking Local Struggles and Transnational Politics*. Routledge, pp 15–33.

Devey, R., Skinner, C. and Valodia, I. (2006) 'Second best?: Trends and linkages in the informal economy in South Africa', *DPRU Working Paper*, 06/102. Development Policy Research Unit.

DiCaprio, A. and Trommer, S. (2010) 'Bilateral graduation: The impact of EPAs on LDC trade space', *The Journal of Development Studies*, 46(9), pp 1607–1627.

Digital Trade Alliance (2024) *A Primer on the Intersection of Labor Rights, Technology and Trade, Digital Trade Alliance*. Available at: https://dtalliance.org/2024/10/01/a-primer-on-the-intersection-of-labor-rights-technology-and-trade/#:~:text=A%20key%20issue%20facing%20workers,decisions%20on%20hiring%20and%20firing

Digital Trade Alliance (2025) *The Development of Digital Trade Agreements*. Available at: https://dtalliance.org/2024/10/03/the-development-of-digital-trade-agreements/

D'Ignazio, C. and Klein, L.F. (2023) *Data Feminism*. The MIT Press.

Domínguez, E. (2002) 'Continental transnational activism and women workers' networks within NAFTA', *International Feminist Journal of Politics*, 4(2), pp 216–239.

Domínguez-Villalobos, L. and Brown-Grossman, F. (2010) 'Trade liberalization and gender wage inequality in Mexico', *Feminist Economics*, 16(4), pp 53–79.

Dommen, C. (2021) 'How can WTO talks on e-commerce benefit women? If only we know'. Human Rights Economics. Available at: https://humanrightseconomics.ch/2021/gender-equality/gendered-impacts-of-wto-e-commerce-talks/).

Dommen, C. (2022) 'WTO ministerial declaration on trade and gender on indefinite hold', *SDG Knowledge Hub*. Available at: https://sdg.iisd.org/commentary/policy-briefs/wto-ministerial-declaration-on-trade-and-gender-on-indefinite-hold/

Dommen, C. (2023) *Gender Equality in WTO Trade Policy Reviews: The Case of Germany*. Friedrich-Ebert-Stiftung.

Döpfner, M. (2025) 'The downfall of the World Trade Organization', *Politico*. Available at: https://www.politico.eu/article/trade-war-donald-trump-downfall-of-the-world-trade-organization-wto/

Dorobantu, C., Ostmann, F. and Hitrova, C. (2021) 'Source code disclosure: A primer for trade negotiators', in I. Borchert and A. Winters (eds) *Addressing Impediments to Digital Trade*. Center for Economic Policy Research, pp 105–140.

Dorsey, T. (2007) 'IMF survey: What is aid for trade?'. Available at: https://www.imf.org/en/news/articles/2015/09/28/04/53/sopol0523a

Doss, C., Meinzen-Dick, R., Quisumbing, A. and Theis, S. (2018) 'Women in agriculture: Four myths', *Global Food Security*, 16, pp 69–74.

dos Santos, T. (1970) 'The structure of dependence', *American Economic Review*, 60(2), pp 231–236.

Dosso, A.A.A. (2019) 'Women in informal cross-border trade in sub-Saharan Africa: An untapped potential to feed, integrate and industrialize Africa', African Development Bank Group. Available at: https://blogs.afdb.org/investing-gender/women-informal-cross-border-trade-sub-saharan-africa-untapped-potential-feed

Dowling, E. (2022) 'Platform care as care fix', in A. Strüver and S. Bauriedl (eds) *Platformization of Urban Life*. Transcript, pp 103–118.

Downes, G. (2004) 'TRIPs and food security: Implications of the WTO's TRIPs Agreement for food security in the developing world', *British Food Journal*, 106(5), pp 366–379.

Drake, W.J. and Nicolaïdis, K. (1992) 'Ideas, interests, and institutionalization: "Trade in services" and the Uruguay Round', *International Organization*, 46(1), pp 37–100.

Dumas, J.A. (2008) 'WSIS gender and ICT policy', in *Information Communication Technologies: Concepts, Methodologies, Tools, and Applications*. IGI Global Scientific Publishing, pp 496–503.

Dür, A. and de Bièvre, D. (2007) 'Inclusion without influence? NGOs in European trade policy', *Journal of Public Policy*, 27(1), pp 79–101.

Du Toit, A and Neves, D. (2007) 'In search of South Africa's second economy: Chronic poverty, economic marginalisation and adverse incorporation in Mt. Frere and Khayelitsha', *Chronic Poverty Research Centre Working Paper*, No. 102, University of the Western Cape.

Eagleton-Pierce, M. (2017) 'All the trader's men: Professionals in international trade policymaking', in L. Seabrooke and L. Folke Henriksen (eds) *Professional Networks in Transnational Governance*. Cambridge University Press, pp 115–129.

ECLAC (2002) *Globalization and Development*, 29th session, Brasilia, Brazil. Economic Commission for Latin America and the Caribbean, United Nations.

ECLAC (2019) *Women's Autonomy in Changing Economic Scenarios* (LC/CRM.14/3), Santiago. Economic Commission for Latin America and the Caribbean, United Nations.

ECLAC (2020) *International Trade Outlook for Latin American and the Caribbean: Regional Integration is Key to Recovery After the Crisis,* (LC/PUB.2020/21-P), Santiago. Economic Commission for Latin America and the Caribbean, United Nations.

ECLAC (2021) *Reorient International Trade towards a Transformative Socio-economic Recovery with Gender Equality: What Role for the WTO?* Presentation in the WTO IWG on Trade and Gender, 28 April. Available at: https://www.wto.org/english/tratop_e/womenandtrade_e/280421_eclac.pdf

ECLAC (2022) *The Care Society: A Horizon for Sustainable Recovery with Gender Equality* (LC/CRM.15/3). Economic Commission for Latin America and the Caribbean, United Nations.

ECOWAS (2014) *Plan of Action for Gender and Trade 2015–2020*. Economic Community of West African States.

ECOWAS (2015) *Supplementary Act A/SA.02/05/15 Relating to Equality of Rights between Women and Men for Sustainable Development in ECOWAS Region*. Economic Community of West African States.

ECOWAS (2019) *Trade Facilitation West Africa: Regional Gender Assessment Report*. Economic Community of West African States.

Edholm, F., Harris, O. and Young, K. (1977) 'Conceptualising women', *Critique of Anthropology*, 3(9–10), pp 101–130.

Elias, J. (2013) 'Davos woman to the rescue of global capitalism: Postfeminist politics and competitiveness promotion at the World Economic Forum', *International Political Sociology*, 7(2), pp 152–169.

Elias, J. (2020) *Gender Politics and the Pursuit of Competitiveness in Malaysia: Women on Board*. Routledge.

Elomäki, A. (2015) 'The economic case for gender equality in the European Union: Selling gender equality to decision-makers and neoliberalism to women's organizations', *European Journal of Women's Studies*, 22(3), pp 288–302.
Elson, D. (1987) 'The impact of structural adjustment on women: Concepts and issues', *Manchester Discussion Papers in Development Studies*.
Elson, D. (1994) 'People, development and the international financial institutions', *Review of African Political Economy*, 21(62), pp 511–524.
Elson, D. (1999) 'Gender budget initiatives: Background paper', Commonwealth Secretariat.
Elson, D. (2009) 'Gender equality and economic growth in the World Bank World Development Report 2006', *Feminist Economics*, 15(3), pp 35–59.
Elson, D. and Pearson, R. (1981) '"Nimble fingers make cheap workers": An analysis of women's employment in third world export manufacturing', *Feminist Review*, 7(1), pp 87–107.
Elson, D. and Çağatay, N. (2000) 'The social content of macroeconomic policies', *World Development*, 28(7), pp 1347–1364.
Elson, D., Grown, C. and van Staveren, I. (2007a) 'Introduction: Why a feminist economics of trade?', in I. van Staveren, D. Elson, C. Grown and N. Çağatay (eds) *The Feminist Economics of Trade*. Routledge, pp 1–10.
Elson, D., Grown, C. and Çağatay, N. (2007b) 'Mainstream, heterodox and feminist trade theory', in I. van Staveren, D. Elson, C. Grown and N. Çağatay (eds) *The Feminist Economics of Trade*. Routledge, pp 33–52.
England, P. (2003) 'Separative and soluble selves', in M.A. Ferber and J.A. Nelson (eds) *Feminist Economics Today: Beyond Economic Man*. University of Chicago Press, pp 37–53.
Esquivel, V. (2016) 'Power and the sustainable development goals: A feminist analysis', *Gender & Development*, 24(1), pp 9–23.
Evenett, S.J. and Meier, M. (2008) 'An interim assessment of the US trade policy of "competitive liberalization"', *World Economy*, 31(1), pp 31–66.
FAO (2020) *Intra-Africa Trade in Food and Agriculture: Issues, Challenges and Prospects in the Context of the African Continental Free Trade Area (AfCFTA)*, ARC/20/INF/10. Food and Agriculture Organization of the United Nations.
FAO (2023) *Agrifood Trade and Gender Equality: Exploring Key Linkages*. Trade Policy Technical Notes No. 22. Food and Agriculture Organization of the United Nations.
FAO, International Fund for Agricultural Development (IFAD), the United Nations Children's Fund (UNICEF), World Food Programme (WFP) and World Health Organization (WHO) (2020) *The State of Food Security and Nutrition in the World 2020: Transforming Food Systems for Affordable Healthy Diets*. Food and Agriculture Organization of the United Nations.
Federici, S. (1974) *Wages against Housework*. Falling Wall Press.
Federici, S. (2004) *Caliban and the Witch*. Autonomedia.

Ferber, M.A. and Nelson, J.A. (eds) (2003) *Feminist Economics Today: Beyond Economic Man*. University of Chicago Press.

Ferguson, L. (2015) 'This is our gender person', *International Feminist Journal of Politics*, 17(3), pp 380–397.

Folbre, N. (2001) *The Invisible Heart: Economics and Family Values*. The New Press.

Fontana, M. (2004) 'Modelling the effects of trade on women, at work and at home: Comparative perspectives', *Economie Internationale*, 3(99), pp 49–80.

Fontana, M. (2007) 'Modelling the effects of trade on women, at work and at home: Comparative perspectives', in I. van Staveren, D. Elson, C. Grown and N. Çağatay (eds) *The Feminist Economics of Trade*. Routledge, pp 117–140.

Fontana, M. and Wood, A. (2000) 'Modelling the effects of trade on women, at work and at home', *World Development*, 28(7), pp 1173–1190.

Footer, M. (1993) 'GATT and the multilateral regulation of banking services', *The International Lawyer*, pp 343–367.

Ford, A., de Tongi, G. and Miller, L. (2021) 'Hormonal health: Period tracking apps, wellness, and self-management in the era of surveillance capitalism', *Engaging Science, Technology, & Society*, 7(1), pp 48–66.

Frank, A. (1967) *Capitalism and Underdevelopment in Latin America*. New York University Press.

Fraser, N. (1989) 'Women, welfare and the politics of need interpretation' in N. Fraser (ed) *Unruly Practices: Power, Discourse and Gender in Contemporary Social Theory*. University of Minnesota Press, pp 144–160.

Fraser, N. (2016) 'Contradictions of capital and care', *New Left Review*, 100, pp 99–117.

Freitag, C., Berners-Lee, M., Widdicks, L., Knowles, B., Blair, G.S. and Friday, A. (2021) 'The real climate and transformative impact of ICT: A critique of estimates, trends, and regulations', *Patterns*, 2(9), pp 100–340.

Friel, S., Hattersley, L. and Townsend, R. (2015) 'Trade policy and public health', *Annual Review of Public Health*, 36(1), pp 325–344

Fuchs, C. (2014) *Digital Labour and Karl Marx*. Routledge.

Fuchs, N. and Hoffmann, U. (2013) 'Ensuring food security and environmental resilience: The need for supportive agricultural trade rules', *UNCTAD Trade and Environment Review*, pp 266–275.

Fukuda-Parr, S. (2023) 'Sustainable Development Goals (SDGs) and the promise of a transformative agenda', in T.G. Weiss and R. Wilkinson (eds) *International Organization and Global Governance*. Routledge, pp. 708-723.

Gabriel, C. and Macdonald, L. (1994) 'NAFTA, women and organising in Canada and Mexico: Forging a "feminist internationality"', *Millennium: Journal of International Studies*, 23(3), pp 535–562.

Gabriel, C. and Macdonald, L. (2005) 'Managing trade engagements? Mapping the contours of state feminism and women's political activism', *Canadian Foreign Policy Journal*, 12(1), pp 71–88.
Galbraith, J. and Lu, B. (2019) 'Gender identity protection, trade, and the Trump administration: A tale of reluctant progressivism', *Yale Law Journal Forum*, 129, pp 45–63.
Gammage, C. and Momodu, M. (2020) 'The economic empowerment of women in Africa: Regional approaches to gender-sensitive trade policies', *African Journal of International Economic Law*, 1, pp 1–40.
Gao, H. (2018) 'Digital or trade? The contrasting approaches of China and US to digital trade', *Journal of International Economic Law*, 21(2), pp 297–321.
Geneva Trade Platform (2023) 'Trade and gender'. Available at: https://wtoplurilaterals.info/plural_initiative/trade-and-gender/
Gereffi, G. (1994) 'Capitalism, development and global commodity chains', in L. Sklair (ed) *Capitalism and Development*. Routledge, pp 225–245.
Gereffi, G. (2015) 'Global value chains in a post-Washington Consensus world', in J. Neilson, B. Pritchard and H.Y. Wai-Chung (eds) *Global Value Chains and Global Production Networks*. Routledge, pp 9–37.
Ghorashi, R. (1995) 'Marx on free trade', *Science & Society*, 59(1), pp 38–51.
Gill, S. (1995) 'Globalization, market civilization, and disciplinary neoliberalism', *Millennium: Journal of International Studies*, 23(3), pp 399–423.
Glipo, A. (2003) *An Analysis of WTO - AoA Review from the Perspectives of Rural Asian Women: paper presented at the International Workshop in the Review of the WTO-AoA (Geneva, February 19–21)*. Available at: https://www.ctc-n.org/resources/analysis-wto-aoa-review-perspective-rural-women-asia
Goff, P. (2021) 'Inclusive trade: Justice, innovation, or more of the same?', *Ethics & International Affairs*, 35(2), pp 273–301.
Gonzalez, C.G. (2000) 'Beyond eco-imperialism: An environmental justice critique of free trade', *Denver University Law Review*, 78(4), pp 979–1000.
Gonzalez, C.G. (2002) 'Institutionalizing inequality: The WTO Agreement on Agriculture, food security, and developing countries', *Columbia Journal of Environmental Law*, 27, pp 433–480.
Gonzalez, C.G. (2006) 'Markets, monocultures and malnutrition: Agricultural trade policy through an environmental justice lens', *Michigan State Journal of International Law*, 14(2), pp 345–382.
Gore, E. (2025) 'Colonial afterlives in the global cocoa supply chain: Sharecropping, labour exploitation, and gendered (re)production', *Review of International Political Economy*, pp 1–30.
Gore, E. and LeBaron, G. (2019) 'Using social reproduction theory to understand unfree labour', *Capital & Class*, 43(4), pp 561–580.
Graeub, B., Chappell, M., Wittman, H., Ledermann, S., Bezner Kerr, R., and Gemmill-Herren, B. (2015) 'The state of family farms in the world', *World Development*, 87, pp 1–15.

Graz, J.-C. (2016) 'The Havana Charter: When state and market shake hands', in E.S. Reinert, J. Ghosh and R. Kattel (eds) *Handbook of Alternative Theories of Economic Development*. Edward Elgar, pp 281–290.
Gregoratti, C., Roberts, A. and Tornhill, S. (2018) 'Corporations, gender equality and women's empowerment: Feminism co-opted?', in C. May and A. Nölke (eds) *Handbook of the International Political Economy of the Corporation*. Edward Elgar, pp 93–105.
Griffin, P. (2009) *Gendering the World Bank*. Palgrave.
Griffin, P. (2010) 'Gender, governance and the global political economy', *Australian Journal of International Affairs*, 64(1), pp 86–104.
Griffin, P. (2013) 'Gendering global finance: Crisis, masculinity, and responsibility', *Men and Masculinities* 16(1), pp 934.
Grown, C., Elson, D. and Çağatay, N. (2000) 'Introduction', *World Development*, 28(7), pp 11451156.
GTC (2020) 'Public letter to the European Commission to support during WTO negotiations: Waiver in regard to TRIPS for the prevention, containment and treatment of COVID-19'. Available at: https://wideplus.org/wp-content/uploads/2020/11/WIDE-Demand-a-TRIPS-Waiver-for-COVID-19–18-Nov-2020.pdf
GTC (2021) 'Gender justice requires a broad mandate for UNCTAD'. Available at: https://owinfs.org/2021/Gender_justice_UNCTAD.pdf
GTC (2022) 'Open letter from the Gender and Trade Coalition to the Director-General and Honorable Delegates of the World Trade Organization (WTO) ahead of MC12'. Available at: https://www.wto.org/english/thewto_e/minist_e/mc12_e/gtc_open_letter.pdf
GTC (2024) 'Feminist trade explainer 4: Climate'. Available at: https://gendertradecoalition.org/publications/explainer-4-climate/
GTC (2025) *Gender and Trade Coalition: A Feminist Trade Agenda*. Available at: https://gendertradecoalition.org/wp-content/uploads/2025/06/Feminist-Trade-Agenda-Gender-and-Trade-Coalition.pdf
Guérin, I., Kumar, S. and Venkatasubramanian, G. (2023) *The Indebted Woman: Kinship, Sexuality, and Capitalism*. Stanford University Press.
Guha-Khasnabis, B., Kanbur, R. and Ostrom, E. (eds) (2006) *Linking the Formal and Informal Economy*. Oxford University Press.
Gurumurthy, A. and Chami, N. (2021) *Building Back Better with E-Commerce: A Feminist Roadmap*. IT for Change.
Gurumurthy, A. and Chami, N. (2024) 'The global digital compact is here: What now for civil Society?', *Bot Populi*. Available at: https://botpopuli.net/?post_type=post&p=8130
Hajjar, R., Ayana, A.N., Rutt, R., Hinde, O., Liao, C., Keene, S., et al (2019) 'Capital, labor, and gender: The consequences of large-scale land transactions on household labor allocation', *Journal of Peasant Studies*, 47(3), pp 566–588.

Hall, R., Scoones, I. and Tsikata, D. (2017) 'Plantations, outgrowers and commercial farming in Africa: Agricultural commercialization and implications for agrarian change', *Journal of Peasant Studies*, 44(3), pp 515–537.

Hannah, E., Scott, J. and Trommer, S. (2015) *Expert Knowledge in Global Trade*. Routledge.

Hannah, E. (2016) *NGOs and Global Trade: Non-State Voices in EU Trade Policymaking*. Routledge.

Hannah, E. and Trommer, S. (2017) 'What does gender mean at the WTO, and who benefits?', *Policy@Manchester Blog*. Available at: https://blog.policy.manchester.ac.uk/posts/2017/10/gender-trade-wto-who-benefits/

Hannah, E., Roberts, A. and Trommer, S. (2018) 'Gendering global trade governance through Canada-UK trade relations', Knowledge Synthesis Grant Final Report. Available at: https://research.manchester.ac.uk/en/publications/gendering-global-trade-governance-through-canada-uk-trade-relatio/

Hannah, E., Roberts, A. and Trommer, S. (2021a) 'Towards a feminist global trade politics', *Globalizations*, 18(1), pp 70–85.

Hannah, E., Scott, J., Trommer, S. and Harman, S. (2021b) 'The global approach to vaccine equity is failing: Additional steps that would help', *The Conversation*, 14 April. Available at: http://theconversation.com/the-global-approach-to-vaccine-equity-is-failing-additional-steps-that-would-help-158711

Hannah, E., Roberts, A. and Trommer, S. (2022) 'Gender in global trade: Transforming or reproducing trade orthodoxy?', *Review of International Political Economy*, 29(4), pp 1368–1393.

Haraway, D.J. (1991) *Simians, Cyborgs, and Women: The Reinvention of Nature*. Routledge.

Hardaker, S. (2025) 'Platformizing structural policy instruments? Fostering (infrastructural) power in the context of Digital Free Trade Zones', *Geoforum*, 160, Article 104218.

Hardefeldt, S. (2017) 'Free trade is bad for women: A WTO declaration won't change that', *openDemocracy*. Available at: https://www.opendemocracy.net/en/opendemocracyuk/free-trade-is-bad-for-women-wto-declaration-won-t-change-that/

Harding, L. (1992) 'Les grands commerçants africains en Afrique de l'Ouest: Le cas du Sénégal et de la Côte d'Ivoire. Essai de synthèse', in L. Harding and P. Kipre (eds) *Commerce et Commerçants en Afrique de l'Ouest: La Côte d'Ivoire*. Edition L'Harmattan, pp 5–27.

Harriss-White, B. and Gooptu, N. (2001) 'Mapping India's World of Unorganized Labour' *Socialist Register* 37, pp 89–118.

Helleiner, E. (2014) *Forgotten Foundations of Bretton Woods: International Development and the Making of the Postwar Order*. Cornell University Press.

Helleiner, E. (2023a) 'Silences of Bretton Woods: Gender inequality, racial discrimination and environmental degradation', *Review of International Political Economy*, 30(5), pp 1701–1722.

Helleiner, E. (2023b) *The Contested World Economy: The Deep and Global Roots of International Political Economy*. Cambridge University Press.

Hinchliffe, E. and Ajemian, N. (2025) 'While Trump's tariffs crash the markets, women-led businesses are outperforming the downturn—so far', *Fortune*, 7 April, https://fortune.com/2025/04/07/while-trumps-tariffs-crash-the-markets-women-led-businesses-are-outperforming-the-downturn-so-far/

Hocking, B. and McGuire, S. (2004) *Trade Politics*. Routledge.

Hoekman, B.M. and Kostecki, M.M. (2009) *The Political Economy of the World Trading System: The WTO and Beyond*. Oxford University Press.

Hoekman, B.M. and Mattoo, A. (2013) 'Liberalizing trade in services: Lessons from regional and WTO negotiations', *International Negotiation*, 18(1), pp 131–151.

Hofmann, C., Osnago, A. and Ruta, M. (2017) 'Horizontal depth: A new database on the content of preferential trade agreements', *Policy Research Working Paper*, No. 7981, World Bank Group.

Hopewell, K. (2016) *Breaking the WTO: How Emerging Powers Disrupted the Neoliberal Project*. Stanford University Press.

Hopewell, K. (2022) 'Heroes of the developing world? Emerging powers in WTO agriculture negotiations and dispute settlement', *The Journal of Peasant Studies*, 49(3), pp 561–584.

Hopkins, T.K. and Wallerstein, I. (1986) 'Commodity chains in the world-economy prior to 1800', *Review (Fernand Braudel Center)*, 10(1), pp 157–170.

Hoskyns, C. and Rai, S.M. (2007) 'Recasting the global political economy: Counting women's unpaid work', *New Political Economy*, 12(3), pp 297–317.

Hudec, R. (1990) *The GATT Legal System and World Trade Diplomacy*. Butterworth Legal Publishers.

Hudec, R. (1992) 'GATT and the developing countries', *Columbia Business Law Review*, pp 67–80.

ICC (2025) 'The WTO moratorium on customs duties on electronic transmissions: Global factsheet', International Chamber of Commerce.

IGC (2025a) 'Impact: Trade. Trade impact working group'. Available at: https://genderchampions.com/impact/trade

IGC (2025b) 'About: Who we are'. Available at: https://genderchampions.com/about

ILO (2002) *Decent Work and the Informal Economy*. International Labour Organization.

ILO (2023) *Women and Men in the Informal Economy: A Statistical Update*. International Labour Organization. Available at: https://www.ilo.org/sites/default/files/wcmsp5/groups/public/%40ed_protect/%40protrav/%40travail/documents/publication/wcms_869188.pdf

ISDB (2021) 'The 2nd phase of Aid for Trade Initiative for the Arab States (AfTIAS 2.0 Program) and gender equality & women's empowerment', presentation to the WTO IWG on Trade and Gender, 16 July. Available at: https://www.wto.org/english/tratop_e/womenandtrade_e/16july21/item_3.2.c._islamic_development_bank.pdf

Ismail, F. (2009) 'An assessment of the WTO Doha round July–December 2008 collapse', *World Trade Review*, 8(4), pp 579–605.

Ismail, Y. (2020) *E-commerce in the World Trade Organization: History and Latest Developments in the Negotiations under the Joint Statement*. International Institute for Sustainable Development and CUTS International.

ITC (2015) *Unlocking Markets for Women to Trade*. International Trade Centre.

ITC (2020a) *Mainstreaming Gender in Free Trade Agreements*. International Trade Centre.

ITC (2020b) *Delivering on the Buenos Aires Declaration on Trade and Women's Economic Empowerment*. International Trade Centre.

ITC (2022) *Evaluation of the ITC SheTrades Initiative*. International Trade Centre Independent Evaluation Unit.

ITC (2025a) 'Trailblazers call to action'. Available at: https://www.intracen.org/sites/default/files/uploadedFiles/intracen.org/Content/About_ITC/Press/Articles/Call_to_Action_Final_document.pdf

ITC (2025b) 'Women Exporters in the Digital Economy (WEIDE) Fund'. Available at: https://www.intracen.org/our-work/partnerships/women-exporters-in-the-digital-economy-weide-fund

ITC (2025c) 'Digital growth with digital payments'. Available at: https://www.shetrades.com/event/digital-growth-with-digital-payments/

ITC (2026) 'She Trades initiative: Expanding women's opportunities in global trade'. Available at: https://www.shetrades.com/

IT for Change (2022). 'Women's rights organisations and allies oppose the gender "upskilling initiative" as an IPEF carrot', 12 December. Available at: https://www.bilaterals.org/?women-s-rights-organisations-and

ITU (2021) *Digital Technologies to Achieve the UN SDGs*. International Telecommunication Union. Available at: https://www.itu.int:443/en/mediacentre/backgrounders/Pages/icts-to-achieve-the-united-nations-sustainable-development-goals.aspx

Jaffe, S. (2020) 'Social reproduction and the pandemic, with Tithi Bhattacharya', *Dissent*, 2 April. Available at: https://dissentmagazine.org/online_articles/social-reproduction-and-the-pandemic-with-tithi-bhattacharya/

James, D. (2021) *Trade and Development Backstory: The Struggle Over the UNCTAD 15 Mandate*. Institute for New Economic Thinking.

Jane, E. (2017) *Misogyny Online: A Short (and Brutish) History*. SAGE.

Jarrett, K. (2016) *Feminism, Labour and Digital Media: The Digital Housewife*. Routledge.

Jawara, F. and Kwa, A. (2004) *Behind the Scenes at the WTO: The Real World of International Trade Negotiations*. Zed Books.

Joekes, S. (1999) 'A gender-analytical perspective on trade and sustainable development', in UNCTAD (ed) *Trade, Sustainable Development and Gender*. United Nations, pp 33–59.

Johnston, L. (2020) 'COVID-19 pushes forward Jack Ma's plans for a World Trade Revolution', China Institute, SOAS University of London. Available at: https://blogs.soas.ac.uk/china-institute/2020/08/25/covid-19-pushes-forward-jack-mas-plans-for-a-world-trade-revolution/

Jones, E. (2023) 'Digital disruption: Artificial intelligence and international trade policy', *Oxford Review of Economic Policy*, 39(1), pp 70–84.

Jones, E. and Adam, C. (2023) 'New frontiers of trade and trade policy: Digitalization and climate change', *Oxford Review of Economic Policy*, 39(1), pp 1–11.

Jones, K. (2010) *The Doha Blues: Institutional Crisis and Reform in the WTO*. Oxford University Press.

Josling, T. (2012) 'New trade issues in food, agriculture, and natural resources', in A. Narlikar, M. Daunton and R.M. Stern (eds) *The Oxford Handbook on the World Trade Organization*. Oxford University Press, pp 655–673.

Juhn, C., Ujhelyi, G. and Villegas-Sanchez, C. (2013) 'Trade liberalization and gender inequality', *American Economic Review*, 103(3), pp 269–273.

Kabeer, N. (1994) *Reversed Realities: Gender Hierarchies in Development Thought*. Verso.

Kabeer, N. (1999) 'Resources, agency, achievements: Reflections on the measurement of women's empowerment', *Development and Change*, 30(3), pp 435–464.

Karim, L. (2011) *Microfinance and Its Discontents: Women in Debt in Bangladesh*. University of Minnesota Press.

Kay, T. and Evans, R.L. (2018) *Trade Battles: Activism and the Politicization of International Trade Policy*. Oxford University Press.

Keasbey, L.M. (1898) 'L'Evolution du Commerce dans les Diverses races Humaines by Ch. Letourneau', *Political Science Quarterly*, 13(3), pp 540–542.

Kelsey, J. (2018) 'How a TPP-Style e-commerce outcome in the WTO would endanger the development dimension of the GATS Acquis (and potentially the WTO)', *Journal of International Economic Law*, 21(2), pp 273–295.

Kelsey, J. (2022) 'The illegitimacy of Joint Statement Initiatives and their systemic implications for the WTO', *Journal of International Economic Law*, 25(1), pp 2–24.

Keohane, R.O. and Nye, J.S. (2003) 'The club model of multilateral cooperation and problems of democratic legitimacy', in R.O. Keohane (ed) *Power and Governance in a Partially Globalized World*. Routledge, pp 219–244.

Kleinwächter, W. (2004) 'WSIS: A new diplomacy? Multistakeholder approach and bottom up policy in global ICT governance', *Information Technology and International Development*, 1(3–4), pp 3–14.

Kofman, E. and Raghuram, P. (eds) (2015) *Gendered Migrations and Global Social Reproduction*. Palgrave Macmillan.

Kokalitcheva, K. (2015) 'Female executives are Alibaba's "secret sauce", founder Jack Ma says', *Fortune*, 20 May. Available at: https://time.com/3891666/female-executives-are-alibabas-secret-sauce-ceo-jack-ma-says/.

Korjan, A. (2023) 'Navigating the Global Digital Compact: Digital cooperation, historical fault lines, and the Global South agenda', *DAWN Informs*, December, pp 65–70.

Krugman, P. (1987) 'Is free trade passé?', *Journal of Economic Perspectives*, 1(2), pp 131–144.

Kucera, D. and Milberg, W. (2007) 'Gender segregation and gender bias in manufacturing trade expansion: Revising the "Wood asymmetry"', in I. van Staveren, D. Elson, C. Grown and N. Çağatay (eds) *The Feminist Economics of Trade*. Routledge, pp 185–214.

Kugler, K. (2025) 'The great disconnect in India's digital trade policy', Council on Foreign Relations, 10 February. Available at https://www.cfr.org/articles/great-disconnect-indias-digital-trade-policy

Kuhlmann, K. (2021) 'Mapping inclusive law and regulation: A comparative agenda for trade and development', *African Journal of International Economic Law*, 2, pp 48–87.

Kvangraven, I.H. (2021) 'Beyond the stereotype: Restating the relevance of the dependency research programme', *Development and Change*, 52(1), pp 76–112.

Lang, A. (2007) 'Reflecting on "linkage": Cognitive and institutional change in the international trading system', *The Modern Law Review*, 70(4), pp 523–549.

Lang, A. (2011) *World Trade Law after Neoliberalism: Reimagining the Global Economic Order*. Oxford University Press.

La Via Campesina (2013) 'Social movements remind the WTO about the death of Korean farmer Kee Kyung Hae inside the official ministerial conference through a powerful action', *La Via Campesina*. Available at: https://viacampesina.org/en/social-movements-remind-the-wto-about-the-death-of-korean-farmer-lee-kyung-hae-inside-the-official-ministerial-conference-through-a-powerful-action/

La Via Campesina (2021) 'Food sovereignty, a manifesto for the future of our planet', 13 October, *La Via Campesina*. Available at: https://viacampesina.org/en/2021/10/food-sovereignty-a-manifesto-for-the-future-of-our-planet-la-via-campesina/

La Via Campesina (2024) '26–29 February: La Via Campesina calls for a week of mobilization against the WTO', 9 February, *La Via Campesina*. Available at: https://viacampesina.org/en/2024/02/26-29-february-la-via-campesina-calls-for-a-week-of-mobilization-against-the-wto/

La Via Campesina (2025) 'About La Via Campesina', *La Via Campesina*. Available at: https://viacampesina.org/en/international-peasants-voice/

LeBaron, G. (2021) 'Wages: An overlooked dimension of business and human rights in global supply chains', *Business and Human Rights Journal*, 6(1), pp 1–20.

LeBaron, G. and Gore, E. (2020) 'Gender and forced labour: Understanding the links in global cocoa supply chains', *The Journal of Development Studies*, 56(6), pp 1095–1117.

LeBaron, G., Edwards, R., Hunt, T., Sempéré, C. and Kyritsis, P. (2022) 'The ineffectiveness of CSR: Understanding garment company commitments to living wages in global supply chains', *New Political Economy*, 27(1), pp 99–115.

Lesavage, H. (2025) 'How Trump's tariffs will affect your closet, explained', *Marie Claire*, 9 April. Available at: https://www.marieclaire.com/fashion/trump-tariffs-explained/

Levasseur, E. (1892) 'The recent commercial policy of France', *Journal of Political Economy*, 1(1), pp 20–49.

Levien, M. (2017) 'Gender and land dispossession: A comparative analysis', *Journal of Peasant Studies*, 44(6), pp 1111–1134.

Liebowitz, D.J. (2008) 'Governing globalization: Feminist engagements with international trade policy', in S. Rai and G. Waylen (eds) *Global Governance: Feminist Perspectives*. Palgrave Macmillan, pp 207–233.

Lighthizer, R. (2020) 'How to Make Trade Work for Workers', *Foreign Affairs*, 99, pp 78–92.

Lind, A. (2010) *Development, Sexual Rights and Global Governance*. Routledge.

Littler, J. (2017) 'Desperate success: Managing the mumpreneur', in J. Littler (ed) *Against Meritocracy: Culture, Power and Myths of Mobility*. Routledge, pp 179–211.

Lodefalk, M. (2017) 'Servicification of firms and trade policy implications', *World Trade Review*, 16(1), pp 59–83.

Lombardozzi, L. (2024) 'The social reproduction of (and through) food: Agrarian change in Uzbekistan', *Journal of Agrarian Change*, 24(3), e12580.

Lugones, M. (2007) 'Heterosexualism and the colonial/modern gender system', *Hypatia*, 22(1), pp 186–209.

Luxton, M. (2006) 'Feminist political economy in Canada and the politics of social reproduction', in K. Bezanson and M. Luxton (eds) *Social Reproduction: Feminist Political Economy Challenges Neo-liberalism*. Queens University Press, pp 11–44.

Macdonald, L. (2002) 'Globalization and social movements: Comparing women's movements' responses to NAFTA in Mexico, the U.S. and Canada', *International Feminist Journal of Politics*, 4(2), pp 151–172.

Macdonald, L.C. (2024) 'Inclusion of gender and labour standards in preferential trade agreements: Evidence from North American and Canada-Chile agreements', *Globalizations*, 21(8), pp 1421–1438.

Mahon, R. (2019) 'Broadening the social investment agenda: The OECD, the World Bank and inclusive growth', *Global Social Policy*, 19(1–2), pp 121–138.

Manley, S. (2021) 'World Trade Organization General Council, November 2021: UK statements', *GOV.UK*. Available at: https://www.gov.uk/government/speeches/world-trade-organization-general-council-november-2021-uk-statements

Manyika, J., Lund, S., Bughin, J., Woetzel, J., Stamenov, K. and Dhingra, D. (2016) *The New Era of Global Flows*. McKinsey Global Institute. Available at: https://www.mckinsey.com/~/media/mckinsey/business%20functions/mckinsey%20digital/our%20insights/digital%20globalization%20the%20new%20era%20of%20global%20flows/mgi-digital-globalization-full-report.pdf

Marfaing, L. and Sow, M. (1999) *Les opérateurs économiques au Sénégal: Entre le formel et l'informel (1930–1996)*. Karthala.

Margulis, M. (2014) 'Trading out of the global food crisis? The World Trade Organization and the geopolitics of food security', *Geopolitics*, 19(2), pp 322–350.

Margulis, M. (2017) 'The forgotten history of food security in multilateral trade negotiations', *World Trade Review*, 16(1), pp 25–57.

Margulis, M. (2023) *Shadow Negotiators: How UN Organizations Shape the Rules of World Trade for Food Security*. Stanford University Press.

Martineau, H. (1837) *Society in America*, Vol. 2. Baudry's European Library.

Martínez-Torres, M.E. and Rosset, P.M. (2010) 'La Vía Campesina: The birth and evolution of a transnational social movement', *The Journal of Peasant Studies*, 37(1), pp 149–175.

Marx, K. and Engels, F. (1888) 'On the Question of Free Trade'. Available at: https://www.marxists.org/archive/marx/works/1848/free-trade/

May, C. and Sell, S.K. (2005) *Intellectual Property Rights: A Critical History*. Lynne Rienner Publishers.

McMichael, P. (1997) 'Rethinking globalization: The agrarian question revisited', *Review of International Political Economy*, 4(4), pp 630–662.

Meagher, K. (2009) 'Trading on faith: Religious movements and informal economic governance in Nigeria', *Journal of Modern African Studies*, 47(3), pp 397–423.

Meagher, K. (2013) 'Unlocking the informal economy: A literature review on linkages between formal and informal economies in developing countries', *WIEGO Working Paper*, No. 27, Women in Informal Employment Globalizing and Organizing.

Melanson, K. (2005) 'An examination of the gendered effects of trade liberalisation', *Policy Perspectives*, 2(1), pp 10–17.

Meltzer, J.P. (2019) 'Governing digital trade', *World Trade Review*, 18(S1), pp S23–S48.

Mengesha, E. (2008) 'Rethinking the rules and principles of the international trade regime: Feminist perspectives', *Agenda*, 22(78), pp 13–26.

Mezzadri, A. (2016) 'Class, gender and the sweatshop: On the nexus between labour commodification and exploitation', *Third World Quarterly*, 37(10), pp 1877–1900.

Mezzadri, A. (2017) *The Sweatshop Regime: Labouring Bodies, Exploitation, and Garments Made in India*. Cambridge University Press.

Mezzadri, A. (2019) 'On the value of social reproduction: Informal labour, the majority world and the need for inclusive theories and politics', *Radical Philosophy*, 2(4), pp 33–42.

Mezzadri, A. (2021) 'A value theory of inclusion: Informal labour, the homeworker, and the social reproduction of value', *Antipode*, 53(4), pp 1186–1205.

Mezzadri, A., Newman, S. and Stevano, S. (2022) 'Feminist global political economies of work and social reproduction', *Review of International Political Economy*, 29(6), pp 1783–1803.

Mezzadri, A., Stevano, S., Ossome, L. and Bargawi, H. (2024) 'The social reproduction of agrarian change: Feminist political economy and rural transformations in the global south. An introduction', *Journal of Agrarian Change*, 24(3), e12595.

Mies, M. (1982) *The Lace Makers of Narsapur: Indian Housewives Produce for the World Market*. Zed Press.

Mies, M. (1996) 'Women and work in a sustainable society', *The Ecumenical Review*, 48(3), pp 354–368.

Mies, M. (1998 [1986]) *Patriarchy and Accumulation on a World Scale: Women in the International Division of Labour*. Zed Books.

Mies, M. and Shiva, V. (1993) *Ecofeminism*. Zed Press.

Mies, M. and Bennholdt-Thomsen, V. (1999) *The Subsistence Perspective: Beyond the Globalised Economy*. Zed Books.

Mies, M., Bennholdt-Thomsen, V. and von Werlhof, C. (1988) *Women: The Last Colony*. Zed Books. (Originally published as *Frauen, die letzte Kolonie*. Rowohlt, 1983)

Migdon, B. (2021) 'US will join WTO joint declaration on gender equality', *The Hill*, 4 December. Available at: https://thehill.com/changing-america/respect/equality/584269-us-will-join-wto-joint-declaration-on-gender-equality/

Minsberg, T. (2025) 'A timeline of Trump's on-again, off-again tariffs', *New York Times*, 13 March. Available at: https://www.nytimes.com/2025/03/13/business/economy/trump-tariff-timeline.html#

Mohanty, C. (1991) 'Under western eyes: Feminist scholarship and colonial discourse', in C. Mohanty, A. Russo and L. Torres (eds) *Third World Women and the Politics of Feminism*. Indiana University Press, pp 51–80.

Monteiro, J.A. (2021) 'The evolution of gender-based provisions in regional trade agreements', *Staff Working Paper*, ERSD-2021–8, World Trade Organization.

Moos, K.A. and Gonalons-Pons, P. (2024) 'A comparison of the socioeconomic and gendered organization of social reproduction in the United States and the United Kingdom, 1973–2013', *Social Politics*, 31(3), pp 502–530.

Mosiane, B. (2011) 'Livelihoods and the transformative potential of cities: Challenges of inclusive development in Rustenburg, North West Province, South Africa', *Singapore Journal of Tropical Geography*, 32(1), pp 38–52.

Murphy, C. (2000) 'Global governance: Poorly done and poorly understood', *International Affairs*, 76(4), pp 789–803.

Murphy, C. (2014) 'Global governance over the long haul', *International Studies Quarterly*, 58(1), pp 216–218.

Muzaka, V. and Bishop, M. (2015) 'Doha stalemate: The end of trade multilateralism?', *Review of International Studies*, 41(2), pp 383–406.

Narlikar, A. and Wilkinson, R. (2004) 'Collapse at the WTO: A Cancun post-mortem', *Third World Quarterly*, 25(3), pp 447–460.

Natile, S. (2020) *The Exclusionary Politics of Digital Financial Inclusion: Mobile Money, Gendered Walls*. Routledge.

National Farmers Union (2023) 'Lee Kyung Hae's dramatic suicide still an inspiration for global action'. Available at: https://www.nfu.ca/kyung-haes-dramatic-suicide-still-an-inspiration-for-global-action/

Nelson, B. (1984) 'Women's poverty and women's citizenship: Some political consequences of economic marginality', *Signs: Journal of Women in Culture and Society*, 10, pp 209–232.

Noble, S.U. (2018) *Algorithms of Oppression*. New York University Press.

O'Connor, J., Orloff, A. and Shaver, S. (1999) *States, Markets, and Families: Gender, Liberalism and Social Policy in Australia, Canada, Great Britain, and the United States*. Cambridge University Press.

O'Donnell, A. and Sweetman, C. (2018) 'Introduction: Gender, development and ICTs', *Gender & Development*, 26(2), pp 217–229.

OECD (2021) *Trade and Gender: A Framework of Analysis*. Organization for Economic Co-operation and Development.

OECD (2023) *The Nature, Evolution and Potential Implications of Data Localisation Measures*. OECD Trade Policy Paper No. 278. Organization for Economic Co-operation and Development.

OECD, WTO and IMF (2019) *Handbook on Measuring Digital Trade, Vol. 1*. Organization for Economic Co-operation and Development, World Trade Organization and International Monetary Fund.

O'Hara, C. (2022) 'Consensus and diversity in the World Trade Organization: A queer perspective', *American Journal of International Law*, 116, pp 32–37.

Okeyo, A.P. (2002) *Globalization and Gender Equity: Perspectives from Africa*. United Nations Development Programme.

Orloff, A. (1993) 'Gender and the social rights of citizenship: The comparative analysis of gender relations and welfare states', *American Sociological Review*, 58(3), pp 303–328.

Ossome, L. (2015) 'In search of the state? Neoliberalism and the labour question for pan-African feminism', *Feminist Africa*, 20, pp 6–25.

Ostry, S. (1997) *The Post-Cold War Trading System*. University of Chicago Press.

Our World is Not For Sale (2017) 'Women's rights groups call on governments to reject the WTO declaration on "women's economic empowerment"'. Available at: https://owinfs.org/2017/R_OWINFS_gender.pdf

Oxfam International (2004) *Trading Away Our Rights: Women Working in Global Supply Chains*. Oxfam.

Pahuja, S. (2000) 'Trading spaces: Locating sites for challenge within international trade law', *Australian Feminist Law Journal*, 14(1), pp 38–54.

Palen, M.-W. (2013) 'The Civil War's forgotten transatlantic tariff debate and the Confederacy's free trade diplomacy', *Journal of the Civil War Era*, 3(1), pp 35–61.

Palen, M.-W. (2016) *The 'Conspiracy' of Free Trade: The Anglo-American Struggle Over Empire and Economic Globalisation, 1846–1896*. Cambridge University Press.

Palen, M.-W. (2020) 'Marx and Manchester: The evolution of the socialist internationalist free-trade tradition, c.1846–1946', *The International History Review*, 43(2), pp 381–398.

Palen, M.-W. (2024) *Pax Economica: Left-Wing Visions of a Free Trade World*. Princeton University Press.

Palen, M.-W. (2025) 'No, Trump's coercive use of tariffs isn't new', *Imperial & Global Forum*, 13 February. Available at: https://imperialglobalexeter.com/2025/02/13/no-trumps-coercive-use-of-tariffs-isnt-new/

Parreñas, R.S. (2001) *Servants of Globalization: Women, Migration and Domestic Work*. Stanford University Press.

Partenio, F. and Weleilakeba, S. (2022) 'Introduction: Feminist challenges in a digital world', *DAWN Informs*, March, pp 4–8.

Partenio, F. and Weleilakeba, S. (2023) 'Introduction: Towards feminist digital justice', *DAWN Informs*, December, pp 6–10.

Pearson, R. (1998) '"Nimble fingers" revisited: Reflections on women and third world industrialisation in the late twentieth century', in C. Jackson and R. Pearson (eds) *Feminist Visions of Development: Gender, Analysis and Policy*. Routledge, pp 171–188.

Pedersen, P.O. and McCormick, D. (1999) 'African business systems in a globalising world', *Journal of Modern African Studies*, 37(1), pp 109–135.

Peres, A. (2024) 'Transience of (in)formality: The role of the joint initiatives in reforming the WTO negotiations', *World Trade Review*, 23(3), pp 385–407.

Peterson, S.V. (2005) 'How (the meaning of) gender matters in political economy', *New Political Economy*, 10(4), pp 499–521.

Picchio, A. (1992) *Social Reproduction: The Political Economy of the Labour Market*. Cambridge University Press.

Piovani, C. (2017) *The Trade and Gender Toolbox: Ex-ante Gender Assessment of Trade Policies*. United Nations Conference on Trade and Development. Available at: https://elearning.unctad.org/pluginfile.php/34371/mod_page/content/20/The%20Trade%20and%20Gender%20Toolbox.pdf

Poinsard, L. (1893) *Libre Échange et Protection*. Firmin Didot et Cie.

Pouliot, V. and Thérien, J.-P. (2018) 'Global governance in practice', *Global Policy*, 9(2), pp 163–172.

Powers, P. (1888) 'The Australian tariff experiment', *Quarterly Journal of Economics*, 3(1), pp 87–98.

Prahalad, C.K. and Hart, S.L. (2002) 'The fortune at the bottom of the pyramid', *Strategy + Business*, 26, pp 54–67.

Prebisch, R. (1950) *The Economic Development of Latin America and its Principal Problems*. UN document no. E/CN.12/89/Rev.1. United Nations.

Price, S. (2018) 'Gender rights and trade agreements', in R.E. Looney (ed) *Handbook of International Trade Agreements*. Routledge, pp 112–121.

Price, S. (2025) 'Gendering Pan-African trade: Exploring the transformational potential of the African continental free trade agreement', *Review of International Political Economy*, pp 1–31.

Prügl, E. (2004) 'Gender orders in German agriculture: From the patriarchal welfare state to liberal environmentalism', *Sociologia Ruralis*, 44(4), pp 349–372.

Prügl, E. (2010) *Gendered Knowledge in the Postmodern State: The Case of Agricultural Trade Liberalization in Europe*. Nomos Verlagsgesellschaft mbH & Co. KG.

Prügl, E. (2015) 'Neoliberalising feminism', *New Political Economy*, 20(4), pp 614–631.

Prügl, E. (2017) 'Neoliberalism with a feminist face: Crafting a new hegemony at the World Bank', *Feminist Economics*, 23(1), pp 30–53.

Prügl, E. (2021) 'Smart economics', in G. Berik and E. Kongar (eds) *The Routledge Handbook of Economics*. Routledge, pp 468–476.

Prügl, E. and True, J. (2014) 'Equality means business? Governing gender through transnational public-private partnerships', *Review of International Political Economy*, 21(6), pp 1137–1167.

Prügl, E. and Joshi, S. (2021) 'Productive farmers and vulnerable food securers: Contradictions of gender expertise in international food security discourse', *The Journal of Peasant Studies*, 48(7), pp 1439–1458.

Prügl, E., Reysoo, F. and Tsikata, D. (2021) 'Agricultural and land commercialization: Feminist and rights perspectives', *The Journal of Peasant Studies*, 48(7), pp 1419–1438.

Public Citizen (2026) 'Statement for the Record: The President's 2026 Trade Policy Agenda', 6 May. Available at: https://www.citizen.org/article/statement-for-the-record-the-presidents-2026-trade-policy-agenda/

Quiroga-Villamarín, D.R. (2020) 'Normalising global commerce: Containerisation, materiality, and transnational regulation (1956–68)', *London Review of International Law*, 8(3), pp 457–477.

Rai, S.M. (2004) 'Gendering global governance', *International Feminist Journal of Politics*, 6(4), pp 579–601.

Rai, S. (2018) 'Gender and development', in J. Elias and A. Roberts (eds) *Handbook on the International Political Economy of Gender*. Edward Elgar, pp 142–158.

Rai, S. (2024) *Depletion: The Human Costs of Caring*. Oxford University Press.

Rai, S.M. and Waylen, G. (2008) *Global Governance: Feminist Perspectives*. Springer.

Rai, S.M., Hoskyns, C. and Thomas, D. (2013) 'Depletion: The cost of social reproduction', *International Feminist Journal of Politics*, 16(1), pp 86–105.

Ranganathan, J., Vennard, D., Waite, R., Dumas, P., Lipinski, B. and Searchinger, T. (2016) *Shifting Diets for a Sustainable Food Future: Creating a Sustainable Food Future, Installment Eleven*. World Resources Institute. Available at: https://www.wri.org/research/shifting-diets-sustainable-food-future

Ranis, G. and Stewart, F. (1999) 'V-goods and the role of the urban informal sector in development', *Economic Development and Cultural Change*, 47(2), pp 259–288.

Rankin, K. (2001) 'Governing development: Neoliberalism, microcredit, and rational economic woman', *Economy and Society*, 30(1), pp 18–37.

Rankin, K (2013) 'A critical geography of poverty finance', *Third World Quarterly* 34(4), pp 547–568.

Ravenhill, J. (2014) 'Global value chains and development', *Review of International Political Economy*, 21(1), pp 264–274.

Razavi, S. (2012) 'World development report 2012: Gender equality and development – a commentary', *Development and Change*, 43(1), pp 423–437.

Rice, J. (2010) 'Viewing trade liberalization through a feminist lens: A content analysis of the counterhegemonic discourse of gender and trade advocacy groups', *Sociological Spectrum*, 30(3), pp 289–316.

Roberts, A. (2015a) 'Gender, financial deepening and the production of embodied finance: Towards a critical feminist analysis', *Global Society*, 29(1), pp 107–127.

Roberts, A. (2015b) 'The political economy of "Transnational Business Feminism": Problematizing the corporate-led gender equality agenda', *International Feminist Journal of Politics*, 17(2), pp 209–231.

Roberts, A. and Soederberg, S. (2012) 'Gender equality as "smart economics"? A critique of the 2012 World Development Report', *Third World Quarterly*, 33(5), pp 949–968.

Roberts, A. and Zulfiqar, G.M. (2019) 'The political economy of women's entrepreneurship initiatives in Pakistan: Reflections on gender, class, and "development"', *Review of International Political Economy*, 26(3), pp 410–435.

Roberts, A. and Trommer, S. (2026) 'Gendered Trade Governance during COVID-19', *Revue Interventions économiques / Papers in Political Economy*, 75, pp 1–25.

Roberts, A., Trommer, S. and Hannah, E. (2019) *Gender Sensitive Trade Policy*, Women's Budget Group. Available at: https://www.wbg.org.uk/publication/gender-impacts-of-trade-and-investment-agreements/

Robinson, C.J. (2021 [1983]) *Black Marxism: The Making of the Black Radical Tradition*. University of North Carolina Press.

Robinson, J. (1973) 'The need for a reconsideration of the theory of international trade', in M. Connolly and A. Swoboda (eds) *International Trade and Money*. George Allen & Unwin, pp 15–25.

Robinson, J. (1974) *Reflections on the Theory of International Trade: Lectures Given in the University of Manchester*. Manchester University Press.

Roemer, M.I. and Roemer, J.E. (1982) 'The social consequences of free trade in health care: A public health response to orthodox economics', *International Journal of Health Services*, 12(1), pp 111–129.

Rosenberg, J. (2006) 'Why is there no international historical sociology?', *European Journal of International Relations*, 12(3), pp 307–340.

Rosset, P.M. (2006) *Food is Different: Why We Must Get the WTO Out of Agriculture*. Fernwood Publishing.

Rothstein, R.L. (2015) *Global Bargaining: UNCTAD and the Quest for a New International Economic Order*. Princeton University Press.

Roy, A. (2010) *Poverty Capital: Microfinance and the Making of Development*. Routledge.

Ruggie, J.G. (1982) 'International regimes, transactions, and change: Embedded liberalism in the postwar economic order', *International Organization*, 36(2), pp 379–415.

Ryu, D. and Nam, H.-J. (2024) 'Impacts of gender inequality on international trade and innovation', *Finance Research Letters*, 63, Article 105366.

Sachs, W. (1992) *The Development Dictionary: A Guide to Knowledge as Power*. Bloomsbury Publishing.

Sairam, E.S. (2025) *How Trump's New Tariffs Will Impact Women's Wallets*, *Forbes*, 2 April. Available at: https://www.forbes.com/sites/erinspencer1/2025/04/02/how-trumps-new-tariffs-will-hurt-womens-wallets/

Sardenberg, C.M.B. (2016 [2008]) 'Liberal vs. liberating empowerment: A Latin American feminist perspective on coneptualising women's empowerment', [IDS Bulletin 393] *IDS Bulletin*, 47(1A), pp 18–27.

Sauvant, K.P. (1993) 'The tradability of services', in K.P. Sauvant and P. Mallampally (eds) *Transnational Corporations in Services*, United Nations Library on Transnational Corporations, pp 300–315.

Scasserra, S. (2023) 'Discourses of inclusion and forms of instrumentalisation of women to drive digital capitalism', in DAWN (ed) *Towards Feminist Digital Justice*. DAWN Informs, pp 55–60. Available at: https://www.dawnfeminist.org/wp-content/uploads/2023/12/DI-on-FDJ-2023.pdf

Schuberth, H. and Young, B. (2011) 'The role of gender in governance of the financial sector', in B. Young, I. Bakker and D. Elson (eds) *Questioning Financial Governance from a Feminist Perspective*. Routledge, pp 132–154.

Scott, C. (2021) 'The gender of dependency theory: Women as workers, from neocolonialism in West Africa to the implosion of contemporary capitalism', *Review of African Political Economy*, 48(167), pp 66–81.

Scott, J. (2017) 'The future of agricultural trade governance in the World Trade Organization', *International Affairs*, 93(5), pp 1167–1184.

Scott, J. and Wilkinson, R. (2012) 'The poverty of the Doha round and the least developed countries', in R. Wilkinson and J. Scott (eds) *Trade, Poverty, Development*. Routledge, pp 17–36.

Scott, J. and Harman, S. (2013) 'Beyond TRIPS: Why the WTO's Doha Round is unhealthy', *Third World Quarterly*, 34(8), pp 1361–1376.

Scott, J. and Trommer, S. (2024) 'The cultural foundations of trade policy: Competitive free trade and the UK–Australia free trade agreement', *Review of International Studies*, pp 1–20.

Seguino, S. (2000) 'Gender inequality and economic growth: A cross-country analysis', *World Development*, 28(7), pp 1211–1230.

Sell, S. (2003) *Private Power, Public Law: The Globalization of Intellectual Property Rights*. Cambridge University Press.

Selwyn, B. and Leyden, D. (2022) 'Oligopoly-driven development: The World Bank's trading for development in the age of global value chains in perspective', *Competition & Change*, 26(2), pp 174–196.

Sen, G. and Grown, C. (1987) *Development, Crises and Alternative Visions: Third world women's perspectives*. Earthscan Publications Limited.

Shava, E. (2021) 'Gender equality in information communication technology (ICT) for attaining Sustainable Development Goal number 5 in South Africa', *Gender and Behaviour*, 19(2), pp 17906–17917.

Shaw, A. and Jobes, K. (2019) *Integrating Gender and Inclusion into Prosperity Fund Trade Programmes*. WOW Helpdesk Query 20. UK Aid. Available at: https://assets.publishing.service.gov.uk/media/5f43a412e90e0752aae59029/Query-20-Gender-Inclusion-Trade-Brief.pdf

Shields, S. and Wallin, S. (2015) 'The European Bank for Reconstruction and Development's gender action plan and the gendered political economy of post-communist transition', *Globalizations*, 12(3), pp 383–399.

Shilliam, R. (2018) *Race and the Undeserving Poor: From Abolition to Brexit.* Agenda Publishing.

Shiva, V. (2001) *Protect or Plunder?* Fenwood Publishing Ltd.

Shiva, V. (2005) *Globalization's New Wars: Seed, Water & Life Forms.* Women Unlimited.

Siles-Brügge, G. (2014) 'Explaining the resilience of free trade: The Smoot–Hawley myth and the crisis', *Review of International Political Economy*, 21(3), pp 535–574.

Singh, J.P. (2017) *Sweet Talk: Paternalism and Collective Action in North-South Trade Relations.* Stanford University Press.

Singh, J.P. (2021) 'Race, culture, and economics: An example from North–South trade relations', *Review of International Political Economy*, 28(2), pp 323–335.

Singh, J.P. and Gupta, S. (2016) 'Agriculture and its discontents: Coalitional politics at the WTO with special reference to India's food security interests', *International Negotiation*, 21(2), pp 295–326.

Smith, J. (2001) 'Globalizing resistance: The battle of Seattle and the future of social movements', *Mobilization: An International Quarterly*, 6(1), pp 1–19.

Smith, R.D., Chanda, R. and Tangcharoensathien, V. (2009) 'Trade in health-related services', *The Lancet*, 373(9663), pp 593–601.

Srnicek, N. (2017) *Platform Capitalism.* Polity Press.

Standing, G. (1999) 'Global feminization through flexible labour: A theme revisited', *World Development*, 27(3), pp 583–602.

Stanford University (2024) *GATT Digital Library.* Available at: https://exhibits.stanford.edu/gatt

Stevano, S. (2025) 'Ultra-processed food, depletion, and social reproduction: A conceptual intervention', *Antipode*, 57(2), pp 515–535.

Stevano, S., Ali, R. and Jamieson, M. (2021) 'Essential for what? A global social reproduction view on the re-organisation of work during the COVID-19 pandemic', *Canadian Journal of Development Studies / Revue canadienne d'études du développement*, 42(1–2), pp 178–199.

Stolper, W. and Samuelson, P. (1941) 'Protection and real wages', *Review of Economic Studies*, 9(1), pp 58–73.

Strange, S. (1985) 'Protectionism and world politics', *International Organization*, 39(2), pp 233–259.

TaPP (2025) 'The environmental effects of digital trade: How to monitor, measure and mitigate', *TaPP Insights.* Available at: https://tappnetwork.org/wp-content/uploads/2025/07/TaPP_Environmental_Effects_of_Digital_Trade_April_2025.pdf.

Taussig, F. (1889) 'Some aspects of the tariff question', *Quarterly Journal of Economics*, 3(3), pp 259–292.

Taussig, F. (1904) 'Schmoller on protection and free trade', *Quarterly Journal of Economics*, 19(3), pp 501–511.

Taylor, W. (1903) 'The relative importance of our foreign trade', *Journal of Political Economy*, 12(1), pp 18–33.

Titeca, K. and De Herdt, T. (2010) 'Regulation, cross-border trade and practical norms in West Nile, north-western Uganda', *Africa*, 80(4), pp 573–594.

Tornhill, S. (2019) *The Business of Women's Empowerment: Corporate Gender Politics in the Global South*. Rowman & Littlefield.

Trade Experettes (2023) *The E-Commerce Moratorium and Women: How the WTO E-Commerce Moratorium Impacts Women Across the World*. Available at: https://static1.squarespace.com/static/5d7025a4a7115800013abe24/t/64fd2059b48a5e6f727ee101/1694310493858/The+E-Commerce+Moratorium+%26+Women.pdf

Trentmann, F. (1998) 'Political culture and political economy: Interest, ideology and free trade', *Review of International Political Economy*, 5(2), pp 217–251.

Trommer, S. (2014) *Transformations in Trade Politics: Participatory Trade Politics in West Africa*. Routledge.

Trommer, S. (2017) 'The WTO in an era of preferential trade agreements: Thick and thin institutions in global trade governance', *World Trade Review*, 16(3), pp 501–526.

Trommer, S. (2022) 'Trade, health and social reproduction in a COVID world', *Globalizations*, 19(3), pp 397–407.

True, J. (2008) 'Gender mainstreaming and regional trade governance in Asia-Pacific Economic Cooperation (APEC)', in S. Rai and G. Waylen (eds) *Global Governance: Feminist Perspectives*. Palgrave Macmillan, pp 129–159.

True, J. (2009) 'Trading-in gender equality: Gendered meanings in EU trade policy', in E. Lombardo, P. Meier and M. Verloo (eds) *The Discursive Politics of Gender Equality*. Routledge, pp 141–157.

True, J. and Parisi, L. (2013) 'Gender mainstreaming strategies in international governance', in G. Caglar, E. Prügl and S. Zwingel (eds) *Feminist Strategies in International Governance*. Routledge, pp 37–56.

Tsikata, D. and Yaro, J.A. (2014) 'When a good business model is not enough: Land transactions and gendered livelihood prospects in rural Ghana', *Feminist Economics*, 20(1), pp 202–226.

UN (2020) 'What does "build back better" really mean? One of the world's top CEOs give us his take', *UN News*. Available at: https://news.un.org/en/story/2020/06/1066152

UN (2023) '"Widening digital gap between developed, developing – states threatening to exclude world's poorest from next industrial revolution", speakers tell Second Committee', UN Meetings Coverage and Press Releases, GA/EF/3587, 6 October. Available at: https://press.un.org/en/2023/gaef3587.doc.htm

UN (2024) *Global Digital Compact*, A/79/L.2. United Nations. Available at: https://www.un.org/global-digital-compact/sites/default/files/2024-09/Global%20Digital%20Compact%20-%20English_0.pdf

UNCTAD (1964) *Proceedings of the United Nations Conference on Trade and Development*. E/CONF.46/141, Vol. II. United Nations Conference on Trade and Development.

UNCTAD (1999) *Trade, Sustainable Development and Gender: Papers Prepared in Support of the Themes Discussed at the Pre-UNCTAD X Expert Workshop on Trade, Sustainable Development and Gender (Geneva, 12–13 July 1999)*. United Nations Conference on Trade and Development. Available at: https://unctad.org/system/files/official-document/poedmm78.en.pdf

UNCTAD (2014) *Looking at Trade Policy through a 'Gender Lens': Summary of Seven Country Case Studies*. United Nations Conference on Trade and Development.

UNCTAD (2015a) *Ensuring Gender-Sensitive Implementation of the Post-2015 Development Framework*. United Nations Conference on Trade and Development.

UNCTAD (2015b) 'On-line course on trade and gender launched by UNCTAD', United Nations Conference on Trade and Development. Available at: https://unctad.org/news/line-course-trade-and-gender-launched-unctad

UNCTAD (2015c) *Entrepreneurship for Sustainable Development: Fostering Small Enterprises as Engines of Inclusive Growth*. United Nations Conference on Trade and Development.

UNCTAD (2016) *Implementing Gender-Aware Ex Ante Evaluations to Maximize the Benefits of Trade Reforms for Women*. United Nations Conference on Trade and Development.

UNCTAD (2017a) *Trade and Gender Toolbox: How Will the Economic Partnership Agreement between the European Union and the East African Community Affect Kenyan Women?* United Nations Conference on Trade and Development.

UNCTAD (2017b) *Rising Product Digitalisation and Losing Trade Competitiveness*. United Nations Conference on Trade and Development.

UNCTAD (2019a) *Trade Deals Can Be a Tool for Women's Empowerment*. United Nations Conference on Trade and Development. Available at: https://unctad.org/news/trade-deals-can-be-tool-womens-empowerment

UNCTAD (2019b) *Entrepreneurship for Sustainable Development: Fostering Small Entreprises as Engines of Inclusive Growth*. United Nations Conference on Trade and Development. Available at: https://unctad.org/system/files/official-document/tc2015d1rev2_S04_P02.pdf

UNCTAD (2020) *Teaching Material on Trade and Gender Linkages: The Gender Impact of Technological Upgrading in Agriculture*. United Nations Conference on Trade and Development.

UNCTAD (2021a) *Trade, Gender and Development Programme: Advocating Inclusive and Gender-Responsive Economic Development on a Global Level.* United Nations Conference on Trade and Development.

UNCTAD (2021b) *The Inaugural Gender and Development Forum at the Fifteenth Session of the United Nations Conference on Trade and Development, Bridgetown Declaration.* United Nations Conference on Trade and Development.

UNCTAD (2021c) *Ministerial Declaration of the Group of 77 and China to UNCTAD XV: From Inequality and Vulnerability to Prosperity for All.* United Nations Conference on Trade and Development.

UNCTAD (2021d) *Policy Options to Support Women Farmers to Benefit from Strengthened Linkages Between Agriculture and Tourism.* United Nations Conference on Trade and Development.

UNCTAD (2022a) *UNCTAD 15 Outcome: The Spirit of Speightstown and the Bridgetown Covenant.* United Nations Conference on Trade and Development.

UNCTAD (2022b) *Linking Trade and Gender towards Sustainable Development: An Analytical and Policy Framework.* United Nations Conference on Trade and Development.

UNCTAD (2022c) *UNCTAD Partners with DHL to Empower Women in E-Commerce.* United Nations Conference on Trade and Development. Available at: https://unctad.org/news/unctad-partners-dhl-empower-women-e-commerce

UNCTAD (2022d) *Fostering Women Entrepreneurship in the Digital Economy.* United Nations Conference on Trade and Development.

UNCTAD (2023a) *Towards Better Trade Opportunities for Female Farmers in Myanmar: A Guidebook to Improve Agricultural Practices, Food Safety, and Access to Credit.* United Nations Conference on Trade and Development.

UNCTAD (2023b) *E-Commerce from a Gender and Development Perspective.* United Nations Conference on Trade and Development.

UNCTAD (2024) *Empowering Women Leaders for Gender Equality in the Digital Economy.* United Nations Conference on Trade and Development. Available at: https://unctad.org/news/empowering-women-leaders-gender-equality-digital-economy

UNCTAD (2025) 'eTrade for Women', United Nations Conference on Trade and Development. Available at: https://unctad.org/topic/ecommerce-and-digital-economy/etrade-for-women

UNCTAD (2026) *Strait of Hormuz Disruptions: Implications for Global Trade and Development.* United Nations Conference on Trade and Development.

UNDP (1999) 'World Survey on the Role of Women in Development: Globalization, Gender and Work.' United Nations Development Programme.

UNECA (2017) *Women's Economic Empowerment: Boosting Women's Entrepreneurship in Africa.* United Nations Economic Commission for Africa.

UNECA (2021a) *Gender-Responsive Implementation of the Agreement Establishing the African Continental Free Trade Area: Defining the Role of the Regional Economic Communities.* United Nations Economic Commission for Africa.

UNECA (2021b) *The Mauritian Strategy to Leverage Opportunities in the African Continental Free Trade Area (AfCFTA).* Report Strategy Produced by International Economics Consulting Ltd. Available at: https://repository.uneca.org/bitstream/handle/10855/49336/b1202319x.pdf?sequence=1&isAllowed=y

UNECA (2022a) *Agricultural Value Chains and Transformation in Southern Africa: Opportunities Stemming from the African Continental Free Trade Area.* United Nations Economic Commission for Africa.

UNECA (2022b) 'A guide to gender mainstreaming in African Continental Free Trade Area (AfCFTA) national AfCFTA strategies'. United Nations Economic Commission for Africa. Available at: https://knowledge.uneca.org/idep/node/114

UNECA and FES (2017) *The Continental Free Trade Area (CFTA) in Africa: A Human Rights Perspective.* United Nations Economic Commission for Africa and Friedrich-Ebert-Stiftung.

UNECA and ATPC (2022) 'Addressing the trade facilitation challenge in the context of the AfCFTA: View from West Africa', *Essay Series on Gender and Trade. Series 1: Trade Facilitation.* United Nations Economic Commission for Africa. Available at: https://repository.uneca.org/bitstream/handle/10855/49479/b12027777.pdf?sequence=1&isAllowed=y

UNICEF (2007) *State of the World's Children: Investing in Women's Rights to Advance the Rights of Both Women and Children.* United Nations Children's Fund.

UNIDO/GTZ (2008) *Creating an Enabling Environment for Private Sector Development in Sub-Saharan Africa.* United Nations Industrial Development Organization.

UN Women (2022) *A toolkit on paid and unpaid care work: From 3Rs to 5Rs.* United Nations.

United Nations High Commissioner for Human Rights (2015) *UN Experts Voice Concern Over Adverse Impact of Free Trade & Investment Agreements on Human Rights.* Office of the High Commissioner for Human Rights.

US Mission Geneva (2025) 'Withdrawing the United States from and ending funding to certain United Nations organizations and reviewing United States support to all international organizations'. Available at: https://geneva.usmission.gov/2025/02/05/executive-order-on-certain-un-organizations-and-all-international-organizations/

Valodia, I. (2001) 'Economic policy and women's informal work in South Africa', *Development and Change*, 32(5), pp 871–892.

Valodia, I. and Devey, R (2010) 'Formal-informal economy linkages: What implications for poverty in South Africa?' *Law, Democracy and Development* 14(1), p 26.

van Ommeren, E. (2025) *Pro Trade, Against Competition: Firms and the Politics of Selective Trade Protection*. Edward Elgar.

van Staveren, I., Elson, D., Grown, C. and Çağatay, N. (eds) (2007) *The Feminist Economics of Trade*. Routledge.

Vertommen, S. (2025) 'Housewifization', *Kohl: A Journal for Body and Gender Research*, 11(1), np.

Vijaya, R. (2007) 'Trade, job losses and gender: A policy perspective', *Forum for Social Economics*, 36(2), pp 73–85.

Villegas Plá, B. (2024) 'Dependency theory meets feminist economics: A research agenda', *Third World Quarterly*, 45(8), pp 1325–1342.

von Bülow, M. (2010) *Building Transnational Networks: Civil Society and the Politics of Trade in the Americas*. Cambridge University Press.

von Werlhof, C. (2007) 'No critique of capitalism without a critique of patriarchy! Why the left is no alternative', *Capitalism Nature Socialism*, 18(1), pp 13–27.

Wallerstein, I. (1974) *The Modern World System*. Academic Press.

Wallerstein, I. (1989) *The Modern World-System, Vol. III: The Second Great Expansion of the Capitalist World-Economy, 1730–1840s*. Academic Press.

Walsh, V.C. (1979) 'Ricardian foreign trade theory in the light of the classical revival', *Eastern Economic Journal*, 5(3), pp 421–427.

Watkins, K. (1996) 'Free trade and farm fallacies: From the Uruguay Round to the World Food Summit', *The Ecologist*, 26(6), pp 253–279.

Watson, M. (2017) 'Historicising Ricardo's comparative advantage theory, challenging the normative foundations of liberal international political economy', *New Political Economy*, 22(3), pp 257–272.

Watson, V. (2009) 'Seeing from the South: Refocusing urban planning on the globe's central urban issues', *Urban Studies*, 46(11), pp 2259–2275.

Waylen, G. (2022) 'Gendering global economic governance after the global financial crisis', *Review of International Political Economy*, 29(4), pp 1007–1026.

Webb, P., Benton, T.G., Beddington, J., Flynn, D., Kelly, N.M. and Thomas, S.M. (2020) 'The urgency of food system transformation is now irrefutable', *Nature Food*, 1(10), pp 584–585.

Weber, M. (2001) 'Competing political visions: WTO governance and green politics', *Global Environmental Politics*, 1(3), pp 92–113.

WEF (2020) *E-Commerce is Globalization's Shot at Equality*. World Economic Forum. Available at: https://www.weforum.org/stories/2020/01/e-commerce-sme-globalization-equality-women/

Weinhardt, C. (2020) 'Emerging powers in the world trading system: Contestation of the developing country status and the reproduction of inequalities', *Global Society*, 34(3), pp 388–408.

Weis, T. (2010) 'The accelerating biophysical contradictions of industrial capitalist agriculture', *Journal of Agrarian Change*, 10(3), pp 315–341.

Weiss, T. and Wilkinson, R. (2014) 'Rethinking global governance? Complexity, authority, power, change', *International Studies Quarterly*, 58(1), pp 207–215.

Wilkinson, R. (2009) 'Language, power and multilateral trade negotiations', *Review of International Political Economy*, 16(4), pp 597–619.

Wilkinson, R. (2012) 'Of butchery and bicycles: The WTO and the "death" of the Doha Development Agenda', *The Political Quarterly*, 83(2), pp 1–7.

Wilkinson, R. (2013) *The WTO: Crisis and the Governance of Global Trade*. Routledge.

Wilkinson, R. (2017) 'Back to the future: "Retro" trade governance and the future of the multilateral order', *International Affairs*, 93(5), pp 1131–1147.

Wilkinson, R. and Scott, J. (2008) 'Developing country participation in the GATT: A reassessment', *World Trade Review*, 7(3), pp 473–510.

Wilkinson, R., Hannah, E. and Scott, J. (2016) 'The WTO in Nairobi: The demise of the Doha Development Agenda and the future of the multilateral trading system', *Global Policy*, 7(2), pp 247–255.

Williams, A. (2026) 'Donald Trump's 10% global tariff ruled illegal by US court', *Financial Times*, 7 May. Available at: https://www.ft.com/content/a53ed6cc-bbef-4527-a19c-8041118e3661?syn-25a6b1a6=1

Williams, M. (2007) 'Gender issues in the multilateral trading system', in I. van Staveren, D. Elson, C. Grown and N. Çağatay (eds) *The Feminist Economics of Trade*. Routledge, pp 277–291.

Williams, M. (2013) 'A perspective on feminist international organizing from the bottom up: The case of the ITGN and the WTO', in G. Caglar, E. Prügl and S. Zwingel (eds) *Feminist Strategies in International Governance*. Routledge, pp 92–108.

Winters, L.A. and Martuscelli, A. (2014) 'Trade liberalization and poverty: What have we learned in a decade?', *Annual Review of Resource Economics*, 6(1), pp 493–512.

Wolf, D.L. (1992) *Factory Daughters: Gender, Household Dynamics and Rural Industrialisation in Java*. Oxford University Press.

Wolfenden, A. (2023) 'A strategy to where? The Pacific Regional E-Commerce Strategy and the need to put data sovereignty first', *DAWN Informs*, December, pp 61–64.

Women at the Table (2025) 'Our story'. Available at: https://www.womenatthetable.net/our-story/

Wood, A. (1991) 'North-South trade and female labour in manufacturing: An asymmetry', *Journal of Development Studies*, 27(2), pp 168–189.

Wood, L. (2020) 'The Seattle model', *Socialism and Democracy*, 34(1), pp 51–65.

World Bank (1995) *Enhancing Women's Participation in Economic Development*. World Bank.

World Bank (2006) *Gender Equality as Smart Economics: A World Bank Group Gender Action Plan (Fiscal Years 2007–10)*. World Bank Group.

World Bank (2007) *The Next 4 Billion: Market Size and Business Strategy at the Base of the Pyramid*. Study published by World Resources Institute (WRI) and International Finance Corporation (IFC).

World Bank (2016) *Feminization of Agriculture in the Context of Rural Transformations: What is the Evidence?* World Bank Group.

World Bank and WTO (2020) *Women and Trade: The Role of Trade in Promoting Women's Equality*. World Bank Group and World Trade Organization.

Wright, S. (1995) 'Women and the global economic order: A feminist perspective', *American University International Law Review*, 10(2), pp 861–887.

WTO (2017a) *Buenos Aires Declaration on Trade and Women's Economic Empowerment*. Available at: https://www.wto.org/english/tratop_e/womenandtrade_e/buenos_aires_declaration_e.htm

WTO (2017b) *WTO Action Plan on Trade and Gender 2017–2019: Building the Trade and Gender Foundations in the WTO*. World Trade Organization.

WTO (2017c) *Work Programme on Electronic Commerce: Statement by the African Group*, WT/MIN(17)/21. World Trade Organization.

WTO (2018a) *Aid for Trade and Women's Economic Empowerment: It's an Easy Win and it Works*. Women's Day Leaflet. World Trade Organization. Available at: https://www.wto.org/english/tratop_e/womenandtrade_e/womensday_e.pdf

WTO (2018b) *World Trade Report 2018: The Future of World Trade – How Digital Technologies are Transforming Global Commerce*. World Trade Organization.

WTO (2019a) *Women's Economic Empowerment: An Inherent Part of Aid for Trade*. Staff Working Paper ESRD-2019–07. World Trade Organization.

WTO (2019b) 'Session 73: What do women need? WTO reform for a comprehensive gender-friendly trading system'. World Trade Organization. Available at: https://www.wto.org/english/forums_e/public_forum19_e/public_forum19_e.htm

WTO (2019c) *Trade Policies Supporting Women's Economic Empowerment: Trends in WTO Members*. Staff Working Paper ERSD-2019–07. World Trade Organization.

WTO (2020a) *The Economic Impact of COVID-19 on Women in Vulnerable Sectors and Economies*. Information Note. World Trade Organization. Available at: https://www.wto.org/english/news_e/news20_e/info_note_covid_05aug20_e.pdf

WTO (2020b) *Draft Work Plan for Implementing Activities under the Informal Working Group on Trade and Gender*, INF/TGE/W/1. World Trade Organization.

WTO (2020c) *The E-Commerce Moratorium and Implications for Developing Countries: Communication from India and South Africa*, WT/GC/W/798 (20–1899), 3 March. World Trade Organization. Available at: https://docs.wto.org/dol2fe/Pages/FE_Search/FE_S_S009-DP.aspx

WTO (2021a) *WTO Action Plan on Trade and Gender 2021–26: Building a Gender-Responsive WTO*. World Trade Organization.

WTO (2021b) *Progress Report on WTO Members and Observers Technical Work on Women's Economic Empowerment*. INF/TGE/R/1. World Trade Organization.

WTO (2021c) *Australia Experiences with Gender-Related Practices and Processes: Communication from Australia*. INF/TGE/COM/1. World Trade Organization.

WTO (2021d) 'Empowering South Asian women entrepreneurs through trade and technology', presentation to the WTO IWG on Trade and Gender by Association of Lady Entrepreneurs of India. World Trade Organization. Available at: https://www.wto.org/english/tratop_e/womenand trade_e/16july21/item_3.4.e._sheel a_bhide.pdf

WTO (2021e) 'Asociación de mujeres Waorani de la Amazonía ecuatoriana'. World Trade Organization. Available at: https://www.wto.org/english/tratop_e/womenandtrade_e/280421_ecua dor.pdf

WTO (2021f) 'Capacity building in trade and gender', presentation by Simonetta Zarrilli, Trade Gender and Development Programme. World Trade Organization. Available at: https://www.wto.org/english/tratop_e/womenandtrade_e/16july21/item_3.4.c._unctad.pdf.

WTO (2021g) 'WTO Informal Working Group on Trade and Gender: Aid for Trade – Supporting the work programme delivery on gender', Presentation by Australian Gender Equality Ambassador, Julie-Ann Guivarra. Available at https://www.wto.org/english/tratop_e/womenandtrade_e/16july21/item_3.2.a._presentation_by_australia.pdf

WTO (2021h) *The Legal Status of 'Joint Statement Initiatives' and Their Negotiated Outcomes*. WT/GC/W/819/Rev.1. World Trade Organization.

WTO (2022a) *Making Trade Work for Women: Key Findings from the 2022 World Trade Congress on Gender*. World Trade Organization.

WTO (2022b) *MC12 Outcome Document*. WT/MIN(22)/24. World Trade Organization.

WTO (2022c) *Aid for Trade Global Review*. World Trade Organization.

WTO (2023a) *Informal Working Group on MSMEs: Access to Finance for Women-Led Micro, Small and Medium-Sized Enterprises*. INF/MSME/W/46, INF/TGE/W/7. World Trade Organization.

WTO (2023b) *Biennial Technical Assistance and Training Plan 2024–2025.* WT/COMTD/W/273. World Trade Organization.

WTO (2023c) *Informal Working Group on Trade and Gender: Trade and Gender-Related Provisions in Regional Trade Agreements.* INF/TGE/COM/4. World Trade Organization.

WTO (2024a) *Joint Statement on Promoting Inclusive and Sustainable Trade through Gender Equality and Building a Gender-Responsive WTO by the Co-Chairs of the Informal Working Group on Trade and Gender.* WT/MIN(24)/6. World Trade Organization.

WTO (2024b) 'Informal Working Group on Trade and Gender reviews 2024 achievements on advancing equality', World Trade Organization, 18 November. Available at: https://www.wto.org/english/news_e/news24_e/iwgtg_18nov24_e.htm

WTO (2024c) 'Practical Integration of Inclusivity in Trade and Investment Policy: Sharing Experiences from APEC and the San Francisco Principles' *Informal Working Group on MSMEs and Informal Working Group on Trade and Gender,* INF/TGE/COM/7, INF/MSME/W/50. World Trade Organization.

WTO (2024d) *Access to Finance for Women-Led Micro, Small and Medium-Sized Enterprises (MSMEs): A Compendium for Financial Inclusion Initiatives.* INF/TGE/W/7/Rev.1. World Trade Organization.

WTO (2024e) *Abu Dhabi Ministerial Declaration.* WT/MIN(24)/DEC. World Trade Organization.

WTO (2024f) *Incorporation of the Agreement on Electronic Commerce into Annex 4 of the WTO Agreement: Communication from the Members Parties to the Agreement on Electronic Commerce.* WT/GC/W/955. World Trade Organization.

WTO (2024g) *Proposal on a Compendium on Educational Programmes for Women Entrepreneurs: Communication from the Russian Federation.* INF/TGE/COM/11. World Trade Organization.

WTO (2025a) 'Public forum'. Available at: https://www.wto.org/english/forums_e/public_forum_e/public_forum_e.htm

WTO (2025b) 'WTO gender research hub'. Available at: https://www.wto.org/english/tratop_e/womenandtrade_e/gender_research_hub_e.htm

WTO (2025c) 'Informal working group on trade and gender'. Available at: https://www.wto.org/english/tratop_e/womenandtrade_e/iwg_trade_gender_e.htm

WTO (2025d) 'Capacity building on trade and gender for WTO members'. Available at: https://www.wto.org/english/tratop_e/womenandtrade_e/iwg_trade_gender_e.htm

WTO (2025e) *Informal Working Group on Trade and Gender Work Plan 2025–2026.* INF/TGE/W/10. World Trade Organization.

WTO (2025f) *Proposal for a New Compendium on 'Empowering Women to Trade through Digitalisation: Policy Insights'*. INF/TGE/COM/13. World Trade Organization.

WTO (2026a) 'WTO chairs programme'. Available at: https://wtochairs.org/index.php/

WTO (2026b) *Informal Working Group on Gender and Trade*. Available at: https://www.wto.org/english/tratop_e/womenandtrade_e/iwg_trade_gender_e.htm#Documents

WTO (2026c) *Declaration on Interim Arrangements for the Agreement on Electronic Commerce*. WT/MIN(26)/W/26. World Trade Organization.

WTO and OECD (2024) *Aid for Trade at a Glance 2024*. World Trade Organization and Organization for Economic Co-operation and Development. Available at: https://doi.org/10.1787/7a4e356a-en

Yeates, N. (2004) 'Global care chains', *International Feminist Journal of Politics* 6(3), pp 369–391.

Young, A. and Peterson, J. (2006) 'The EU and the new trade politics', *Journal of European Public Policy*, 13(6), pp 795–814.

Young, B. and Hoppe, H. (2003) 'The Doha Development Round, gender and social reproduction', *Dialogue on Globalization*, 7.

Yunus, M. (2010) *Building Social Business: The New Kind of Capitalism that Serves Humanity's Most Pressing Needs*. Public Affairs.

Zakaria, S. (2018) 'Fair trade for women, at last: Using a sanctions framework to enforce gender equality rights in multilateral trade agreements', *Georgetown Journal of Gender and the Law*, 20, pp 241–264.

Zeleza, P. (1993) *A Modern Economic History of Africa: The Nineteenth Century*. East African Educational Publishers.

Zirpoli, C. (2026) Supreme Court Rules Against Tariffs Imposed Under the International Emergency Economic Powers Act (IEEPA), Congressional Research Service, LSB11398, US Congress.

Zuboff, S. (2019) *The Age of Surveillance Capitalism*. Profile Books.

Zulfiqar, G. M. (2016) 'Does microfinance enhance gender equity in access to finance? Evidence from Pakistan', *Feminist Economics*. 23(1), pp 160–185.

Index

References to figures appear in *italic* type; those in **bold** type refer to tables.
References to endnotes show the page and chapter number and the note number (160ch2n4).